The Sterilization Movement and Global Fertility in the Twentieth Century

The Sterilization Movement and Global Fertility in the Twentieth Century

IAN DOWBIGGIN

OXFORD
UNIVERSITY PRESS

2008

OXFORD
UNIVERSITY PRESS

Oxford University Press, Inc., publishes works that further
Oxford University's objective of excellence
in research, scholarship, and education.

Oxford   New York
Auckland   Cape Town   Dar es Salaam   Hong Kong   Karachi
Kuala Lumpur   Madrid   Melbourne   Mexico City   Nairobi
New Delhi   Shanghai   Taipei   Toronto

With offices in
Argentina   Austria   Brazil   Chile   Czech Republic   France   Greece
Guatemala   Hungary   Italy   Japan   Poland   Portugal   Singapore
South Korea   Switzerland   Thailand   Turkey   Ukraine   Vietnam

Copyright © 2008 by Oxford University Press.

Published by Oxford University Press, Inc.
198 Madison Avenue, New York, New York 10016
www.oup.com

Oxford is a registered trademark of Oxford University Press

Library of Congress Cataloging-in-Publication Data
Dowbiggin, Ian Robert, 1952–
The sterilization movement and global fertility in the twentieth century / Ian R. Dowbiggin.
p. ; cm.
Includes bibliographical references and index.
ISBN-13: 978-0-19-518858-5
1. Sterilization (Birth control)–
United States–History–20th century.   I. Title.
[DNLM: 1. Sterilization, Reproductive–history.   2. Contraception Behavior–history.
3. History, 20th Century.   4. Socioeconomic Factors. WP 11.1 D744s 2008]
HQ766.5.U5D69 2008
304.6'66–dc22
2007036920

1 3 5 7 9 8 6 4 2

Printed in the United States of America
on acid-free paper

To my father

Acknowledgments

First and foremost, this book is the culmination of numerous visits over several years to the Social Welfare History Archives at the University of Minnesota, where I benefited from the unstinting assistance of David Klaassen and Linnea Anderson. I am also grateful to Barbara Floyd, Kimberly Brownlee, and University of Toledo President Dan Johnson for their gracious help and hospitality when I visited the University of Toledo's Ward Canaday Center. The same can be said for Sarah Hutcheon at Radcliffe Institute's Schlesinger Library and Leslie Shores at the University of Wyoming's American Heritage Center. John Cusack and Peter Rankin, as student assistants, were invaluable in performing library and Internet searches, as was my administrative assistant Sharon Currie.

I am indebted to the Social Science and Humanities Research Council of Canada, the Hannah Institute for the History of Medicine, and the University of Prince Edward Island for helping to fund the research behind this book. Without their financial assistance, this book would not have been possible.

Contents

Prologue

As he watched urban civilization steadily close in on his cabin in New York State's Adirondack Mountains, environmentalist Bill McKibben made a big personal decision: shortly after the birth of his only child, he chose to have a vasectomy. As McKibben confessed in his 1998 best-seller *Maybe One*, he underwent the operation to help slow population growth and prevent global warming.

What a difference twenty years make. Had McKibben announced the same news in the 1970s, he would have been lauded for his cutting-edge, selfless behavior. Back then, limiting one's family size in the interests of the planet was one of the noblest acts imaginable.

Today, however, growing numbers of people aren't so sure Bill McKibben did the right thing. To present-day pundits such as Phillip Longman, the real danger facing many developed and developing countries around the world is *depopulation*, not overpopulation. Longman states, "[N]ot since the fall of the Roman Empire has the world ever experienced anything on the scale of today's loss of fertility."[1] From the pages of *The New York Times*, the *Wall Street Journal*, and *Foreign Affairs* to a rash of new books, social scientists predict this "birth dearth" or "demographic winter" will soon trigger a crisis that will cripple future generations. As the baby boomers approach retirement age, anxious governments wonder how, in the coming years, taxpayers will pay the bills for costly social programs such as Medicare and social security. In Europe, where low fertility rates and an aging population coincide with stagnant economies, policy makers believe the status quo is unsustainable but worry that the political will to change it is missing.[2]

Other experts warn that the drop in fertility in countries such as China and India, where roughly 40% of the world's population resides, has produced a gender imbalance heavily skewed in favor of males. Some forecast that the millions of unmarried, underemployed, unhappy, and rootless surplus men in the world's two most populous countries will threaten domestic stability and endanger international security.[3] If these forecasts come true, the birth dearth will likely rival global warming as an issue of international concern in the twenty-first century.

What, then, accounts for the birth dearth?

The plummeting fertility rates of the late twentieth century are due to factors such as abortion, economic development, sexually transmitted diseases, and changes in the status of women, but the most important cause is the widespread use of contraceptives.[4] In fact, over the past thirty years, the world has undergone a contraceptive revolution. Today, surveys show that about 65% of American women between the ages of fifteen and forty-four use artificial contraception, with an increase from 30 million to 39 million women between 1982 and 1995 alone.[5] This contraceptive revolution, cutting across class, race, and religious lines, has given Americans a sense of omnipotence never experienced by earlier generations— a belief in their ability and right to control their own bodies, to free themselves from what birth control pioneer Margaret Sanger once called "biological slavery." Many Americans want the whole world to enjoy this same freedom.

The impact of the oral contraceptive, or "Pill," is a matter of historical record, but few realize that as the twentieth century came to a close, the preferred instrument of birth control in the United States was actually sterilization, in the form of vasectomy for men or tubal ligation for women.[6] Estimates are that roughly a quarter of all American women practicing contraception between the ages of fifteen and forty-five have chosen tubal ligation, making it the most popular female birth control method. One in ten reported male sterilization as their favorite form of contraception. Forty percent of ever-married women or their husbands have had a sterilization operation; fully 65% of women with three or more children have opted for surgical sterilization.[7]

The rise in sterilization's popularity as a contraceptive measure during the twentieth century was nothing less than a "revolution in public and medical opinion," in the words of one U.S. birth control proponent.[8] In 1973, for example, American public health officials were talking openly about a "vasectomania" sweeping the nation.[9] By the late 1970s, surgical contraception was the *world's* foremost method for controlling fertility.

According to one U.S. official, sterilization, once "the 'ugly duckling' among contraceptive methods," had become "the 'lovely swan' of the seventies."[10] At the turn of the twenty-first century, sterilization was still the most popular form of contraception worldwide, with roughly a quarter of all couples relying on it.[11]

In other words, the history of the sterilization movement is the untold story of the twentieth-century birth control movement, more important than the history of the Pill and rivaling the significance of the history of abortion. The future of the sterilization movement remains to be written, but if its past is any indication, its impact will be felt deeply over the course of the twenty-first century.

If the popularity of sterilization did so much to produce the birth dearth, who made it so popular in the first place? The answer, revealed in this book for the first time, is a group of dedicated men and women who ended up changing the course of history. These individuals helped to launch nothing less than a revolution in contraceptive behavior and sexual mores, first in the United States and later in other developed and developing countries overseas. Their rhetoric during the Cold War led to "the decision [in the 1960s] to link U.S. foreign-policy objectives with the subsidy of family planning and population control," a "truly exceptional" enterprise "in that it explicitly aimed at altering the demographic structure of foreign countries through long-term intervention. No nation had ever set in motion a foreign-policy initiative of such magnitude."[12] In other words, U.S. foreign aid for family planning was an attempt to disseminate the belief "in the fundamentally disruptive effect of too many children being born of the wrong women in the wrong places."[13] Present-day governments around the world are just beginning to grapple with the consequences of these momentous Cold War–era events.

The revolutionaries behind this turning point in history included such luminaries of the birth control movement as Margaret Sanger, Alan Guttmacher, Robert Latou Dickinson, John Rock, and Mary Calderone. They also included biologist Paul Ehrlich; advice columnist Abigail "Dear Abby" Van Buren; science-fiction writer Isaac Asimov; and show business celebrities Arthur Godfrey, Shirley MacLaine, and ex–major league ballplayer Jim Bouton, author of the best-selling *Ball Four*.

Prominent non-Americans also played important roles in helping to launch this revolution. The list includes Canadian Brock Chisholm, the first director-general of the World Health Organization (1948–1952), and Sripati Chandrasekhar, Indian Minister of Health under Prime Minister Indira Gandhi from 1967 to 1970. It was Chandrasekhar's belief in the virtues of mass sterilization as a population control measure that paved the way for Indira Gandhi's controversial eighteen-month sterilization program of 1976–1977, described in harrowing detail in Rohinton Mistry's best-selling 1996 novel *A Fine Balance.*

Like most revolutions, this contraceptive revolution was accomplished in the teeth of fierce opposition. Until the mid-twentieth century, vasectomy and tubal ligation were highly controversial medical procedures. The medical establishment, mirroring conventional values, made it difficult for many Americans to obtain a sterilization. Condemned by the Roman Catholic Church for violating natural law, and opposed by countless Americans on similar religious and ethical grounds, these operations also suffered from the stigma of eugenics. *Eugenics,* a term coined by Charles Darwin's cousin Francis Galton in 1883, derives from the Greek word for "well-born" and normally refers to selective human breeding in order to improve the health of future generations. Eugenicists in a wide variety of countries spent much of the early twentieth century advocating policies designed either to encourage the "fit" to marry and have children ("positive eugenics") or discourage the "unfit" from reproducing ("negative eugenics"). Negative eugenics included state sterilization laws targeting the mentally and physically handicapped. The most notorious example of eugenic sterilization was the Third Reich's 1933 law that led to the sterilization of some 400,000 Germans by 1939.[14]

So, when sterilization became the most popular contraceptive method for Americans by the 1990s, it signaled the end of one of modern history's most powerful taboos. Yet for the most part, historians have either ignored the full history of this revolution in Americans' contraceptive behavior or failed to recognize its formidable impact on birth rates and mores regarding sex and gender.[15] The primary purpose of this book is to tell, for the first time, the full story of this pivotal chapter in history. At the heart of the story is the group EngenderHealth, to which Sanger, Guttmacher, Dickinson, Chisholm, Chandrasekhar, Ehrlich, and many other notable opinion makers belonged in its earlier incarnations. Today, EngenderHealth is a nongovernmental organization (NGO) with a budget of $40 million providing maternal and reproductive health-care services in over thirty developing countries.[16] In 2002, it received the United Nations Population Award, and Mayor Michael Bloomberg proclaimed July 1, 2002, "EngenderHealth Day" in New York City. EngenderHealth is hardly a household name today, but, given its impact on history, it should be.

This book relies heavily on EngenderHealth's rich archival records, housed at the University of Minnesota. But it also relies on other key archival collections in the United States and Canada, including the Hugh Moore papers at Princeton, the Brock Chisholm records at the National Archives of Canada, the Sripati Chandrasekhar papers at the University of Toledo, the Lawrence Lader papers at the New York City Library, the Robert Latou Dickinson and Clarence Gamble papers at Harvard Medical School, and the Ruth Proskauer Smith and Emily Mudd collections at the Radcliffe Institute's Schlesinger Library. In so doing, it provides a unique glimpse into the history of this long-neglected chapter of American history. It is much more than an institutional history. Just as the story of the birth control movement is much more than the history of the Planned Parenthood Federation of America, so the story of the sterilization movement during the Cold War is a tale of remarkable individuals whose vision, ambition, dedication, and energy transcended the activities of a single organization.

Since its origins in the eugenics movement of the 1930s, EngenderHealth has undergone a series of transformations: from advocating compulsory to voluntary sterilization, from private to public funding, from lay to professional leadership, from appeals to welfare cost-cutting to environmental and women's rights issues. When it was founded, in 1937, as the Sterilization League of New Jersey (SLNJ), its leadership lobbied assiduously but unsuccessfully for a eugenic sterilization statute in the Garden State. In 1943, the SLNJ became a national, private, nonprofit organization and changed its name to Birthright, Inc. In 1950, having moved its headquarters from Princeton, New Jersey, to Manhattan, Birthright became the Human Betterment Association of America (HBAA), then the Human Betterment Association for Voluntary Sterilization (HBAVS) in 1962, the Association for Voluntary Sterilization (AVS) in 1965, the Association for Voluntary Surgical Contraception (AVSC) in 1984, AVSC International in 1994, and finally EngenderHealth in 2001. EngenderHealth's many name changes indicate how reform groups that seek to influence public policy and public opinion on sensitive social issues try mightily to adapt to changes in government, corporate culture, and society's mores and behavior.[17]

EngenderHealth's metamorphosis over the second half of the twentieth century also reveals the intimate historical links among the environmental, civil liberties, eugenics, euthanasia, population control, sex education, marriage counseling, and birth control movements. Because sterilization has been variously advocated for defusing "the population bomb," lowering welfare costs, expanding individual choice, liberating women from the fear of pregnancy, strengthening marriage, improving the quality of life for retarded persons, and reducing the incidence of hereditary disorders, it is understandable how much support it has enjoyed from American opinion makers.

On a more personal level, this book constitutes the third volume of an ongoing history of twentieth-century U.S. reform movements.[18] The chronicle of the activists who labored to break down popular, religious, and medical resistance to sterilization is closely intertwined with the tale of the reformers who struggled to convince Americans to accept a right to die as well as abortion and birth control rights. Indeed, what strikes the historian is how membership in these different movements has so often overlapped. For example, it was not uncommon for the same individuals to serve on the boards of the AVS, Planned Parenthood Federation of America, the National Association for the Repeal of Abortion Laws, the Sex Information and Education Council for the United States, and the Euthanasia Society of America. They formed what one abortion rights activist in 1966 called "the stage army of liberal causes," a familiar cast of characters from America's elite, East Coast social circles whose names showed up on the letterheads of numerous reform groups.[19] However, I follow sociologist James Davison Hunter in calling these individuals "progressivists" rather than liberals. Progressivists, according to Hunter, reject appeals to "external, definable, and transcendent [moral] authority" and tend to view authority in terms of "the spirit of the modern age, a spirit of rationalism and subjectivism." To progressivists, truth is a "process" that unfolds in history and remains open to multiple interpretations derived from science or personal experience.[20] From a historical standpoint, support for free and unfettered access to sterilization services, despite the opposition it has aroused in some circles, was a certifiably "progressivist" cause in post–World War II America.

The fact that sterilization enjoyed the backing of so many noted American progressivists is particularly relevant to the ongoing debate over the history of eugenics. Edwin Black and other historians claim that the similarities between U.S. and Nazi eugenics help to define the political nature of eugenics.[21] Yet scholars such as Daniel Kevles, Wendy Kline, Molly Ladd-Taylor, and Alexandra Minna Stern have correctly maintained that U.S. eugenics did not disappear with the collapse of Hitler's regime in Germany at the end of World War II, nor was eugenics solely based on theories of race hatred. American eugenics continued to thrive in the Cold War era, albeit under new labels. For example, between the Great Depression and the 1960s, the emerging field of marriage and family counseling was heavily affected by eugenic considerations. Paul

Popenoe, a sterilization proponent and marriage counseling pioneer, exploited the pronatalist cultural climate of America in the 1950s to make the eugenic argument that marriage and the family could be strengthened by men and women selecting mates with "sound minds and sound bodies."[22]

The history of the activists involved with EngenderHealth and other social reform groups reveals that, indeed, eugenics did not peter out after 1945. It also reveals that the notion of a "reform eugenics," which rejects the racism and faulty science of earlier eugenics while defending the same basic reproductive goals, tends to fit U.S. eugenics after World War II.[23] American eugenics, although sometimes defended by people who drew invidious distinctions between different racial groups, at the same time was supported by many people whose political views tended to be progressive and liberal. As Christine Rosen has shown, eugenics attracted numerous U.S. religious leaders animated by the teachings of the social gospel.[24]

Another thing that the history of sterilization after World War II demonstrates is how the same group of reformers helped to alter traditional notions of gender and sexuality. The majority of pre–World War II eugenicists (men and women) regarded women as the "mothers of the race," whose destiny was limited to their biological capacity to produce hale and hardy future citizens. Yet as early as the 1930s, eugenically minded birth control pioneers such as Dickinson and Sanger were praising sterilization as a means of freeing women from the anxiety of unwanted pregnancies, enabling them to enjoy sexual pleasure for its own sake. As obstetrician H. Curtis Wood, a longtime member of the sterilization movement, wrote in 1969, a major benefit for the individual patient was that after tubal section "she could have all the sex she desired—without also having babies." This theme of sexual fulfillment through sterilization ("sterilization without unsexing," in Dickinson's words) became increasingly evident long before the 1960s, when women ostensibly began to reap the benefits of detaching sex from motherhood. By celebrating the virtues of female sexual desire for its own sake, sterilization advocates were early exponents of the theory that gender roles were socially constructed. They helped to pave the way for the remarkable strides women took in the 1960s and 1970s to emancipate themselves from conventional roles as homemakers and baby-makers. By promoting vasectomy, sterilization advocates also bolstered the feminist demand that men, too, take responsibility for reproductive decisions, in the process altering gendered notions of masculinity. Not all sterilization advocates endorsed these pivotal social changes to the status of women, but in crafting their message that sterilization was a fundamental birth control right, they either intentionally or "inadvertently contributed to a 'discourse of discontent' that laid the groundwork for women's liberation."[25] Thus, historians who differentiate earlier generations of birth control reformers from more recent reproductive-rights activists are drawing distinctions that the past cannot support. Continuity, more than discontinuity, governs the history of the family-planning movement in the twentieth century. While much about this history has changed, much has remained the same.

As Chapter 1 shows, the history of voluntary sterilization began in the depths of the Great Depression of the 1930s. The surgical procedures of vasectomy and tubal ligation had been pioneered around the turn of the twentieth century, but by the 1930s, acceptance of sterilization had been largely limited to its eugenic usefulness. Thirty states had passed laws permitting the sterilization of handicapped persons, but in the 1930s the eugenics movement was undergoing an unsettling transition. The movement was reeling from criticism that it smacked of Nazi-like "Nordic" thinking. Biologists also argued that the eugenic emphasis on the inheritability of many mental and physical traits was unscientific. Additionally, pro-sterilization eugenicists faced powerful cultural and political opposition in the form of the Roman Catholic Church. It was at this unpropitious moment in the history of eugenics that the social worker Marian Olden decided to agitate for such a law in New Jersey. Her role in founding the SLNJ and her eventual failure to persuade the state's legislators to enact a sterilization law signaled the end of one era and the beginning of another in the history of eugenics.

Chapter 2 describes the difficulties of American sterilization advocates in the post–World War II years. Besides Roman Catholic opposition and divisions within their own ranks, they encountered resistance from the medical profession. Even though sterilization as a surgical operation was legal in all but two American states, most physicians and hospitals refused to perform the procedure when asked. Sterilization proponents decided that, in the wake of revelations about Nazi atrocities during the war, it was impossible to convince state legislators to pass additional eugenic sterilization laws. Instead, reformers concluded that the best course of action was to persuade the medical profession to liberalize its attitudes toward sterilization and the mainstream birth control movement to support sterilization as a contraceptive method. To do so, however, sterilization advocates concluded that Marian Olden's virulent anti-Catholicism, abrasive personality, and open fondness for coercive sterilization measures were public-relations liabilities. Olden's subsequent marginalization cleared the way for other, less controversial birth control reformers, such as the esteemed gynecologist Alan Guttmacher, to assume leadership of the movement to improve access to sterilization services for the American public.

While trying to break down public, professional, and religious resistance to sterilization in the 1950s, these reformers contended that wider access to sterilization could help low-income couples avoid unwanted pregnancies and thus reduce poverty, as Chapter 3 shows. Yet in advancing the case that sterilization was a welfare measure, they found it difficult to avoid targeting the poor and the mentally challenged in economically depressed regions of the country such as Appalachia. As H. Curtis Wood[26] confided in 1948,

> if the half wits and morons could be talked into sterilization after the birth of a few children, instead of making no attempt to limit their numbers at all, we could at least be getting somewhere. I and several of my friends are doing them quite often on these women on a strictly voluntary basis and it is not hard to talk most of them into it during their pregnancies. They do not want to be bothered with a lot of children and when it is explained to them are only too happy to have it done. We need to educate the doctors to educate their patients.

Comments such as these indicated that eugenic sentiments were still alive and well among sterilization advocates during the early part of the Cold War.

In the 1950s, however, the crusade to liberalize attitudes regarding sterilization received a major boost with the rise of the population control movement, the topic of Chapter 4. More and more American opinion makers began warning about the consequences of rapid population growth, both domestically and abroad. Thanks to this key development, attention shifted quickly to sterilization as the best method for curbing global fertility. Even the introduction of the oral contraceptive pill in the early 1960s did not undermine the support for sterilization as a birth control technique.

Benefiting from this trend was the then HBAA. In 1964, Hugh Moore, millionaire inventor of the Dixie Cup and the most outspoken American advocate of population control, became the HBAA president, infusing the organization with his money and energy. Reflecting the fact that the respectability of sterilization was on the rise, Moore, who coined the term "the population bomb" before it was popularized in 1968 by biologist Paul

Ehrlich, changed the HBAA's name to the Association for Voluntary Sterilization. By the end of the turbulent 1960s, amidst the widespread countercultural ferment of that era, Moore had generated enormous publicity for sterilization in general and the AVS in particular. His success was crowned in 1972 when, for the first time, the AVS began receiving funding from the U.S. Agency for International Development. By then, the AVS had emerged as not only America's most effective lobbying group for U.S. funding for sterilization programs in the developing world but also the nation's foremost think tank for policy discussions about sterilization's impact on global fertility. Moore and the AVS stressed that they endorsed only voluntary sterilization, but their catastrophist predictions of what would happen if population growth were not seriously curtailed hinted darkly that coercive sterilization might be necessary.

Chapter 4 also covers the rise in popularity of sterilization as a contraceptive measure in developing countries such as India during the 1960s and 1970s. Among sterilization proponents on the international stage, few enjoyed as much power and prestige as Sripati Chandrasekhar, India's U.S.-educated Minister for Health and Family Planning. Thanks to Chandrasehkar, between the 1950s and the 1980s, India's birth rate dropped from six per woman to three. Yet in part this was accomplished through authoritarian methods, which ultimately led to the defeat of Indira Gandhi's government in 1977. Countless Indians were rounded up and herded into "family planning camps" where deception, financial incentives, and outright bullying were often used to meet sterilization quotas imposed on health-care workers by the central and state governments. But Chandrasekhar's impact did not end at India's borders: the international media repeatedly broadcast his message that sterilization was the "only salvation for mankind's survival" in countries throughout the developed and developing world. Arguably, no single individual did more to popularize sterilization as a birth control method than Chandrasekhar.

Domestically, as Chapter 5 illustrates, the pro-sterilization campaign was making similarly impressive progress as the 1970s dawned. As early as 1961, the American Medical Association had stated that sterilization posed no greater danger of civil liability than any other medical or surgical procedure. Later, private insurers such as Blue Cross/Blue Shield began covering voluntary sterilizations. In 1969, the American College of Obstetricians and Gynecologists (ACOG) declared that sterilization could be performed on anyone who was legally capable of giving consent. (Prior to 1969, ACOG had used an age/parity formula based on a woman's age and number of children as its criterion for sterilizing a female patient.)

In the early 1970s, AVS allied with the American Civil Liberties Union and the conservationist group Zero Population Growth in a successful campaign to threaten hospitals with litigation if they refused to perform elective sterilizations.

On another front, amid fears about complications stemming from use of the Pill, women's rights activists openly celebrated the virtues of sterilization. Self-described feminists also urged men to undergo vasectomies as a further way of emancipating women from the "biological subjugation" of unwanted pregnancy. Within this context, vasectomy could be a "revolutionary and feminist action for a man." The result of these and countless other declarations was an annual national sterilization rate that in the early 1970s reached about 1 million operations for men and women.

Yet, as we see in Chapter 6, at the very peak of the sterilization movement's success in the 1970s, changes in America's political and cultural climate compelled its advocates to shift their principal attention overseas. In 1971, the U.S. Office of Economic Opportunity began providing funding for voluntary sterilization services, a major victory for the AVS. But in the 1970s, scandals erupted over the sterilization of low-income, minority women without informed consent. The AVS, which had helped to draw up the guidelines regulating federal services, swiftly became the target of interest groups that accused it of abetting racial genocide. Then a series of court cases made it virtually impossible for concerned parents to have their retarded children legally sterilized. Feeling deserted by many of their traditional allies, AVS leaders decided to devote the bulk of their efforts to providing sterilization services in the Third World, where governments, courts, and funding agencies were much less hostile to the notion of curbing fertility through sterilization.

Chapter 7 describes the era since Ronald Reagan's election as president in 1980. Over these years, sterilization proponents, like the family-planning movement in general, have had to cope with periodic attempts by a conservative White House and Congress to cut federal funding for overseas programs. In their approach to strategic planning, they have faced the challenges of a global environment characterized by opposition from resourceful and well-funded interest groups. This opposition has profoundly affected their approaches to research, policy development, and issue advocacy. As long as countries such as India and the People's Republic of China enacted strict fertility control programs, sterilization advocates could plausibly maintain that a population "bomb" threatened the very survival of the globe.

But, recently, more and more governments are saying they need to *increase* birth rates. So compelling is this argument that, in 2004, the People's Republic of China reportedly was reconsidering its policy of restricting Chinese couples to a single child. Besides the fear that there may not be a tax base in the future to fund government programs, the Chinese are motivated by another worry: because most Chinese deem sons to be more valuable than daughters, especially in rural areas, male births surpass female births. The surplus of males without prospects for life partners has led to rising rates of prostitution, rape, trafficking of women, and gang violence in the streets of China. Now that the same concerns are being expressed about the "free-fall" in the number of female babies born in India, questions about the past efforts of groups such as EngenderHealth are bound to multiply.[27]

A historical perspective demonstrates that the past has weighed heavily on the efforts of family planners to translate their mission statements into reality. For years, the ghosts of eugenics have haunted their campaign, no thanks to the random statements of various outspoken activists. Sterilization advocates have been hamstrung by a chronic problem afflicting all policy attempts to lower fertility rates, no matter what their intentions: when the supposed beneficiaries of such programs have a different skin color, or suffer from poverty, or live with disabilities, the boundaries between "voluntary" and "involuntary" inevitably become blurred, no matter how many safeguards are in place. When calls for expanded family-planning services throughout the developing world are couched in alarmist language that highlights runaway population growth, similar confusion between coercion and consent is bound to flourish. The United Nations now deems family planning to be a human right, but historically the right to limit family size and one's "duty" to save the planet and revolutionize the status of women through family planning have often been conflated. As this book reveals, groups like EngenderHealth have frequently found it difficult to separate improving access to surgical contraception from propagandistic efforts to increase the sterilization rate among the poor and powerless. All too often, population control organizations have operated on the assumption that they knew best which pregnancies were wanted and which were not.

This ambiguity surrounding the fine line between choice and compulsion has a special relevance in the early twenty-first century, when some political philosophers are hailing a "liberal eugenics" based on the remarkable advances in reproductive and genetic technology. Notable liberal philosophers such as John Rawls invoke the doctrine of personal autonomy to defend the right of parents to use whatever technological means at their disposal to "insure for their descendants the best genetic endowment." Yet Rawls himself admits that there are social justifications for voluntary eugenics, such as easing public financial burdens by preventing the spread of genetic defects throughout the community. The trouble is that in a society that accepts elective eugenics, children with imperfections (and the parents who brought them into the world) would feel as stigmatized as ever.[28] They could also suffer discrimination at the hands of the insurance industry or medical providers. The growing talk in America and throughout the industrialized world about the future affordability of health care makes the possibility of such illiberal consequences all too real. The history of population control is a reminder that not so long ago, "voluntary" sterilization was all the rage because it was considered to be the responsible thing to do in a crisis-filled world of rapidly escalating scarcity.

Put another way, it is supremely difficult, if not impossible, to pursue personal autonomy in reproductive matters without affecting the quality of life for other people. Personal choices inevitably have social consequences. Yet the history of the sterilization movement teaches that determining where involuntarism ends and pure freedom begins is not a new problem for today's bioethicists. Whether it is Bill McKibben opting for a vasectomy or infertile couples shopping at sperm banks, removing overt coercion does not mean that such practices necessarily cease to be eugenics. The mounting media attention to recent advances in genetics and technologies like cloning and gene therapy ensures that the debate over reproductive ethics will intensify as the twenty-first century continues to unfold.

Notes

1. Longman P. *The Empty Cradle: How Falling Birthrates Threaten World Prosperity and What to Do About It.* New York: Basic, 2004; Wattenberg B. *Fewer: How the New Demography of Depopulation Will Shape Our Future.* Chicago: Ivan R. Dee, 2004.
2. Samuelson RJ. "The end of Europe." *Washington Post*, June 15, 2005, p. A25; "Making babies." *Wall Street Journal*, June 2, 2006, p. W13.
3. Hudson V, Den Boer A. *Bare Branches: The Security Implications of Asia's Surplus Male Population.* Cambridge, MA: MIT Press, 2004.
4. On the factors that have affected the fall in fertility, see Wattenberg B. *Fewer: How the New Demography of Depopulation Will Shape Our Future.* Chicago: Ivan R.

Dee, 2004, pp. 94–109. A 1998 RAND study estimated that 40% of the decline in fertility in the developing world from the 1960s to the 1990s was due to the impact of family programs alone (http://www.engenderhealth .org/pubs/enews/wt02.html).

5. Piccinino LJ, Mosher WD. Trends in contraceptive use in the United States. *Family Planning Perspectives.* 1998;30:4–10. See also Current Contraceptive Status and Method for Women, United States, 1995, National Center for Health Statistics, http://www.cdc.gov/nchs/datawh/statab/pubd/2319; and Sollom T, Benson Gold R, Saul R. Public funding for contraceptive, sterilization, and abortion services. *Family Planning Perspectives.* 1996;28:167–173.

6. See Marks LV. *Sexual Chemistry: The History of the Contraceptive Pill.* New Haven and London: Yale University Press, 2001. See also Tone A. *Devices and Desires: A History of Contraceptives in America.* New York: Hill and Wang, 2002.

7. Piccinino LJ, Mosher WD. Trends in contraceptive use in the United States. *Family Planning Perspectives.* 1998;30:4–10.

8. Lader L (Ed.). *Foolproof Birth Control: Male and Female Sterilization.* Boston: Beacon Press, 1972, p. 2.

9. Wolfers D, Wolfers H. Vasectomania. *Family Planning Perspectives.* 1973;5:196–199.

10. Landman LC. Fourth International Conference on Voluntary Sterilization. *Family Planning Perspectives.* 1979;11:241–247.

11. Ross JA. Sterilization: past, present, future. *Studies in Family Planning.* 1992;23:187–198.

12. Sharpless J. World population growth, family planning, and American foreign policy. In Critchlow DT (Ed.), *The Politics of Abortion and Birth Control in Historical Perspective.* University Park: The Pennsylvania State University Press, 1996, pp. 72–102. See also Donaldson PJ. *Nature Against Us: The United States and the World Population Crisis, 1965–1980.* Chapel Hill: University of North Carolina Press, 1990.

13. Donaldson PJ. *Nature Against Us: The United States and the World Population Crisis, 1965–1980.* Chapel Hill: University of North Carolina Press, 1990, p. 26.

14. For the history of U.S. eugenics, see Haller M. *Eugenics: Hereditarian Attitudes in American Thought.* New Brunswick: Rutgers University Press, 1963; Pickens DK. *Eugenics and the Progressives.* Nashville: Vanderbilt University Press, 1969; Ludmerer KM. *Genetics and American Society: A Historical Appraisal.* Baltimore and London: Johns Hopkins University Press, 1972; Kevles DJ. *In the Name of Eugenics: Genetics and the Uses of Human Heredity.* New York: Knopf, 1985; Mehler BA. *A History of the American Eugenics Society, 1921–1940.* University of Illinois at Urbana-Champaign: Unpublished doctoral dissertation, 1988; Larson EJ. *Sex, Race, and Science: Eugenics in the Deep South.* Baltimore and London: Johns Hopkins University Press, 1995; Hasian MA. *The Rhetoric of Eugenics in Anglo-American Thought.* Athens: University of Georgia Press, 1996; Dowbiggin IR. *Keeping America Sane: Psychiatry and Eugenics in the United States*

and Canada, 1880–1940. Ithaca: Cornell University Press, 1997; Rafter NH. *Creating Born Criminals: Biological Theories of Crime and Eugenics.* Urbana: University of Illinois Press, 1997.

15. Philip R. Reilly discusses at length the history of sterilization, but he is principally interested in the history of *involuntary* sterilization. See his *The Surgical Solution: A History of Involuntary Sterilization in the United States.* Baltimore and London: The Johns Hopkins University Press, 1991. Thomas M. Shapiro's *Population Control Politics: Women, Sterilization, and Reproductive Choice* (Philadelphia: Temple University Press, 1985) is useful for its attention to the conflicts over sterilization in the 1970s. See also Trombley S. *The Right to Reproduce: A History of Coercive Sterilization.* London: Weidenfeld and Nicholson, 1988.

16. The only history of EngenderHealth is William R. Vanessendelft's 1978 University of Minnesota unpublished doctoral dissertation, *A History of the Association for Voluntary Sterilization, 1935–1964.* As the title indicates, he covered only the period in the group's history up to the mid-1960s.

17. For an insightful analysis of this and other factors shaping modern U.S. policy history, see Critchlow DT. *Intended Consequences: Birth Control, Abortion, and the Federal Government in Modern America.* New York and Oxford: Oxford University Press, 1999.

18. Dowbiggin IR. *Keeping America Sane* (see Note 14); Dowbiggin IR. *A Merciful End: The Euthanasia Movement in Modern America.* New York and Oxford: Oxford University Press, 2003.

19. Moya Woodside to Ruth Smith, December 23, 1966, RPS, Box 1, Folder 3.

20. Hunter JD. *Culture Wars: The Struggle to Define America.* New York: Basic, 1991, pp. 44–45.

21. See Black E. *The War Against the Weak: Eugenics and America's Campaign to Create a Master Race.* New York: Four Walls and Eight Windows, 2003. For other accounts of the history of American eugenics that stress the same theme, see Kuhl S. *The Nazi Connection: Eugenics, American Racism, and German National Socialism.* New York and Oxford: Oxford University Press, 1994; Mehler B. Beyondism: Raymond B. Cattell and the New Eugenics. *Genetica.* 1997; 99:153–165; Winston AS. Science in the service of the Far Right: Henry E. Garrett, the IAAEE, and the Liberty Lobby. *Journal of Social Issues.* 1998; 54:179–210.

22. Ladd-Taylor M. Eugenics, sterilization and modern marriage in the USA: The strange career of Paul Popenoe. *Gender and History.* 2001;13:298–327; Kline W. *Building a Better Race: Gender, Sexuality and Eugenics from the Turn of the Century to the Baby Boom.* Berkeley: University of California Press, 2001, pp. 54–56, 81–84, 140–156, 161–164; Stern AM. *Eugenic Nation: Faults and Frontiers of Better Breeding in Modern America.* Berkeley: University of California Press, 2005, pp. 156–164, 193–199.

23. Paul D. *Controlling Human Heredity: 1865 to the Present.* Atlantic Highland, NJ: Humanities Press, 1995, pp. 117–121.

24. Rosen C. *Preaching Eugenics: Religious Leaders and the American Eugenics Movement.* New York and Oxford: Oxford University Press, 2003.

25. Ladd-Taylor M. Eugenics, sterilization, and modern marriage in the USA: The strange career of Paul Popenoe. *Gender and History.* 2001;3:322.

26. H. Curtis Wood to Robert Latou Dickinson, November 22, 1948, AVS, Box 2, folder 15.

27. Azizur Rhaman S. Where the girls aren't. *The Globe and Mail,* October 16, 2004, p. F2; Aborting female fetuses distorts India's sex ratio. *National Post,* August 5, 2005, p. A11; China's boy trouble. *Globe and Mail,* December 11, 2004, p. F5.

28. For a searching criticism of Rawls, see Sandel M. The case against perfection. *The Atlantic Monthly.* April 2004, pp. 51–62.

Chapter 1

Up From Eugenics

The Great Depression of the 1930s was a dismal time for millions around the world. Yet to Marian Olden (1888–1981), a volunteer social worker and wife of a Princeton University professor, the Depression was the best of times for realizing her great goal in life.[1]

For Olden, the most pressing need in Depression-era America was the enactment of laws permitting the sterilization of people with mental disabilities, notably in her home state of New Jersey. By the mid-1930s, over thirty American states, two Canadian provinces, and numerous countries around the world had already passed comparable legislation. Opinion polls told her that many Americans supported these kinds of laws. Throughout the United States and across the globe, countless scientists, physicians, academics, intellectuals, and journalists also endorsed the sterilization of the mentally handicapped and other eugenic policies. *Eugenics*, a term coined in 1883 by Francis Galton, Charles Darwin's cousin, referred to the scientific study of ways to improve human breeding. George Bernard Shaw, H. G. Wells, H. L. Mencken, Teddy Roosevelt, Jack London, Helen Keller, Margaret Sanger (see center insert), and Alexander Graham Bell are some of the luminaries who at one time or another expressed support for eugenics. As she studied social conditions during the Depression, Olden could be forgiven for thinking that she was riding the crest of a massive international wave of informed opinion.

Events would soon prove that Marian Olden had misread the precise temper of her times, but even if she had somehow known beforehand that a sterilization law in New Jersey would fail, it is still doubtful that this knowledge would have deterred her from pursuing her goal. As she admitted many years later, "My difficulty was that I'm not a compromiser," a major reason New Jersey declined to enact her proposed sterilization bill.[2] Olden's refusal to compromise also prompted the group she founded in 1937, the Princeton-based Sterilization League of New Jersey (SLNJ), to expel her unceremoniously some ten years later. By then, however, Olden's vision of sterilization as the remedy for poverty-stricken and unhealthy people had helped to set in motion a series of events that ultimately touched the lives of millions of men and women throughout the world over the course of the twentieth century.

The Birth of Eugenics

Just as Marian Olden began planning a campaign to persuade New Jersey's elected officials to pass a sterilization law, the word "eugenics" was starting to fall out of favor, in a steady decline that reached its nadir in the 1970s. Yet until World War II, eugenics was one of the most fashionable social reform movements in American history. A major accomplishment of the eugenics movement was its success during the early twentieth century in breaking down resistance to both vasectomy for men and tubal ligation for women, the first phase of the crusade to curb global fertility that spanned the Cold War era.

Eugenics dated back to the nineteenth-century interest in biological theories about the natural history of the human race. Since the early nineteenth century, leading naturalists such as Jean-Baptiste de Lamarck (1744–1829) and Georges Cuvier (1769–1832) had been documenting how much species changed over long stretches of time. By the mid-nineteenth century, most biologists agreed that species were mutable, but there was little agreement as to what caused them to change and which (if any) species were descended from a common ancestor. To account for the modification of species, biologists studied the hereditary transmission of features from generation to generation. Gregor Mendel, a monk who conducted pioneering experiments with pea plants, had published his findings in the 1860s that heredity was determined by fixed factors (or "genes"). Yet his results were ignored until the early twentieth century, and in the meantime speculation abounded about exactly what offspring inherited from their ancestors.

A popular theory that stimulated scientific interest in heredity was that of degeneration. Introduced by the French psychiatrist Bénédict-Augustin Morel (1809–1871) in 1857, the theory of degeneration stated that in unhealthy living conditions, human beings could acquire a wide range of pathological traits, including emotional disorders and mental retardation, and then pass them on to their progeny. Morel's theory not only spread among physicians and scientists around the world but also shaped the views of writers such as Emile Zola, whose twenty-volume *Rougon-Macquart* series of novels (1869–1893) evocatively depicted how degeneration routinely destroyed countless families caught up in the vicious cycle of poverty, depravity, sickness, and drunkenness. Adherents to degeneration theory frequently differed over its details, but the common denominator to all versions of degeneration theory was the belief that late-nineteenth-century civilized society was threatened by a hereditary plague of mental, physical, and behavioral deviance. The danger was that the human race would become less biologically robust as time went on, unless steps were taken to curtail the breeding of "degenerates."[3]

At roughly the same time, another major development in the history of science sparked similar interest in the effects of human reproduction on the human race. Two years after Morel published his findings on degeneration, Charles Darwin's *Origin of Species* (1859) introduced a new and persuasive explanation for the immense diversity of flora and fauna on earth. Darwin (1809–1882), using data that he had gathered during his voyage on the British ship the *Beagle* (1831–1836) and inspired by his reading of Thomas Malthus's *Essay on the Principle of Population* (1798), hypothesized that throughout natural history, species were modified because the fittest individuals survived the fierce struggle for existence over nature's limited food supply. Those who survived tended to transmit their favored traits through heredity more often than supposedly "unfit" individuals, thus accounting for the changes species underwent over time. Darwin called the whole process "natural selection," claiming it dispensed with the need to invoke the special creation of species by God. In Darwin's eyes, natural selection was even sufficient to bring about new species. The overall message of Darwin's theory was optimistic, implying that natural laws were slowly but steadily working to modify species in a generally progressive direction. The evolution of the human race, with its gradual ascent from barbarism to civilization, seemed to vindicate Darwin.[4]

Yet, in his less optimistic *Descent of Man* (1871), Darwin argued that the evolutionary progress of the human race was not an "invariable rule." Ironically, the very growth of civilization increased the risk of degeneration, according to Darwin. Hospitals, asylums, welfare programs, and therapeutic medicine interfered with natural selection, enabling the "weak members" of society to survive and reproduce their own kind. Worse, "the reckless, degraded, and often vicious members of society tend to increase at a quicker rate than the provident and generally virtuous members," Darwin wrote. Unless some way was found to prevent the so-called "unfit" from breeding, civilization faced a nightmare of historic proportions: eventually the unfit classes would swamp the fit classes through sheer weight of numbers. The political consequences of a teeming, fertile underclass of lawless, drunken, and immoral "degenerates" caused many sleepless nights for respectable Victorians.[5]

Darwin, although impressed with the results of animal breeding himself, shrank from endorsing the deliberate breeding of humans as a way of combating degeneration. His cousin, the brilliant amateur scientist Francis Galton (1822–1911), was not as reluctant. In 1883, Galton invented the term "eugenics" (from the Greek for "good birth") to describe his plan for improving the human race through "judicious mating" and the control of "all influences that tend in however remote degree to give the more suitable races or strains of blood a better chance of prevailing speedily over the less suitable than they otherwise would have had."[6] A convinced evolutionist himself, Galton believed that it was time to replace the "purposelessness" of natural selection with eugenics. "What nature does blindly, slowly, ruthlessly, man may do providently, quickly, and kindly," Galton wrote.[7] Eugenics, he maintained, could be divided into either positive eugenics, encouraging the fit to breed, or negative eugenics, preventing the unfit from reproducing. U.S. President Theodore Roosevelt captured the spirit of positive eugenics in 1910 when he exclaimed that "some day we will realize that the prime duty, the inescapable duty, of the *good* citizen of the right type is to leave his or her blood behind him in the world."[8] Initially Galton preferred positive eugenics, but late in life he stated that "the first object of eugenics is to check the birth rate of the unfit, instead of allowing them to come into being."[9] Galton never advocated sterilization as a form of negative eugenics. Yet in the long term he helped to kindle keen interest in exploring different ways of translating negative eugenics into clinical medicine and public policy.

Surgical Sterilization

At the same time as eugenics was catching fire as a social reform movement, developments in medicine pointed to revolutionary methods for putting Galton's theories into practice. Medicine was undergoing a "therapeutic revolution" at the end of the nineteenth century as physicians increasingly emphasized localized disease processes as the source of illness and searched for curative treatments for each pathological condition. Prior to the therapeutic revolution, physicians and the general public held that illness was due to an imbalance in "humours," or bodily fluids thought to determine temperament and health. To restore humoral balance, physicians resorted to a variety of therapies, including purgatives, emetics, and bloodletting. As the twentieth century dawned, the focus of therapeutics was shifting from individual patients to specific diseases caused by anatomical or physiological lesions. Doctors of the therapeutic revolution typically sought to discover what disease was ailing each patient and to devise a particular treatment that was best for each medical condition.[10]

Surgical sterilization was one such treatment that emerged during the therapeutic revolution. Sterilization became a feasible medical option thanks to striking developments in surgical practice. The introduction of anesthesia (first demonstrated in 1846 at the Massachusetts General Hospital) and the widespread acceptance of Joseph Lister's aseptic techniques for preventing infection in the 1880s and 1890s meant that surgeons could undertake bodily cavity operations that had long been "associated with scenes of anguish and terror." As one U.S. surgeon exclaimed in 1888, "Abdominal surgery is now the field where the most brilliant successes are to be attained. . . . No branch of surgery can compare with it for a moment."[11]

Following fast on the heels of such breakthroughs was the emergence of gynecology as a medical specialty. For centuries, doctors had treated women suffering from a wide range of conditions afflicting their reproductive and sexual organs, including vaginal fistulas; prolapsed uterus (the falling of the womb); and uterine cancers, cysts, and hemorrhaging.[12] The mounting interest in pathological anatomy in the early nineteenth century generated new knowledge about women's bodies and encouraged clinicians to focus on internal organs as the sites of disease. Yet it was the advent of modern surgery that chiefly led to the professionalization of gynecology in the late nineteenth century. Before then, most physicians had been reluctant to operate on women for fear of the pain they would inflict on patients. Once surgery became much safer and less traumatic, doctors recognized that it would prove to be "the pivot around which is to revolve the gynecology of the future," as an American physician declared in 1879. Ten years later, an Alabama doctor exclaimed, "Operative gynecology is now sweeping the world" (p. 99).[13]

As gynecological surgery became more acceptable in the late nineteenth century, physicians either developed new operations or performed old procedures with unprecedented enthusiasm and regularity. Among the operations that ended women's fertility were ovariotomy (excision of the ovaries), hysterectomy (removal of the uterus), and tubal ligation (bilateral cutting and tying of the fallopian tubes). Between 1701 and 1851 there were 222 recorded ovariotomies in Europe and the United States combined. The high death rate (two out of every three patients) due to shock, infection, or hemorrhage dictated that the procedure was usually a last resort to save extremely sick women from certain death. But once fears about patient mortality began to subside, ovariotomies and hysterectomies became more and more frequent. Physicians recommended surgery even when there was no evidence that a woman's organs were diseased. Surgeon Robert Battey gained notoriety for removing healthy ovaries as a treatment for menstrual problems and sexual nervous disorders. "Battey's operation" sparked such an alacrity for pelvic surgery on women that one practitioner dubbed it a "fad" of the late nineteenth century.[14]

The popularity of ovariotomy had a significant impact on the incidence of hysterectomy. "After you have laid hands on the ovaries," a U.S. physician stated in 1895, "it matters not what becomes of the uterus" (p. 81).[15] Removal of the uterus through the vagina dated back to classical antiquity, and a handful of skilled, early-nineteenth-century surgeons even managed to save some of their patients when performing hysterectomies. The first abdominal hysterectomy was performed by the American Charles Clay in 1844, but by the 1860s operative mortality was still as high as 90%. Then, thanks to anesthesia and antisepsis, the number of hysterectomies began to climb dramatically, until the operation became commonplace in the twentieth century. As one British physician predicted in 1904, "Hysterectomy has a wonderful future."[16] He was right: by the 1980s, millions of U.S. women had undergone the operation.[17]

Some physicians, including Elizabeth Blackwell, America's first formally educated woman physician, criticized their colleagues for "reckless" operations on women based on "inadequate and erroneous conceptions of pathological conditions" (p. 110).[13] In 1936, a Georgia internist reminisced about how late-nineteenth-century ovariotomies were often "instances of the bias that money-mindedness can give."[18] Opponents lashed back that some patients badgered surgeons to have their sexual organs removed.[19] Nor did Blackwell's attempts to rally female physicians against the sterilization of women succeed. Mary Putnam Jacobi, another pioneering woman physician, replied that there was no "special sanctity to the ovary." If male doctors supported Blackwell, it was often for reasons such as those cited by the U.S. gynecologist who in 1906 stated that "[a] woman's ovaries belong to the commonwealth . . . [S]he is simply their custodian" (p. 108).[13] As the rate of gynecological surgery soared over the course of the twentieth century, to whom a woman's reproductive organs belonged was a question that sparked livelier and livelier debate.

Amid the ferment within medicine surrounding gynecological surgery, physicians began experimenting with tubal ligation. Until the 1880s, the only method of asexualization for both men and women was castration—removing the ovaries, womb, or testes. Tubal sterilization would later become the most popular form of contraception in various countries around the world, including the United States. Meanwhile, it faced a steeper uphill battle for acceptance than either ovariotomy or hysterectomy. While the latter two operations could be justified on the basis of their curative value, especially in cases of cancer, it was difficult to hide the fact that tubal ligation was chiefly intended to prevent pregnancy. In fact, tubal sterilization was initially proposed, in 1823, by the British physician James Blundell as a way of avoiding repeated cesarean section. The first successful tubal sterilization was performed in 1880 by the U.S. surgeon Samuel Lungren, but the German doctor Madlener did the most to develop the procedure by operating on eighty-nine women between 1910 and 1920, with only three postoperative deaths. Madlener's technique of ligation and crushing proved to be the most popular method of tubal sterilization until the 1970s.[20]

Operations on the sex organs of men also became more numerous during the ascendancy of surgery at the end of the nineteenth century. Physicians were the first to admit that men were extremely averse to operations on their genitals, but male circumcision (excising the prepuce, or foreskin of the penis) enjoyed a vogue at the time (p. 94).[21] The earliest American report of vasectomy, or the severing of the vas deferens through a slit in the scrotum, was published in 1897 by A. J. Ochsner, a Chicago surgeon who was treating two patients suffering from prostate problems. Ochsner claimed that both patients improved after the operation. Yet, in a sign of things to come, Ochsner also advocated male sterilization for "chronic inebriates, imbeciles, perverts, and paupers," as well as criminals. To him, vasectomy was a simple, reliable means of stemming the tide of degeneracy. Vasectomy was clearly superior to outright castration, a more controversial form of sterilization. Indeed, only a few years prior to Ochsner's report, Hoyt Pilcher, medical superintendent of the Asylum for Idiots and Feeble-Minded Youths in Winfield, Kansas, had lost his job after it was revealed he had castrated 14 girls and 44 boys at his institution. The discovery of a less mutilating form of sterilization that seemingly did not rob patients of their sexual desire captured the imagination of other physicians who were growing increasingly concerned about the fertility of society's "unfit" groups.

One such physician was Harry C. Sharp, surgeon for the Indiana Reformatory, a penal institution for boys. In 1902, he reported he had performed the operation on 42 prison inmates ranging in age from 17 to 25. The results, he claimed, were impressive. The patients "feel that they are stronger, sleep better, their memory improves, the will becomes stronger, and they do better in school." Every male who entered a reformatory, insane asylum, prison, or home for the mentally retarded should be sterilized, Sharp advised. His announcement was "virtually a manifesto for a sterilization movement," in the words of one historian.[22]

As the nineteenth century drew to a close, operations whose primary aim was to end male and female fertility were still considered radical procedures and enjoyed the support of only a tiny fraction of the medical profession and general public. Sterilization for medical purposes was not against the law, but surgeons understandably worried that by operating they might be charged with "mayhem," the "unlawful and malicious removal of a member of a human being or the disabling or disfiguring thereof or rendering it useless." This old English law made it a felony to "castrate or maim another" with the "intent to render impotent." The fear of being charged with mayhem was borne out in 1936, when a San Francisco heiress filed a $500,000 damage suit against her mother and the two surgeons who had sterilized her without her knowledge in 1934.[23] Surgeons who sterilized men or women for contraceptive purposes alone might be liable to legal action and could forfeit their medical malpractice insurance, leaving them to pay for their own defense and any fines levied against them.[24]

Meanwhile, however, the nineteenth century marked the most significant watershed in the entire history of medicine. Innovations in gynecological surgery meant French historian Jules Michelet had not been far wrong when, in 1868, he called the nineteenth century "the age of the womb," ushering in a new era filled with hope that the quality of life for women would improve dramatically (p. 64).[15] The introduction of vasectomy, though less heralded at the time, would prove to be another noteworthy surgical advance. As the twentieth century wore on, opposition to sterilization would gradually melt away as surgical contraception became a reality for millions of men and women around the world.

Eugenic Sterilization

Nothing accelerated the acceptance of surgical sterilization more than the rise of eugenics. In the first two decades of the twentieth century, eugenics went from being an idea with limited backing in scientific and medical circles to a concept that tended to dominate debate over public health policy in country after country[25]—and no nation was more receptive to eugenics than the United States. Most of America's geneticists, biologists, physicians, and social scientists embraced eugenics, a trend that culminated in the founding of the American Eugenics Society (AES) in 1923.[26] Eugenics pervaded college, university, and high school curricula. The Carnegie and Rockefeller Foundations funded eugenic research. Eugenics seeped into popular culture, too, evident in the "better baby contests" and numerous movies and stage dramas about the dangers of sexually transmitted diseases. Until the 1930s, America vied with Germany for international leadership of the eugenics movement, including the enactment of laws permitting the sterilization of people with mental and physical disabilities.

Twentieth-century advocacy in favor of sterilizing the mentally ill and other vulnerable social groups spanned continents. The British physician Robert Rentoul wrote in 1903 that degenerates "should be sterilized, and so rendered unable to beget offspring."[27] The science fiction author H. G. Wells similarly urged the "sterilization of [society's] failures," whether they wished it or not.[28] Early-twentieth-century support for sterilization also emerged in Germany, even though it was still illegal there. Some leading German physicians and scientists, including Ernst Rüdin, professor of psychiatry at the University of Munich, defended compulsory sterilization as the most efficient way of ridding society of "bad heredity."[29] German enthusiasm for involuntary sterilization culminated in 1933, shortly after the Nazis came to power, in the Third Reich's sterilization law, targeting schizophrenics; epileptics; alcoholics; the mentally retarded; and sufferers of manic depression, Huntington's chorea, and hereditary blindness and deafness. By the outbreak of World War II, in 1939, approximately 400,000 Germans had been sterilized under the nation's 1933 law.

In the United States, Indiana was the first state to pass a eugenic sterilization bill (1907). By 1912, eight other states had followed suit. The momentum of the sterilization movement slowed between 1913 and 1918, when seven state laws were constitutionally challenged and each challenge succeeded. Informed opinion may have been growing incrementally more pro-eugenic, but medical and public health experts were divided over the virtues of sterilization. Some thought it inhumane and preferred segregating the handicapped in special institutions as a means of preventing their reproduction. Others believed that by separating sex from reproduction, sterilization would foster immorality and venereal disease. Operations were few under the existing laws and were limited mostly to patients of mental hospitals (pp. 82–83).[28]

Yet in 1923, support for eugenic sterilization in the United States was revived. That year, sterilization laws were enacted in Oregon, Delaware, Montana, and Michigan. In 1924, Virginia joined the bandwagon, as did seven other states, in 1925. By the end of 1925, seventeen states had made eugenic sterilization legal (p. 84).[22]

The ink on Virginia's involuntary sterilization bill was barely dry before the statute's constitutionality was challenged. The now-infamous case involved an eighteen-year-old woman named Carrie E. Buck, an inmate of the State Colony for Epileptics and Feeble-Minded and the illegitimate daughter of a supposedly feeble-minded woman. Carrie Buck had just given birth to a child also diagnosed as feeble-minded, and her medical superintendent decided she should be sterilized to keep her from becoming pregnant again. Carrie Buck's appeal of this decision wound its way through the courts until it reached the U.S. Supreme Court. In 1927, the court (by a vote of eight to one) upheld the constitutionality of Virginia's law in the *Buck v. Bell* ruling. In the haunting words of Justice Oliver Wendell Holmes, who wrote the majority decision, "the principle that sustains compulsory vaccination is broad enough to cover cutting the Fallopian tubes." To Holmes and most of the court, society was entitled to "prevent those who are manifestly unfit from continuing their kind" (pp. 86–87).[22]

Buoyed by the belief that compulsory sterilization was constitutional, state governments took advantage of *Buck v. Bell*. Between 1927 and 1930, twelve states enacted new, or revised old, sterilization statutes. By the end of 1931, the total number of states with enabling laws had climbed to twenty-eight. All the state sterilization legislation after *Buck v. Bell* included procedural safeguards similar to those in the Virginia law, making the bills immune to constitutional attack. By World War II, thirty American states had passed sterilization legislation (Georgia was the last, in 1937). Over the same time period, Denmark, Norway, Sweden, Finland, Iceland, Switzerland, and two Canadian provinces enacted similar legislation. By the 1970s, when most such laws were repealed, the total number of legal sterilizations in the United States had reached 60,000, with about half occurring in California. The totals for Scandinavia were even higher.[30]

However, by the early 1930s, much of the optimism surrounding sterilization laws had evaporated. Initially, the 1933 Nazi sterilization law was hailed by U.S. eugenicists as a step in the right direction, but as the decade wore on and the racial overtones of Hitler's policies became more and more evident, sterilization advocates in America grew increasingly worried that they might be linked to the Third Reich. In 1940, the Californian Ezra Gosney warned fellow eugenicists that "[w]e have little in this country to consider in *racial integrity*. Germany is pushing that. We should steer clear of it lest we be misunderstood."[31] Once the United States entered World War II against Germany, the last thing any eugenicists wanted were reminders of the similarities between Nazi and American sterilization laws.[32]

Opposition to sterilization was also beginning to mount in the Roman Catholic Church. As long as early-twentieth-century eugenicists talked vaguely about responsible marriage, increasing the birth rate, and the public health virtues of "fit" families, some Catholics expressed "wary acceptance" of eugenics.[33] In the 1920s, two prominent American Catholic clerics even joined the American Eugenics Society (AES), but by 1928 one of them had concluded ruefully that the group's leadership was little more than "a crowd of 'nuts,' " "hopelessly entangled in Nordic presuppositions."[34] In Germany, a handful of Catholic theologians argued that sometimes the state was justified in compelling people unfit for parenthood to refrain from bearing children. The German Jesuit scientist Hermann Muckermann reasoned that eugenic public education could improve the health and size of families and also defended sterilization in cases where patients gave their consent. Yet the coming to power of Adolf Hitler altered the political landscape, so much so that Muckermann was forced to resign from the Kaiser Wilhelm Institute for Anthropology, Human Genetics, and Eugenics in 1933 after he disputed the racial theories of the new Nazi government.[35]

By the 1930s, Catholics were implacable foes of artificial contraceptive methods, including sterilization. In states such as New York, Connecticut, and Colorado, Catholic dioceses and lay Catholic groups mobilized to defeat eugenic sterilization laws.[36] The end of any hopes for a Catholic–eugenics rapprochement came in 1930 with *Casti Connubii*, Pope Pius XI's encyclical on Christian marriage. In addition to condemning contraceptives, Pius XI denounced sterilization. The Pope's words galvanized

Catholics in other areas such as Britain, France, Latin America, and the largely French-speaking Canadian province of Quebec, where Church activism scuttled attempts to legalize eugenic sterilization. Catholics objected to the prejudices and unscientific ideas that they believed riddled eugenics, including the reasoning behind the Supreme Court's *Buck v. Bell* decision. In 1940, a Detroit Jesuit pointedly asked the Carnegie Institute, a generous financial supporter of eugenic research, if Carrie Buck and her daughter were really "mental defectives." It was a good question: subsequent research has demonstrated that neither was mentally retarded.[37]

The growth of genetic knowledge also encouraged second thoughts about eugenic sterilization. Beginning in the late nineteenth century, biologist August Weismann argued that the germ cells found in the reproductive organs were unaltered by environmental influences. Consequently, the view grew that traits such as intelligence and emotional stability were transmitted as unit factors and that certain human traits ran in families; in other words, like begat like. Yet, by the 1930s, geneticists were increasingly aware of the distinctions between phenotype and genotype, as well as those between dominant and recessive genes. What mattered in heredity was the genotype—the organism's genes—and not their expression, or the phenotype. Inheritance mostly rested on a polygenic basis: while eye color was a unit character, other traits such as height and intelligence were the products of multiple genes. Similarly, while some conditions, such as Huntington's chorea, were dominant hereditary traits, many others, such as mental retardation, were recessive, meaning both parents would have to carry the hereditary factor for it to be expressed in offspring. If subnormal intelligence was a recessive hereditary factor, then there were countless otherwise normal people who carried the trait. In 1927, geneticist Raymond Pearl of the Johns Hopkins University took issue with the conventional theory "that superior people will have superior children and inferior people inferior children." By subscribing to this theory, Pearl asserted, "orthodox eugenicists" were "going contrary to the best established facts of genetical science" (p. 114).[22]

In other words, sterilizing someone on the basis of a diagnosis of mental disability was unlikely to have much of an effect on its incidence in the next generation. As the *New York Times* editorialized in 1932, "The evidence is clear that normal persons also carry defective genes which may manifest themselves in an insane progeny . . . . Even if we discovered the carriers of hidden defective genes by applying the methods of the cattle-breeder to humanity, the process would take about a thousand years." The hopes of eugenicists that measures like sterilization would "solve the problem of hereditary defects, close up the asylums for feebleminded and insane, [and] do away with prisons" were unrealistic, concluded the geneticist H. S. Jennings.[38]

Nonetheless, the mounting scientific skepticism about the sweeping claims of sterilization proponents did not mean that faith in sterilization as a medical procedure disappeared. The 1930s were actually the heyday of America's sterilization laws. In 1929, the nation's total of sterilizations was just under 11,000. By the end of 1941, it was 38,000. Over that time span, more than 2,000 Americans on average were sterilized each year under the country's eugenic laws. From 1930 to 1944, almost 11,000 patients were sterilized in Californian institutions alone (pp. 97–102).[22]

The American public did not seem to mind. In 1937, a *Fortune* magazine survey, one of the first opinion polls in U.S. history, found that 66% of its readers supported the measure. That same year, according to a Gallup poll, 84% of the American public backed the sterilization of the chronically mentally ill (including 92% in both the Mountain and Pacific regions).[39] As one South Dakota psychologist told Olden in 1939, the major problem facing sterilization advocates was not "opposition to sterilization as such—but to convince courts that high grade morons are feeble-minded."[40] Most Americans agreed that people with mentally disabilities should be sterilized. The big question was how to identify who qualified for sterilization. Defenders of sterilization repeatedly warned that "high grade morons" were not easily detected, yet they abounded in the community. "You can't always tell by appearances," one sterilization publication cautioned, especially in the case of "defective" girls. "[T]rained sufficiently to pass for normal by those with superficial judgement," these girls "were the greatest menace to the race when returned to the community without the protection of sterilization."[41]

Eugenic ideas had also seeped into popular discussions about public health. In 1930, President Herbert Hoover convened a White House Conference on Child Health and Protection, bringing together hundreds of physicians, psychologists, sociologists, eugenicists, and home economists. According to one physician, the conference "put the parents of the United States on trial," particularly mothers. Hoover addressed the nation on radio in November, 1930, summarizing many of the conclusions the conference reached. "There shall be no child in America," he declared, "that has not the complete birthright of a sound mind in a sound body." Hoover's Child's Bill of Rights called on Americans to make the United States "a fitter country in which to bring up children." Parents had to be much more responsible about reproductive choices and better at meeting high standards of parenthood, the president warned. The White House Conference's Committee on Mental Deficiency advised that one important way to ensure the health of future generations of American children was "selective" sterilization—that is, sterilization performed on a case-by-case basis (pp. 101–103).[42]

This new emphasis in the 1930s on "selective" sterilization for both hereditary and environmental reasons compelled eugenicists to subtly alter their message about sterilization. As one eugenicist said in 1938, "[p]arents produce faulty children by bad rearing as well as by bad heredity" (p. 123).[42] By 1940, gone were most references to mass eugenic sterilization laws as the catch-all solution to cleaning up the nation's gene pool and eradicating poverty, crime, disease, and welfare dependence. In their place were statements that sterilization had to be based on the most up-to-date diagnostic precision and most thorough consideration of each patient as a whole. Sterilization supporters asserted that the operation, used judiciously, not only prevented the transmission of genetic disorders but also prevented children from being exposed to the allegedly inferior parenting of mentally handicapped couples. In 1936, the president of the American Association of Mental Deficiency declared that "the most powerful argument for sterilization today is that which urges that no feeble-minded person is fit to be a parent, whether or not his condition is hereditary and therefore likely to be genetically transmitted."[43] An added bonus was that sterilization supposedly saved "the wrong kinds of parents" from the mental stress of trying to raise children.[44]

U.S. psychiatrist Abraham Myerson's 1936 report on sterilization articulated the emerging consensus in sterilization advocacy. Myerson's conclusions, drawn from an American Neurological Association investigation into the conditions of commitment to and sterilization in mental institutions, have often been cited as a crucial turning point in the history of eugenics. Indeed, Myerson cautioned against expecting state sterilization programs to appreciably lower the incidence of mental disability or affect the overall level of intelligence throughout society. He concluded that most of eugenics was "a mess of incomprehensible bias" and empathetically stated that "so far as mental disease is concerned, the race is not rapidly going to the dogs, as has been the favorite assertion for some time." Yet Myerson still supported the selective sterilization of the mentally disabled and even defended the 1933 Nazi statute.[45]

Myerson's findings indicated that by the late 1930s, eugenics was well on its way to becoming what one historian has described as a "dirty word" in post–World War II scientific circles.[46] No longer was it acceptable to justify the mass sterilization of entire minority groups, as earlier eugenicists had sometimes done. Yet the acceptance of sterilization itself as a method of birth control for the mentally and physically handicapped remained strong. Approval of "selective" sterilization based on what was best for the child, the American family, and the nation appeared to be widespread. The *New York Times* spoke for many Americans when it stated that it was "not opposed to sterilization as such," just "the wild talk of the more ignorant eugenists."[47]

Therapeutic Sterilization

Eugenics may have been the most powerful rationale for sterilization in the first half of the twentieth century, but, as has been discussed, from the first, vasectomy was hailed for its beneficial effects on mental and physical health as well as its effectiveness in curtailing fertility. Many psychiatrists working in state hospitals in the early twentieth century stressed how sterilization could alleviate both the medical and social problems of inmates. Up to the 1930s, psychiatrists in the California State Hospital Service tended to justify decisions to sterilize on the basis of how the operation might improve patients' lives and meet individual patients' needs; rarely did they explicitly emphasize eugenic reasons. Acutely aware of psychiatry's failure to discover effective treatments for mental illness in comparison with the impressive strides general medicine was making, psychiatrists in the early twentieth century often invested their hopes in sterilization as a therapeutic procedure.[48] This led some psychiatrists to champion the then-popular theory that vasectomy caused the patient to absorb testicular secretion, a process thought to "rejuvenate" the individual's body and mind. It seemed to work: as a California psychiatrist insisted in 1924, "[I]n talking to male patients who have benefitted from the operation many claim that in about two weeks after the operation they begin to feel better, that is, their mentality improves and they feel stronger both mentally and physically. I have had a number of men at the hospital ask me to sterilize them after they had seen the beneficial effects of the operation on other patients."[49] The testicular-secretion theory soon proved to be incorrect, but in the meantime psychiatrists urged selected male patients to undergo vasectomy because they sincerely believed in its positive biological effects.

Women, even more than men, were caught up in the early-twentieth-century use of sterilization for therapeutic purposes. Sterilization of men, though a simpler and safer procedure, was mainly limited to institutionalized patients whose parole often depended on their consent to the operation. Otherwise, men generally resisted vasectomy. Some gynecologists, after listening to the complaints of their female patients about repeated pregnancies, advised them to suggest vasectomy to their husbands. "My husband isn't in favor" was the standard reply (p. 66).[50] Men frequently mistook vasectomy for castration. They harbored suspicions that any operation on their genitalia would damage their ability to perform sexually and enjoy intercourse. Or they objected on religious grounds, telling social workers that surgical sterilization was "not what God intended."[51] Even comparatively well-informed male doctors shied away from the operation. In 1909, one U.S. physician taunted his colleagues by asking, "How many of *you* would be willing to have a vasectomy done?"[52]

Women, on the other hand, "don't mind [sterilization] as badly as men," according to a North Carolina social worker (p. 66).[50] In a day and age without reliable, safe, and simple birth control methods, many women with large families already viewed sterilization as a realistic option. Writing in 1929, one social worker noted that several women at a Denver birth control clinic "can't be bothered with any kind of contraption and would like to get fixed up safe, once [and] for all" (p. 377).[53] A common refrain was the one expressed by a North Carolina mother of ten who sought the operation: "I've had my pile. I've done my share." Some women in North Carolina were so desperate to undergo sterilization that they asked social workers to petition the state's Eugenics Board for permission to have the operation; they seemingly did not mind being labeled as "defective" as long as they were able to have the surgery (pp. 134–135, 146).[54]

Yet if some women and their doctors saw eye to eye about the desirability of such operations, the cultural standing of medicine and the paternalism rife in the profession at the time ensured that purely elective surgery was rare. The first decades of the new century, what some have called medicine's "golden age," witnessed the dramatic rise in organized medicine's cultural authority.[55] The reputation of physicians and hospitals soared thanks to discoveries such as penicillin and insulin. The profession enjoyed a virtual "mandate" based on the premise that doctors knew best and should be allowed to run their own affairs as they saw fit. Many both inside and outside the profession believed that the more medical care the public received, the better off it was.[56]

Medicine's mandate faltered badly in the 1970s when criticism of the profession's putative greed, impersonality, paternalism, resistance to reform, and overreliance on technology peaked. Meanwhile, however, the medicalization of various conditions, notably obstetrical practice, proceeded apace. As the twentieth century wore on, fewer and fewer women gave birth at home at the hands of midwives, and more and more gave birth in hospitals, where doctors increasingly resorted to operations such as cesarean section. If pregnancy and childbirth were medical conditions, then, many doctors concluded, each was a pathological process that turned women into "invalids" in need of a doctor's care.[57] Women with symptoms of hypertension, heart disease, or tuberculosis were often urged to undergo postpartum tubal ligation so that childbirth would never again compromise their overall health. If a woman was delivered by cesarean section, the thinking went, all the more reason for doctors to sterilize her then and there while her abdomen was open to the surgeon's scalpel. Physicians' counseling under these circumstances often took the form of either subtle or heavy-handed pressure. A doctor at Philadelphia's Obstetrical Society remarked in 1920, "I say to the woman who has had two Caesarean sections with two children, 'why not consider the advisability of not having any more?' Usually our patients follow our advice in such matters." Other physicians utterly disregarded patient consent. "The woman's opinion is not a great thing," insisted one doctor in 1919; "I do not care much what a woman tells me about what she wants or what she does not want. I know what is good and I'm the best judge of that job."[58] Yet issues of patient consent troubled some physicians. One 1928 contributor to the *Journal of the American Medical Association* wondered whether doctors had the "right to suggest it, or even to perform [sterilization] at the request of the patient, or, as one of my friends expressed it, 'to arrogate to ourselves the attributes of the Almighty.'"[59]

The actual incidence of "therapeutic" or "voluntary" sterilizations in the first half of the twentieth century is difficult to determine, but some physicians suspected that the official number of sterilizations performed under existing state laws was just the tip of the iceberg.[60] Hospital statistics are in many cases meaningless, since underreporting appears to have been widespread. Yet in some hospitals the official numbers are high enough to suggest the wide extent of the practice. The head of the obstetrics department of a North Carolina teaching hospital estimated that he alone had performed roughly two hundred sterilizations in the late 1940s (p. 131).[54] In the words of a North Carolina social worker in 1950, "[S]ocial agencies in their desire to lessen some of the many problems presented by continued fertility, ill-health, and poverty, have recourse to the assistance of sympathetic surgeons who will interpret 'therapeutic' in the broadest meaning of the word" (pp. 48–49).[50]

Yet it was not simply poverty-stricken women from vulnerable social groups who ended up being sterilized. A frequent allegation was that affluent, well-educated women requested the operation because they sought the procedure either for themselves or their daughters. Indeed, a major justification for extending sterilization services to the poor was not to "inflict a deprivation" on them "but to confer on them a blessing already enjoyed by the rich" in private clinics.[61]

In actual clinical practice, doctors found it difficult to separate purely medical from social indications. With both male and female patients, most doctors took into consideration a broad range of factors, including physical health, emotional state, level of intelligence, previous pregnancies, family history, socioeconomic status, quality of life, the interests of tax-payers, ability to function independently in the community, and the like. Then (as now), physicians balanced medical criteria and social factors, negotiating patient compliance in a variety of ways. Then (as now), doctors did their best to treat the "whole patient." Yet the historical context of the interwar period, featuring unprecedented prestige of the medical profession and wide belief in eugenics, meant the difference between choice and coercion, so neat and tidy in theory, was repeatedly blurred in everyday encounters between doctor and patient. Ordinarily, it is exceedingly difficult at any one time to disentangle medical and social indications for any therapeutic intervention, or to distinguish compulsion from consent (p. 379).[53] When it came to surgical sterilization in the twentieth century, it was virtually impossible.

Marian Olden

At precisely this transitional moment in the history of sterilization, Marian Olden stepped boldly onto the historical stage. Intelligent, attractive, determined, opinionated, yet at the same time touchingly vulnerable: all these words begin to describe her but ultimately fail to do her justice. She was married four times, changing her given name from Marian to Marion and then back to Marian so correspondents would not mistake her for a man. By 1976, shortly before her death, she had not mellowed. When a University of Minnesota graduate student tried to include what Olden believed was privileged material in his doctoral dissertation, she threatened him with a lawsuit.[62] Undaunted to the day she died, Olden stood out in a movement that was not known for bashful men and women in the first place.

Olden, born in Philadelphia in 1888, was the first of three daughters of Arthur H. Stephenson, a merchant in woolens and worsted yarn. Stephenson was an agnostic and fervent admirer of Henry George, author of *Progress and Poverty* (1879) and well-known proponent of the idea of a "single tax" as a way of reducing the economic gap between rich and poor. Olden admitted later in life that she "adored" her father, who died of typhoid fever in 1902, when she was only fourteen. Up to that time she had been "the queen bee of the home," her beloved father's favorite, and it is not stretching psychological theory to say that for the rest of her life she sought to recreate the dominance over her parents' home that she had enjoyed in childhood.

At the age of 30, she became an adherent of the New Thought movement, an outgrowth of Christian Scientism, and thereafter pledged herself to fulfilling the plan God had for her. Her impressive intellectual and emotional strengths guaranteed that she would always have admirers and followers, but the same qualities tended to scuttle collaboration. Summing up her personality in 1948, she wrote that "[i]f you had known my father you would better know me . . . . He championed a cause that was scorned by all rich men and suffered the ostracism of his whole family . . . . I adored my father . . . . He has shaped my whole life." Said Olden, "people's feelings just don't register with me . . . . Principles are eternal, human relations may not be."[63]

The similarities between Olden and Margaret Sanger, her more famous contemporary in the birth control movement, are uncanny. Both were sensual women whom men found attractive. Both were far closer to their politically progressive and free-thinking fathers than their traditionalist mothers. In words that Olden could have scripted herself, Sanger confided late in life that "it was my father more than any other person, who influenced me through his teachings and his vital belief in truth, freedom, right." Olden's and Sanger's fathers even shared an ardent admiration for the writings of Henry George.[64]

Sanger and Olden also founded separate family-planning organizations that to this day provide contraceptive services around the world. Both came from social worker or nursing backgrounds and had been converted to the cause of birth control after concluding that the mental and physical suffering of poor women was due to their ostensible inability to control their fertility. Olden, like Sanger, had been appalled at doctors' ignorance of birth control methods and was furious to learn that society frowned on active efforts to help women and their spouses avoid unwanted pregnancies. Both Olden and Sanger harbored a virulent antipathy toward the Roman Catholic Church for its opposition to artificial birth control. Olden, again like Sanger, would be eased out of the organization she had founded—Olden from the Sterilization League of New Jersey (SLNJ), Sanger from the Planned Parenthood Federation of America (PPFA)— largely because of the very traits that had enabled their organizations to survive in the first place.[65] Why the world today remembers only one of these two pioneering women is a mystery in light of the powerful impact of the sterilization movement on global reproductive behavior.

It was during her marriage to Princeton University faculty member Paul R. Coleman-Norton that Olden became convinced that sterilization held the key to the eugenic campaign to prevent the mentally handicapped from having children. In 1934, she was asked to form a study group to discuss matters of public health. In the process of organizing her study group, Olden came across eugenic literature, notably Edwin Grant Conklin's *Heredity and Environment in the Development of Man* (1917) and H. S. Jennings's *The Biological Basis of Human Nature* (1930). Careful reading of these and other books turned her into an adherent of eugenics, interested in addressing both the quantitative and qualitative sides to population control through sterilization.

Her reasons for supporting eugenics crystallized when she took her study group on field trips to state institutions for the insane, epileptic, and mentally retarded. There, she learned that many psychiatrists and superintendents of homes for the mentally retarded were in favor of sterilizing patients. Physicians warned Olden that families with tainted heredity were "scattering" throughout New Jersey, "menac[ing] our better stock." Sterilization of patients, she was told, would prevent the genetic transmission of mental disabilities, thus reducing the number of social dependents over time and saving Depression-era governments money.

Yet genetic and economic reasons were not the only justifications for sterilization cited by physicians and scientists. Sterilization of selected patients enabled institutions to discharge inmates into the community. There, ex-patients could live "normal" lives without the fear of pregnancy or the possibility of exposing unborn and possibly healthy children to their inadequate parenting. Discharging patients also enabled hospitals to free up beds in institutions for more severely disabled patients who required hospitalization. Olden came away from her visits to state institutions believing that sterilization was the answer to numerous pressing social and public health challenges facing governments that were trying to provide a measure of public charity in difficult economic times. In Olden's mind, biological, humanitarian, and socioeconomic considerations were part of an overall vision predicated on the remarkable capacity of sterilization to solve some of the nation's most urgent problems.[66]

In 1935, after drafting a model sterilization bill, Olden spearheaded a League of Women Voters campaign to introduce it in the New Jersey Senate. After the legislature failed to take her bill seriously, Olden broke with the League of Women Voters and launched the SLNJ in 1937. Olden, as secretary of the group, was able to build its dues-paying membership from twenty-three to three hundred and seventy-three within its first year of operation. She traveled around the state lecturing and distributing literature she had composed on the basis of her study of eugenic writings.

In 1938, her research took her to Nazi Germany, where officials greeted her warmly. The lawyer Falk Ruttke, a member of both the SS (*Schutzstaffel*) and the Committee for Population and Race Policies in the Third Reich's Ministry of the Interior, welcomed Olden to Germany. She was already well known to Nazi eugenicists, who had been avidly reading her anti-Catholic pamphlets on sterilization since 1935. Politicians in the Third Reich, who faced Catholic objections to the Nazi 1933 sterilization law, found her contention that Catholic attacks on sterilization were unscientific useful in trying to silence Church opposition. Olden was so flattered by Nazi attention that she agreed to collaborate with Ruttke on a German pro-sterilization film. Olden's willingness to collaborate with the Nazis, at a time when most Anglo-American eugenicists had severed ties with German eugenics, spoke volumes about her fierce devotion to sterilization.[67]

Back in the United States in 1939, Olden believed the time was right to try again to get a sterilization bill passed in New Jersey. Two years later, after extensive consultations with legal experts, the SLNJ found a state representative on the verge of retirement willing to introduce the twenty-four-page bill. The legislation empowered a state eugenicist to conduct a survey of all persons in New Jersey who were believed to be unfit for parenthood. The state eugenicist could present petitions to a State Eugenic Council requesting the sterilization of such persons, and, unless they appealed the order for their sterilization, the operation could be performed even if patients or their families objected.

Unfortunately for Olden, the compulsory nature of the statute sparked broad opposition. Even the League of Women Voters, normally supportive of sterilization, withheld its endorsement, as did New Jersey's Birth

Control League and the state's medical, nursing, and social work organizations. Intemperate comments to the press by some SLNJ members did not help. In late 1941, an unnamed official of the group was quoted as saying, "Apparently Germany accomplished in a few days what we hope to accomplish in a few generations."[68]

Additionally, Olden's personality had alienated a good many potential allies, as had her inveterate inability to sugarcoat her public proclamations. One of her booklets began with a picture of a mentally handicapped patient and the caption,

> See the happy moron;
> He doesn't have a care,
> His children and his problems
> Are all for us to bear.

Even when she tried to argue that sterilization was a humane means of preventing people with disabilities from enduring misery, her message was buried by the harsh language she used. Selective sterilization, she contended, would be law if only "every voter saw the squatting, slobber-soaked idiots tied to benches."[69]

Despite attempts to have the SLNJ's bill reported to the floor of the state's legislature, the bill was swiftly referred to the Speaker of the Ways and Means Committee, a Catholic. Later it was referred to the Miscellaneous Business Committee, known as "the morgue," where the bill, predictably, died.

The bill's fate was a terrific disappointment to Olden and the SLNJ, but it confirmed their suspicions about just who their most formidable adversaries were. First and foremost in their minds was the Roman Catholic Church. Catholic electoral clout was powerful in the Northeast states, where almost 10 million of the nation's 19 million Catholics were concentrated. State legislators in this region of the country knew they faced political suicide by backing eugenic statutes. They knew they would draw the ire of some of the most vocal and powerful figures in the Church's hierarchy, such as Cardinals Hayes of New York and Gibbons of Boston.[70] The Church relied on its growing demographic might to stymie groups like the SLNJ, which, in Catholic eyes, were attempting to popularize the idea that ethics, morality, and values were contingent, not absolute. The disadvantaged, Catholic prelates argued, should be "properly housed and protected against the profiteer," not sterilized. To Olden, such arguments were nonsense; the Church was simply "an obstacle to progress in every form."[71]

Olden's trials and tribulations trying to convince New Jersey legislators to enact a compulsory sterilization law signaled that, by the early 1940s, the window of opportunity for enacting such laws, seemingly so wide only ten years earlier, was closing rapidly. Olden's unvarnished rhetoric about "morons" was a throwback to an age in the history of eugenics swiftly fading into the past. The public, while apparently more receptive to sterilization than ever before, increasingly disliked the harsh terminology she used to describe society's less fortunate citizens. Her blunt style of advocacy was a liability in an era that was more and more dominated by the techniques of advertising and public relations.[72] Behaving like a bull terrier on behalf of a controversial cause sharply conflicted with the maxims of advertising, which taught that trust and amiability were necessary to "sell" a product to the American public.

Another formidable obstacle standing in the way of the sterilization movements was organized medicine. As the male-dominated medical profession steadily augmented its autonomy in the early twentieth century, it less and less tolerated nonphysicians (especially if they were women) telling them what they should do for their patients. Until the 1960s, the U.S. medical profession was also a bastion of social conservatism. It tended to resist medical reforms that looked even vaguely radical, such as national health insurance.[73] Birth control was viewed as a similarly subversive cause. In an era when the country's fertility rate was actually dropping, most American doctors believed that women needed to have more, not fewer, children. Physicians reported that their married female patients complained about infertility more than they requested contraceptive advice. Needing public support and confidence, physicians shared the mainstream values of society at large, which for most of the twentieth century remained traditionalist. Olden's endorsement of sterilization as a form of birth control defied customary mores regarding sex and reproduction. The price was the marginalization of her movement for the next two decades.[74]

Nonetheless, Olden left behind a notable and lasting achievement. In the coming years, the SLNJ would undergo name and personnel changes as well as shifts in philosophy. Its influence would wax and wane, but in the 1960s, in the wake of the "baby boom" of the 1950s, it would emerge as an increasingly powerful organization that helped to shape the environmentalist, population control, reproductive rights, and women's movements of the late twentieth century. Olden antagonized friend and foe alike, but in time few doubted that her determination had helped to launch a movement that eventually would change the course of world history.

Notes

1. Marian Olden conducted her professional activities under the name Marion S. Norton (sometimes Coleman-Norton) until 1941 when, after marrying her fourth husband, she began calling herself Marian S. Olden. For simplicity's sake, I shall call her Marian Olden throughout this book.
2. Vanessendelft WR. *A History of the Association for Voluntary Sterilization, 1935– 1964*. University of Minnesota: Unpublished doctoral dissertation, 1978, p. 52.
3. Pick D. *Faces of Degeneration: A European Disorder, c.1848–c.1918*. Cambridge: Cambridge University Press, 1989; Dowbiggin I. *Inheriting Madness: Professionalization and Psychiatric Knowledge in Nineteenth-Century France*. Berkeley and Los Angeles: University of California Press, 1991. This fear of degeneracy spawned a string of family-history studies that, culminating in the post– World War I era, purported to document the cost to society of allowing families to reproduce freely. The best-known family study focused on the "Jukes," whose history was reconstructed by U.S. social reformer Richard Dugdale in 1877. Dugdale calculated that this single family, with its long list of paupers, drunks, criminals, and lunatics, had cost the state $1.25 million over just 75 years. How to prevent similar families from breeding civiliza- tion into "race suicide" was the daunting question confronting politicians and public health officials as the nineteenth century drew to a close. See Haller MH. *Eugenics: Hereditarian Attitudes in American Thought*. New Brunswick, NJ: Rutgers University Press, 1963, pp. 21–25; Reilly P. *The Surgical Solution: A History of Involuntary Sterilization in the United States*. Baltimore and London: The Johns Hopkins University Press, 1991, pp. 9–10, 14–17; Rafter NH. *Creating Born Criminals*. Urbana and Chicago: University of Illinois Press, 1997, pp. 38–39.
4. Larson EJ. *Evolution: The Remarkable History of a Scientific Theory*. New York: Modern Library, 2004, pp. 79–89.
5. Darwin C. *Descent of Man,* I, pp. 205–206, 212–213, 216.
6. Galton F. *Inquiries into Human Faculty and its Development*. London: J. M. Dent and Sons, 1883, pp. 24.
7. Galton F. *Essays in Eugenics*. London: Eugenics Education Society, 1909, pp. 24–25.
8. His emphasis. Quoted in Kevles DJ. *In the Name of Eugenics: Genetics and the Uses of Human Heredity*. New York: Knopf, 1985, p. 85.
9. Trombley S. *The Right to Reproduce: A History of Coercive Sterilization*. London: Weidenfeld and Nicholson, 1988, p. 15. Galton's preference for positive

eugenics was still strong as late as 1901. See Gillham NW. *A Life of Sir Francis Galton: From African Exploration to the Birth of Eugenics.* New York: Oxford University Press, 2001, p. 327.

10. Rosenberg CE. The therapeutic revolution: Medicine, meaning, and social change in nineteenth-century America. In Vogel MJ, Rosenberg CE (eds.), *The Therapeutic Revolution: Essays in the Social History of American Medicine.* Philadelphia: University of Pennsylvania Press, 1979, pp. 3–25.

11. Rosenberg CE. *The Care of Strangers: The Rise of America's Hospital System.* New York: Basic, 1987, pp. 26, 148. The rise of comparatively safe surgery in the late nineteenth century also revolutionized the hospital as a medical institution. The growing complexity of surgery made the hospital operating room the natural center for such procedures and wore down long-standing public reluctance to enter hospital for treatment. By the 1920s, hospital surgery was steadily becoming the norm (Rosenberg, *The Care of Strangers,* p. 149). However, surgery, including the delivery of babies, continued to be performed in private homes well into the twentieth century.

12. For a provocative, controversial history of women's health to the present day, see Shorter E. *A History of Women's Bodies.* New York: Basic Books, 1982. See also Stage S. *Female Complaints: Lydia Pinkham and the Business of Women's Medicine.* New York: Norton, 1979, p. 79.

13. Morantz-Sanchez R. *Conduct Unbecoming a Woman: Medicine on Trial in Turn-of-the-Century Brooklyn.* New York: Oxford University Press, 1999.

14. Shorter E. *From Paralysis to Fatigue: A History of Psychosomatic Illness in the Modern Era.* New York: The Free Press, 1992, pp. 73–81; Morantz-Sanchez R. *Conduct Unbecoming a Woman: Medicine on Trial in Turn-of-the-Century Brooklyn.* New York: Oxford University Press, 1999, p. 106.

15. Stage S. *Female Complaints: Lydia Pinkham and the Business of Women's Medicine.* New York: Norton, 1979.

16. Benrubi GI. History of hysterectomy. *Journal of the Florida Medical Association.* 1988;75:533–538.

17. Sutton C. Hysterectomy: A historical perspective. *Baillière's Clinical Obstetrics and Gynecology.* 1997;11:1–22.

18. Houston WR. *The Art of Treatment.* New York: 1936, p. 50. Quoted in Shorter E. *From Paralysis to Fatigue: A History of Psychosomatic Illness in the Modern Era.* New York: The Free Press, 1992, p. 77.

19. For evidence of this phenomenon, see Shorter E. *From Paralysis to Fatigue: A History of Psychosomatic Illness in the Modern Era.* New York: The Free Press, 1992, pp. 81, 87.

20. Bordahl PE. Tubal sterilization: A historical review. *Journal of Reproductive Medicine.* 1985;30:18–24; Reilly PR. *The Surgical Solution: A History of Involuntary Sterilization in the United States.* Baltimore and London: The Johns Hopkins University Press, 1991, p. 34.

21. Shorter E. *From Paralysis to Fatigue: A History of Psychosomatic Illness in the Modern Era.* New York: The Free Press, 1992.

22. Reilly PR. *The Surgical Solution: A History of Involuntary Sterilization in the United States.* Baltimore and London: The Johns Hopkins University Press, 1991, p. 31.

23. For an account of the Ann Cooper Hewitt case, see Kline W. *Building a Better Race: Gender, Sexuality, and Eugenics from the Turn of the Century to the Baby Boom.* Berkeley and Los Angeles: University of California Press, 2001, pp. 111–123.

24. Elmer Belt to Robert Latou Dickinson, October 28, 1947, AVS, Box 13, folder 108.

25. Pernick MS. Eugenics and public health in American history. *American Journal of Public Health.* 1997;87:1767–1772.

26. Mehler BA. *A History of the American Eugenics Society, 1921–1940.* University of Illinois, Urbana-Champaign: Unpublished doctoral dissertation, 1988.

27. Trombley S. *The Right to Reproduce: A History of Coercive Sterilization.* London: Weidenfeld and Nicholson, 1988, p. 17.

28. Paul DB. *Controlling Human Heredity: 1865 to the Present.* Atlantic Highlands, NJ: Humanities Press, 1995, p. 75.

29. Weikart R. *From Darwin to Hitler: Evolutionary Ethics, Eugenics, and Racism in Germany.* New York: Palgrave Macmillan, 2004, pp. 137–138.

30. For the debate over eugenic sterilization in the U.S. Deep South, see Larson EJ. *Sex, Race, and Science: Eugenics in the Deep South.* Baltimore and London: Johns Hopkins University Press, 1995. For sterilization data in Scandinavia, see Broberg G, Roll-Hansen N (eds.), *Eugenics and the Welfare State: Sterilization Policy in Denmark, Sweden, Norway, and Finland.* East Lansing: Michigan State University Press, 1996.

31. E. S. Gosney to Frank Reid, September 9, 1940, Gosney Papers and the Records of the Human Betterment Foundation, 1.2, California Institute of Technology Archives, Pasadena, CA. Gosney's emphasis. Cited in Kline W. *Building a Better Race: Gender, Sexuality, and Eugenics from the Turn of the Century to the Baby Boom.* Berkeley and Los Angeles: University of California Press, 2001, p. 104.

32. For example, see Clarence Gamble to Robert Latou Dickinson, August 14, 1948, AVS, Box 13, folder 106.

33. Rosen C. *Preaching Eugenics: Religious Leaders and the American Eugenics Movement.* New York and Oxford: Oxford University Press, 2004, p. 140; Leon SM. 'Hopelessly entangled in Nordic pre-suppositions': Catholic participation in the American Eugenics Society in the 1920s. *Bulletin of the History of Medicine.* 2004;59:15.

34. Rosen C. *Preaching Eugenics: Religious Leaders and the American Eugenics Movement.* New York and Oxford: Oxford University Press, 2004, p. 143; Leon SM. 'Hopelessly entangled in Nordic pre-suppositions': Catholic participation in the American Eugenics Society in the 1920s. *Bulletin of the History of Medicine.* 2004;59:28.

35. Weindling P. *Health, Race, and German Politics Between National Unification and Nazism, 1870–1945.* Cambridge, UK: Cambridge University Press, 1989, pp. 508–509.

36. Rosen C. *Preaching Eugenics: Religious Leaders and the American Eugenics Movement*. New York and Oxford: Oxford University Press, 2004, pp. 140–145.

37. McGreevy JT. *Catholicism and American Freedom: A History*. New York: W. W. Norton, 2003, pp. 224–225. Quoted in Reilly PR. *The Surgical Solution: A History of Involuntary Sterilization in the United States*. Baltimore and London: The Johns Hopkins University Press, 1991, p. 117.

38. Jennings HS. *The Biological Basis of Human Nature*. New York: W. W. Norton, 1930, p. 218. See also Editorial, *New York Times*, June 22, 1932, quoted in Kevles DJ. *In the Name of Eugenics: Genetics and the Uses of Human Heredity*. New York: Knopf, 1985, p. 165.

39. *Fortune*, 16 (July 1937), p. 106; Gallup GH. *The Gallup Poll: Public Opinion, 1935–1971*, Vol. 1. New York: Random, 1972, p. 59.

40. J. H. Craft to Olden, September 16, 1939, AVS, Box 1, folder 3.

41. Olden M. *The ABC of Human Conservation*. Princeton: Birthright, Inc., 1946, pp. 6, 9.

42. Kline W. *Building a Better Race: Gender, Sexuality, and Eugenics from the Turn of the Century to the Baby Boom*. Berkeley and Los Angeles: University of California Press, 2001.

43. Doll E. Current thoughts on mental deficiency. *Journal of Psycho-Asthenics*. 1936;41:44.

44. Schwesinger G. "Sterilization and the Child." Paper read at the Sixty-third Annual Meeting of the New Jersey Health and Sanitary Association, December 10, 1937. Quoted in Kline W. *Building a Better Race: Gender, Sexuality, and Eugenics from the Turn of the Century to the Baby Boom*. Berkeley and Los Angeles: University of California Press, 2001, p. 106.

45. Myerson A, et al. *Eugenical Sterilization: A Reorientation of the Problem*. New York: Macmillan, 1936, pp. 4, 6, 22, 177–83. See also Trent JW. "Who Shall Say Who Is a Useful Person?" Abraham Myerson's opposition to the eugenics movement. *History of Psychiatry*. 2001;12:33–57

46. Kevles DJ. *In the Name of Eugenics: Genetics and the Uses of Human Heredity*. New York: Knopf, 1985, p. 251.

47. Waldemar Kaempffert to Olden, February 10, 1936, AVS, Box 1, folder 3.

48. For the growing perception within U.S. psychiatry that its scientific and therapeutic credentials were not as impressive as the rest of organized medicine, see Grob GN. *Mental Illness and American Society, 1875–1940*. Princeton: Princeton University Press, 1983, pp. 108–143.

49. Braslow J. *Mental Ills and Bodily Cures: Psychiatric Treatment in the First Half of the Twentieth Century*. Berkeley and Los Angeles: University of California Press, 1999, p. 61. See also Dowbiggin IR. *Keeping America Sane: Psychiatry and Eugenics in the United States and Canada, 1880–1940*. Ithaca: Cornell University Press, 1997 (paperback edition: 2003).

50. Woodside M. *Sterilization in North Carolina: A Sociological and Psychological Study*. Chapel Hill: University of North Carolina Press, 1950.

51. Woodside M. *Sterilization in North Carolina: A Sociological and Psychological Study.* Chapel Hill: University of North Carolina Press, 1950, pp. 66, 77. See also Schoen J. 'A Great Thing For Poor Folks': Birth control, sterilization, and abortion in public health and welfare in the twentieth century. University of North Carolina at Chapel Hill: Unpublished doctoral dissertation, 1995, p. 148.

52. My emphasis. Gellhorn G. The justifiability of sterilizing a woman after cesarean section with a view to preventing subsequent pregnancies. *Transactions of the American Gynecological Society.* 1909;34:93–94.

53. Lerner B. Constructing medical indications: The sterilization of women with heart disease or tuberculosis, 1905–1935. *Bulletin of the History of Medicine.* 1994;49.

54. Schoen J. *"A Great Thing For Poor Folks": Birth control, sterilization, and abortion in public health and welfare in the twentieth century.* University of North Carolina at Chapel Hill: Unpublished doctoral dissertation, 1995.

55. Burnham JC. American medicine's golden age: What happened to it? *Science.* 1982;215:1474–1479.

56. Starr P. *The Social Transformation of American Medicine.* New York: Basic Books, 1982, p. 379.

57. Leavitt JW. *Brought to Bed: Childbearing in America, 1750 to 1950.* New York: Oxford University Press, 1986, pp. 68, 70.

58. Peterson R. When is sterilization of women justifiable? *Journal of the Michigan Medical Society.* 1919;18:614.

59. Williams JW. Indications for therapeutic sterilization in obstetrics: When is advice concerning the prevention of conception justifiable? *Journal of the American Medical Association.* 1928;91:1238.

60. Butler FO. Sterilization in the United States. *American Journal of Mental Deficiency.* 1951;56:360–363. One researcher stated that prior to 1955, 75,000 Americans had been sterilized "voluntarily," slightly higher than the roughly 60,000 sterilizations performed under state sterilization statutes. Christopher Tietze, minutes of HBAA meeting, January 27, 1959, AVS, Box 4, folder 38.

61. Kline W. *Building a Better Race: Gender, Sexuality, and Eugenics from the Turn of the Century to the Baby Boom.* Berkeley and Los Angeles, University of California Press, 2001, pp. 111–123. See also C. P. Blacker to C. J. Bond, March 20, 1931, SA/EUG/Box 5/C.31. Blacker was a leading British eugenicist.

62. As a result, the dissertation literally has huge gaps in its early pages.

63. Vanessendelft WR. *A History of the Association for Voluntary Sterilization, 1935–1964.* University of Minnesota. Unpublished doctoral dissertation, 1978, pp. 16–19, 25, 131–132. Some of this information on Olden is based on Vanessendelft's series of interviews with Olden in April 1976. See also Marian Olden to H. Curtis Wood, January 4, 1948, Marian Olden Papers, Archibald Steven Alexander Library, State University of New Jersey at Rutgers University, F-1948.

64. Morehouse W. *The Speaking of Margaret Sanger in the Birth Control Movement from 1916 to 1937*. Purdue University: unpublished doctoral dissertation, 1968, p. 38. Cited in Reed J. *From Private Vice to Public Virtue: The Birth Control Movement and American Society since 1830*. New York: Basic, 1978, p. 129. For Henry George's influence on Sanger's father, see Reed, *From Private Vice to Public Virtue,* pp. 70, 129–130.

65. For these aspects of Sanger's life, see Chesler E. *Woman of Valor: Margaret Sanger and the Birth Control Movement in America*. New York: Simon and Schuster, 1992, especially pp. 21– 43.

66. Olden M. "Birthright, Inc.–Its Roots, Fruits, and Objectives," AVS, Box 2, folder 8.

67. Kühl S. *The Nazi Connection: Eugenics, American Racism, and German National Socialism*. New York and Oxford: Oxford University Press, 1994, pp. 28–30, 58–59.

68. Sterilization is discussed. Newark *Evening News*, November 13, 1941.

69. Norton MS. *Selective Sterilization in Primer Form*. Privately published, 1937, passim. Vanessendelft WR. *A History of the Association for Voluntary Sterilization, 1935–1964*. University of Minnesota, unpublished doctoral dissertation, 1978, p. 47.

70. Dolan JP. *The American Catholic Experience: A History from Colonial Times to the Present*. Notre Dame: University of Notre Dame Press, 1992, pp. 191–192.

71. Marian Olden to Charles Potter, February 2, 1947, Partnership for Caring Records, Lewis Advertising, Baltimore, MD, Box C-4.

72. Rorabaugh WJ, Critchlow DT, Baker P. *America's Promise: A Concise History of the United States*, Vol. 2. Lanham, MD: Rowman and Littlefield, 2004, pp. 511, 512.

73. Numbers RL. The third party: Health insurance in America. In Vogel MJ, Rosenberg CE (Eds.), *The Therapeutic Revolution: Essays in the Social History of American Medicine*. Philadelphia: University of Pennsylvania Press, 1979, pp. 178–200.

74. Reed J. Doctors, birth control, and social values, 1830–1970. In Vogel MJ, Rosenberg CE (Eds.), *The Therapeutic Revolution: Essays in the Social History of American Medicine*. Philadelphia: University of Pennsylvania Press, 1979, pp. 109–133.

Chapter 2

A New League

T rue to her indomitable nature, Marian Olden did not let her setback in the New Jersey legislature stop her. In 1943, hard on the heels of her failure to convince state representatives to enact an involuntary sterilization law, she and her allies formed a national, private, nonprofit organization called Birthright, Inc.

Initially, Birthright was a tiny organization, desperately short of funds and headquartered in Olden's home. Religious and medical opposition, as well as Birthright's grave shortfalls in membership and financial backing, left it largely powerless to influence policymaking, shape public opinion, or conduct meaningful research. Yet by the 1970s, after several name changes, Birthright was spearheading a movement that helped to reshape the nation's and the world's attitudes toward sex and reproduction. By the end of the twentieth century, America's sterilization movement had played a pivotal role in the international effort to make contraceptive sterilization respectable and cut global birth rates to their lowest recorded levels in history.

Birthright

In the aftermath of the Sterilization League of New Jersey's (SLNJ) legislative defeat, a bitter conflict broke out within the group. In late 1942, one faction, keen on recasting the SLNJ as a more moderate organization, attempted to wrest control of the group away from Olden. SLNJ infighting was hardly new for Olden, who had fought back a similar attempt in 1940.

"I just couldn't obey," Olden admitted later.[1] After she threatened to resign, other members rallied to her side, and the dissidents left the organization. The stage was set for a new group, this time national in scope.

The new organization was to be a clearinghouse for sterilization information that like-minded individuals from all states could access, "thus creating an effective solidarity among hitherto isolated workers," in Olden's own words.[2] Originally, Olden had hoped that the group would be called the Sterilization League for Human Betterment, named after eugenicist Ezra S. Gosney's Human Betterment Foundation (HBF). HBF, founded in 1929 and based in Pasadena, California, was a nonprofit corporation designed to promote eugenic sterilization.[3] But Gosney died in 1942, and his daughter refused to let the new group use the words "Human Betterment" in its title.

The name "Birthright" was chosen because it felicitously evoked memories of the 1930 White House Conference on Child Health and Protection. As then-president Herbert Hoover had declared, "[T]here shall be no child in America that has not the complete birthright of a sound mind in a sound body, and that has not been born under proper conditions." To many in the sterilization movement, the conference's broad mandate and message, with its references to making America "a fitter country in which to bring up children," was an ideal frame of reference for their advocacy of sterilization. Sterilization, in this view, was less a punitive weapon aimed at society's "misfits" and more a selective, medically approved procedure designed to improve the overall health of tomorrow's children. Birthright, in Olden's words, stood "on the principle that procreation is not a right to be unrestrictedly exercised but that it is a responsibility to be assumed by those capable of producing normal offspring and of giving them necessary care." Officially, in the early 1940s, the goals Olden and others hoped sterilization would achieve were more modest than those espoused by earlier eugenicists, who had talked about both raising the birth rate among the nation's "best stock" and (through mass sterilization) improving the biological quality of the "race."[3]

The risk of such eugenic rhetoric, as Birthright's members well knew, was to strengthen in the public mind the association between them and Nazism. In 1942, Winfred Overholser, head psychiatrist at St. Elizabeths mental hospital in Washington, D.C., frankly told Olden that though he was "not opposed to sterilization as such, I have a feeling that organizations like yours proceed on bases which are not scientifically demonstrated and which, particularly at the present time, savor a good deal of Hitler's eugenic theories."[4] Instead, the official aim of the sterilization movement in the early 1940s, as America mobilized to battle Hitler's Germany, was simply to produce more "normal offspring." Birthright's message for public consumption was that the beneficiaries of sterilization's popularization should be first and foremost the country's children, not the race.[4]

The choice of Birthright as the group's name also indicated that the word "sterilization" itself had a tarnished image once World War II broke out. Olden, characteristically wishing to "call a spade a spade," had favored the title "Sterilization League of America." Other members, more sensitive about public relations, preferred "Birthright" because of its mainstream connotations. Olden ruefully had to admit that many people equated sterilization with Nazi atrocities.[5] Not until 1962, under dramatically different political, social, and cultural conditions, did the organization reintroduce the word "sterilization" to its name (p. 83n).[6]

Yet no matter how much Birthright tried to moderate the public image of the group, behind the scenes Olden and others remained hard-line eugenicists, a source of festering tension. Experience rarely made an impression on Marian Olden unless it confirmed her preconceived notions, so the often tough lessons of birth control politics during the period spanning the Depression and the United States' entry into World War II had not radically changed her mind. She adhered to the cardinal beliefs of early-twentieth-century American eugenics, including the theory that in the first two decades of the twentieth century the United States had become the "dumping ground" for southern and eastern Europe's "subnormal" population. She contended that these kinds of immigrants to America were congenitally prone to crime and mental illness.[7]

Additionally, into the 1940s Olden continued to believe that the fertility of society's "feeble-minded" population presented a grave hereditary threat to the nation's overall intelligence quotient. Civilization, according to Olden, was incessantly "temporizing with natural selection [which] merely aids the survival of the unfit and brings society no ultimate relief." Lamenting that "our best blood was spilled" in World War I, "while the worst stock multiplied without check or hindrance," she predicted that after World War II the nation would awaken to "the need for biological improvement in our youth and the necessity of putting a check upon the breeding of defectives."[8] The tragedy for Olden was that while the birth control movement had given the law-abiding, taxpaying classes the information to enable them to reduce the size of their families, the supposedly fast-breeding poor either were too ignorant to use this information or lacked access to public services that could help them to prevent pregnancy.

Olden's social-Darwinist version of eugenics, coupled with her outspoken anti-Catholicism, put her on a collision course with other members of the movement who favored soft-pedaling sterilization. In their more candid moments, her colleagues shared many of Olden's harsh views, but they believed it was better to keep them to themselves. As one colleague said of her in 1947, Olden had "much to learn about public relations" (p. 128).[6] Her prickly, unyielding personality increasingly posed a serious threat to the unity of the sterilization movement in the 1940s. When she clashed with Clarence Gamble, her best-known rival and a formidable character in his own right, her claim to being the nation's foremost sterilization advocate was in serious jeopardy.

Clarence Gamble

In the politics of birth control advocacy in twentieth-century America, gender, wealth, and professional status were critical factors, and no one's career as a family-planning campaigner illustrated this truth more than Clarence Gamble's. Like Olden and Margaret Sanger, Gamble (1894–1966) was willing to ruffle feathers to achieve his aims. An inveterate maverick, Gamble enjoyed the extra advantage of being a male physician in a movement staffed with numerous nonprofessionals, including many women. Yet the main reason Gamble was able to follow an idiosyncratic style of sterilization activism was his immense wealth. He was an heir to the huge Gamble Ivory Soap fortune, and other proponents in the sterilization movement, no matter how much they disapproved of his tactics, tended to treat him with kid gloves.

Gamble's appearance on the scene in the 1940s underscored the difficulties Birthright had finding affluent donors. With the prestige of eugenics on the wane, the large philanthropies were withdrawing their support for eugenic research. In 1939, the Carnegie Institute closed the Eugenics Records Office at Cold Spring Harbor, New York. Predictably, in 1946, Carnegie turned down Birthright's request for funding. In 1947, Olden's desperate search for donors took her to the home of Wickliffe Draper, a noted benefactor of eugenic research (and founder of the controversial Pioneer Fund).[9] Draper stunned Birthright by offering a $100,000 donation, but, according to Olden, he wanted to finance research that would prevent "miscegenation in the South" and legitimize "racial prejudice." Olden may have been a eugenicist, but placing "racial prejudice" on a scientific basis was going too far, so she declined Draper's offer.[10] When Clarence Gamble approached Birthright with a more modest offer of $10,000 to expand the scope of existing state sterilization laws, its executive committee eagerly accepted. Yet Gamble's relationship with Birthright proved to be as stormy as that of the other rich benefactors who later paid for the group's sterilization programs.

Gamble was born in 1894 in Cincinnati, Ohio, the third son of David Berry Gamble, one of the last Gambles to play an important role in running the Procter & Gamble Corporation. After growing up in a strait-laced Presbyterian family that stressed the social gospel, Gamble headed off to Harvard University, where he received his medical degree in 1920. A career in medical research went nowhere, but in the meantime Gamble fell under the influence of eugenicists such as the Princeton scientist Edward Grant Conklin and the University of Pennsylvania microbiologist Stuart Mudd. In 1933, Gamble was elected president of the Pennsylvania Birth Control Federation (PBCF), one of the country's most activist family-planning groups. By then he had concluded that birth control was the greatest social cause to which he could dedicate himself. He agreed heartily with PBCF propaganda that urged reducing the birth rate of people on welfare. As the Roosevelt New Deal extended public support to millions of underprivileged Americans in the 1930s, Gamble and his birth control allies in Pennsylvania preached that contraception was the key to improving the lives of the indigent and saving taxpayers money (pp. 227–235).[11]

Gamble devoted most of his time, money, and energy to the search for a foolproof contraceptive for women. Yet, from the beginning, it was clear that Gamble was mainly concerned about the women who lacked the desire, education, privacy, and sanitary conditions to practice consistently reliable birth control. A method that caught his attention was the use of a contraceptive foam powder that was applied to a damp sponge and inserted into the vagina. In 1937, he decided to test the foam powder method in North Carolina, with its large population of rural poor and its willingness to operate birth control clinics at the county level as part of its state public health system. With the cooperation of state officials, Gamble's program spread rapidly. By early 1938 there were thirty-six birth control clinics in thirty-three counties. One year later, North Carolina had sixty-two clinics in sixty counties, and by 1946, ninety-three of the state's hundred counties offered birth control services. Besides foam powder, diaphragms, jelly, and condoms were also prescribed (pp. 252–256).[11]

These efforts made North Carolina the first American state to offer contraceptives through its public health clinics on such a large scale (p. 63).[12] But Gamble remained frustrated with North Carolina's birth control services: "[W]e really haven't reached every mother, and until then I won't be content," he wrote in 1940.[13] Gamble always considered his own financial contributions as "seed money," and he soon grew impatient with North Carolina's inability to tap other sources of funding. Finally, in March, 1940, he ceased donating to the state's birth control program (p. 81).[12]

Gamble quickly switched to sterilization projects. In the 1940s, he barnstormed throughout the Midwest and South, starting more than twenty sterilization clinics in Michigan, Indiana, Iowa, Nebraska, Kansas, Missouri, and Florida. His interest in sterilization as a birth control method made cooperation between him and Birthright an obvious step. In exchange for a promise of funding from Gamble, Birthright's board agreed to set up a special "fieldwork" committee to oversee efforts to popularize sterilization around the country. Gamble was named chairman, and the entire committee was given considerable autonomy to operate as he wished. His financial contributions were placed in a separate fund for his fieldwork, and he controlled this money.[14]

North Carolina, selected as the demonstration state for the Birthright–Gamble partnership, stood out as a state that offered family planners unique opportunities to curb fertility rates through sterilization. Alone among the states, it permitted the sterilization of people who lived outside state institutions: between 1929 and 1973, over 8,000 North Carolinians were sterilized under the state's sterilization law (p. 98).[12]

North Carolina's sterilization statute had been enacted in 1933, after its 1929 law had been ruled unconstitutional. The 1933 law set up a statewide Eugenics Board that heard petitions to sterilize epileptic, feeble-minded (IQ below 70), and mentally ill individuals. The heads of county homes, correctional schools, mental institutions, and county public welfare agencies were empowered to begin sterilization proceedings. The first big challenge for Gamble and Birthright was to encourage these officials to do so. Another challenge was to get poor men and women who ordinarily had no access to health-care services to request sterilization (p. 115).[12]

Birthright's fieldwork committee under Clarence Gamble lasted only until 1947, but in the meantime his projects constituted the most significant undertaking in the group's first half-decade. In his first year alone he raised $15,000 for fieldwork, a considerable sum for an organization whose general receipts for 1944 totaled only $4,355. In terms of public education, the efforts of Gamble and his followers boosted the sterilization cause immeasurably. In 1945–1946, North Carolina newspapers carried numerous articles on the virtues of sterilization, generating plenty of publicity for the movement.

In the short term, however, Gamble's social experiment did not trigger a large number of sterilizations. The rate of official sterilizations in the state remained modest, although it rose from three hundred and thirty in 1946–1948 to almost eight hundred in 1950–1952.[15]

Gamble's slash-and-burn style of making sterilization accessible mirrored his eagerness to deprive the poor and people with mental disabilities of their fertility. As he wrote in 1948, his "fundamental objective in the sterilization field" was to "reach the happy though distant year when no child in the United States shall be born to insane or feeble-minded patients."[16] Yet his approach to sterilization did not rule out the health benefits of sterilization for "the tired-out mother from low-income groups." Gamble was responsible for bringing British psychiatric social worker Moya Woodside to the United States, where, with Gamble's support and over the course of a year and a half, she studied sterilization in North Carolina. Sterilization was justified when the operation was in the "best interests, mental, moral or physical, of the individual concerned; or for the public good; or where children who might be born would have tendency to serious physical, mental or nervous disease or deficiency." To Woodside, the foremost goal was "social welfare, especially the welfare of children," not "the reduction of future generations of defectives." The latter was a "long-term and maybe Utopian goal" (pp. 11, 19).[17]

After extensive interviews with physicians, patients, social workers, and public health officials, Woodside concluded that North Carolina's sterilization law needed to be "broaden[ed]." She argued that demand was growing from all social groups, but a "mentally normal person" from the poor classes had "much less chance of assistance, although on every ground her need is likely to be greater." Such women customarily bore numerous children and thus had a right to contraception that would relieve them entirely of the worry about unwanted pregnancies (p. 58).[17] Once sterilized, their marital lives would improve substantially, thanks in large part to their being less "exhausted" from childrearing and "happier about [their] sexual relationships." As one thirty-seven-year-old African American mother of four confided, sex "fe[lt] better" after her sterilization:

"I know I'm not going to get caught," she rejoiced. Woodside claimed that women's orgasmic capacity tended to increase after sterilization (pp. 136–137).[17]

Woodside's findings matched those of other sterilization advocates. Some sterilized women from around the country wrote movingly about the "constant dread of having another child." Thanks to the operation, many claimed their "mentality" was better because they no longer lived with the fear of becoming pregnant again. "Now that conception is impossible," one testified, "I have no worry and can enter into relations with my husband with a freedom and zest I never enjoyed before. I believe sexual impulse is stronger since the operation." "As far as sexual life, it is enjoyed with much more pleasure," another reported.[18]

In all likelihood, these statements reflected the genuine sentiments of some, if not all, sterilized women. What is beyond dispute is that Woodside (and Gamble) believed that sterilization was good not just for society and future generations of children but for the individuals concerned, from both a psychological and a physical standpoint. With Gamble, as with so many of the pre–*Roe v. Wade* pioneers in the birth control movement, on close inspection it is extremely difficult to disentangle the eugenic, biological, socioeconomic, humanitarian, and feminist motives in their thinking about contraception.

Purge

It was a good thing Gamble possessed money and a strong commitment to sterilization, because he had a propensity to annoy Olden and others in the movement. By the late 1940s, Gamble was a notorious lone wolf when it came to birth control strategy. He had already parted company with the American Birth Control League, in 1942, due to conflicts over fieldwork involving birth control clinics. One Birthright member said Gamble was "the type that likes a particular job which is his own and which he can finance and run."[19]

As for Olden, she admitted that "Dr. Gamble and I seldom agree." She bristled at his criticisms of her posters and publications, notably her fondness for drawing statistical correlations between African Americans and low IQ.[20] Gamble was no freethinker on the issue of race, but he was more sensitive than Olden about the need to defuse potential criticism that sterilization programs targeted African Americans (p. 117).[6] Olden also rejected Gamble's grassroots style of sterilization advocacy, which focused on county welfare rolls, preferring to operate through existing state sterilization laws. Last but not least, she viewed his ability to get things done in the field as a threat to her leadership of the sterilization movement. It came down to a choice between her and Gamble, Olden announced. "If I were removed now," she asked, "what would happen to the movement? Be taken over by Dr. Gamble for his own ideas alone?" (p. 116).[6]

In Gamble's opinion, Olden was responsible for "the irritation which I have found that the organization had left in several places."[21] Yet in the final analysis, Olden had most of the executive committee on her side. Gamble's attitude seemed to say that he was more important than the entire sterilization movement. As effective as Gamble was in expanding access to and generating demand for sterilization services at the local level, the consensus among Birthright's leaders was that no individual's agenda should take priority over the task of building a strong national organization.[22]

In 1947, to no one's surprise, Birthright and Gamble parted ways. Over the next decade, lines of communication between the two never closed entirely. In the 1950s, Gamble helped Birthright pay for small items such as mailing costs. The common cause of sterilization advocacy continued to draw Gamble and Birthright together, yet the clash of personalities dictated that close cooperation was no longer possible. After 1957, when Gamble founded The Pathfinder Fund, an organization dedicated to introducing population control programs in Asia, Africa, and Latin America, he and Birthright (by then the Human Betterment Association of America [HBAA]) went their separate ways.

Olden may have been right about Gamble's independent nature, but her own days as the spokesperson for the sterilization movement were numbered. Much had changed for the sterilization movement in only ten years. The day of the amateur was rapidly coming to a close. Colorful individuals such as Olden were being replaced by (nearly always male) professionals in the medical and social science fields. Birthright's executive committee preferred that a more corporate mentality should reign within the movement. Many sterilization advocates remained eugenic in spirit, but they increasingly frowned upon explicitly social or utilitarian rationales for sterilization. The onus was shifting from trying to get sterilization laws passed in state legislatures to convincing the medical profession to be more receptive to sterilization as a family-planning measure. Within this shifting environment, the sterilization movement increasingly looked to physicians such as Robert Latou Dickinson for the polished, respectable leadership that Olden seemingly could not supply.

Robert Latou Dickinson

Among the activists responsible for changing public attitudes toward birth control in twentieth-century America, only Margaret Sanger over-shadowed the contributions of gynecologist Robert Latou Dickinson (1861–1950). Remarkably, Dickinson somehow managed to maintain his professional stature while simultaneously promoting the highly controversial cause of contraception, a tribute to his considerable social skills and scientific reputation. Dickinson was a major reason why the American Medical Association, which long viewed itself as a defender of "civilized morality" and a stalwart opponent of any politically suspicious reform, recognized contraception as a medical service in 1937 (p. 52).[11]

Elected president of the American Gynecological Association in 1920, Dickinson was founder and director of the Committee of Maternal Health (1923), a group dedicated to clinical studies of various contraceptive methods. He pioneered the use of rubber and plastic models for medical teaching purposes and played a vital role in helping to launch the country's marriage counseling movement. His avid interest in sex research caught the eye of University of Indiana scientist Alfred C. Kinsey, author of the best-selling *Sexual Behavior in the Human Male* (1948) and *Sexual Behavior in the Human Female* (1953). Dickinson introduced Kinsey to "Mr. X," the polymorphously erotic man whom Kinsey studied closely and on whom Kinsey based many of his theories about human sexuality.[23]

In the years leading up to his death, in 1950, Dickinson also became an active supporter of the legalization of euthanasia in the form of "mercy killing," and was one of numerous twentieth-century individuals who campaigned for both the right to die and the acceptance of sterilization.[24] Indeed, on several occasions during the post–World War II era, Birthright and the Euthanasia Society of America exchanged membership lists. Both groups believed that those who endorsed sterilization were also philosophically partial to the legalization of euthanasia, and vice versa.[25]

Dickinson's broad interest in sterilization as a birth control technique led him to join Birthright in 1943. Dickinson was a friend of Clarence Gamble and promptly introduced him to Birthright, setting in motion the short-lived Gamble–Birthright partnership. Dickinson was the first chairman of the group's Medical and Scientific Committee, originally formed in 1949. In 1950 (shortly before his death), Birthright changed its name to the Human Betterment Association of America (HBAA), and its headquarters moved from Princeton, New Jersey, to Dickinson's own Manhattan studio at the New York Academy of Medicine.

As a member of the American Eugenics Society, Dickinson never ceased believing in the eugenic merits of sterilization, calling it a means "to preserve our biological heritage."[26] He was convinced that with every successive generation, the average intelligence level in the United States dropped by 3%. In 1947, he urged Americans to pursue "a sound eugenic program" to counter this alleged decline in national intelligence.[27]

Dickinson's career illustrated how advocacy of sterilization often dovetailed with a concern for a woman's right to sexual happiness. Dickinson believed wholeheartedly in the virtues of separating sex from reproduction. As early as 1913, he argued that sterilization left women "as ready or even more ready for promiscuous intercourse."[28] Beginning in 1920, he launched himself into his "second career" as a sex researcher, promoting (as he put it) "sterilization without unsexing" as an ideal way to help women experience sexual pleasure and strengthen marriage as a social institution (p. 148).[11] Time and again, Dickinson contended that mutual sexual satisfaction was key to marital success, and that informed sex counseling and reliable use of contraception made "exalted expressions of love between husband and wife" possible. To achieve this goal, children should be wanted, planned, and spaced (p. 162).[11] Thus he experimented with different methods of tubal ligation, as well as sterilization with cautery wire. His experimentation also included female masturbation with a vibrator and the use of genital stimulation during pelvic examinations for frigid patients.

Dickinson did not advocate the pursuit of female sexual desire outside of marriage, yet he tirelessly preached the liberating benefits for women of sex education and birth control. Sterilization to Dickinson was an important medical means for reaching his overall goal of emancipating human beings, and especially women, from disease, disability, and ignorance about the physiology of sex and reproduction. He never thought there was the slightest inconsistency between sterilization advocacy and enacting "a broad program to improve the quality of life."[29]

Paul Popenoe

Another marriage-counseling pioneer from the sterilization movement was Paul Popenoe. Born in 1888, Popenoe grew up in Topeka, Kansas, and in 1905 moved with his family to California. In 1929, he was awarded an honorary degree by Occidental College and thereafter was known as "Dr. Popenoe," a national expert in heredity, eugenics, marriage, and the family. In later years he appeared as a syndicated newspaper columnist and regular guest on the popular radio and television versions of *Art Linkletter's House Party*. His series in the *Ladies' Home Journal* (titled "Can This Marriage Be Saved?") was still running in 2005, featuring stories of couples whose marriages were rescued by counseling. In the words of the *Journal*, "Can This Marriage Be Saved?" is "the most popular, most enduring women's magazine feature in the world." Little wonder that Popenoe, who died in 1979, was dubbed "the man who saves marriages."

Popenoe's early career was mainly devoted to eugenics and the study of heredity. As he and his co-author E. S. Gosney wrote in *Sterilization for Human Betterment* (1929), "Modern civilization, human sympathy, and charity have intervened in Nature's plan. . . . The weak and defective are now nursed to maturity and produce their kind."[30] Popenoe and Gosney strongly recommended that the "weak and defective" be sterilized before they produced any children.

Yet by the 1930s, Popenoe correctly sensed that enthusiasm for eugenic sterilization laws was waning, and he switched his interests from "negative" eugenics to the "positive" promotion of "fit" families. He was able to persuade his colleague Gosney to bankroll his American Institute of Family Relations (AIFR), the first marriage-counseling institute in the United States. The AIFR soon became known as the "Mayo Clinic of family problems," and by the early 1950s it boasted thirty-seven counselors, published a monthly magazine, offered degree-based training in marriage counseling, and claimed to have helped 20,000 people enjoy a "happily adjusted marriage." By the time Popenoe died, in 1979, the AIFR had opened seven branches in southern California.[31]

Popenoe's career move into marriage counseling did not mean that he himself had lost faith in sterilization as a method of birth control for society's "defectives." In the 1930s, he described the Nazi sterilization law as "well drawn" and likely to do "a great deal of good" if implemented "conservatively, sympathetically, and intelligently."[32] Yet, as time went on, Popenoe tended to stress how surgical sterilization was a safe and handy operation that met the needs of all couples. By helping couples limit family size, it alleviated the pressure on husbands trying to support their families, improved conjugal relations between spouses, and shielded women with medical conditions from the health consequences of repeated pregnancy. All in all, sterilization saved marriages and made families healthier, according to Popenoe.

Like Dickinson, Popenoe was a good example of the kind of marriage counselor who joined Birthright during its formative years. Other pivotal marriage counselors who belonged to Birthright were Emily Hartshorne Mudd (wife of University of Pennsylvania microbiologist Stuart Mudd); New York City psychiatrist Robert Laidlaw; and Hannah and Abraham Stone, husband-and-wife birth controllers who, in 1931, opened a marriage counseling service, shortly after Popenoe's AIFR was established. Laidlaw, chief of psychiatry at New York City's Roosevelt Hospital and a member of the American Eugenics Society, served as the HBAA's president in the early 1960s. In 1962 he stated[33] that

> as a psychiatrist and marriage counselor I have found that tensions created by fear of repeated pregnancies in many instances have resulted in serious nervous disorders and a disruption of marital harmony. A sterilization operation performed on one of the partners is often the best means of relieving this situation and turning a hopeless into a happy marriage.

In 1963, Laidlaw declared that voluntary sterilization contributed to mental health by easing the fear felt by parents about unwanted pregnancies and "allowing the retarded to marry and lead more normal lives."[34]

Laidlaw's views on sterilization coincided with those of Medora Steedman Bass, born September 8, 1909, in Ardmore, Pennsylvania (see insert). Married to manufacturer George Bass, Medora Bass was the daughter of George Fox Steedman, who had amassed a fortune in the foundry business. During the Depression, she worked as a volunteer with Planned Parenthood and at New Jersey's Vineland Training School. In New Jersey, she met Marian Olden and became a member of the SLNJ. Bass, herself a mother of four, asserted that "most American women want only two or three children."[35] At age forty, having raised her children, she went to back to school and obtained a master's degree in social psychology from Bryn Mawr College. By 1951 she was HBAA vice-president, a fitting post for someone who believed sterilization for "lower socio-economic parents" was a "privilege."[36] Bass wanted to extend this "privilege" to the mentally retarded, who she felt deserved the right to marry but not the right to have children.

Emily Mudd, also a member of the American Eugenics Society, joined HBAA's Medical and Scientific Committee in 1961. Mudd, born September 6, 1898, in Merion, Pennsylvania, was an exceptionally prolific writer on marriage, sexuality, divorce, contraception, the family, and women's rights. Credited with playing "a role in the development of marriage counseling in the United States analogous to that played by

Margaret Sanger in contraception," Mudd had opened the Marriage Counsel of Philadelphia (MCP) in 1933 (renamed the Council for Relationships in 2005) after she and her husband Stuart Mudd had helped to found Pennsylvania's first birth control clinic, in 1927.[37] The Mudds became "devoted" friends of Clarence Gamble, and both served for many years on the board of directors for Gamble's Pathfinder Fund.[38]

Mudd became only the third woman to join the University of Pennsylvania's Medical School and was instrumental in making the MCP the first of its kind in the country to be affiliated with a medical school. She also collaborated with sex researchers William Masters and Virginia Johnson and worked closely with Alfred Kinsey on the research and writing of his second best-seller, *Sexual Behavior in the Human Female* (1953).[39] Mudd, Laidlaw, and Abraham Stone helped to found the American Association of Marriage Counselors (AAMC) in 1945 (renamed the American Association for Marriage and Family Therapy by the early twenty-first century), representing about 23,000 therapists in the United States, Canada, and abroad.[40]

Mudd, Dickinson, Laidlaw, Popenoe, and Stone were key founders of the U.S. marriage counseling profession, whose origins stretched back to Weimar Germany (1919–1933), where centers had been established to provide advice on how to contract "a quality marriage." By 1932, forty-nine out of ninety-eight German cities with more than 50,000 inhabitants had marriage-counseling centers. Originally intended to dispense information on marrying "eugenically," these centers were accessed mainly by men and women looking instead for information on sex and contraception.[41]

In the United States, a similar process unfolded. Even counselors such as Popenoe who favored a eugenic approach to marriage counseling increasingly emphasized women's right to sexual pleasure (albeit within marriage) and greater sexual openness and communication between husbands and wives. In the interest of saving marriages, Popenoe attacked the sexual double standard that privileged male pleasure, instead encouraging husbands to be more sensitive to their wives' sexual needs and more willing to assume parental and housekeeping chores. As a contraceptive method, sterilization was normally granted to couples who had all the children they wanted and were "mentally capable of understanding the situation."[42]

The intersection between the sterilization and marriage-counseling movements, notably after World War II, pointed to the diversity of motives behind the campaign to make sterilization a popular form of birth control. Marriage counselors such as Dickinson, Popenoe, and Mudd sought to strengthen marriages by advocating sex education and information about contraception, including sterilization. Their support for male sterilization anticipated the mounting approval over the next several decades of men taking increasing responsibility for contraception. They never ceased being interested in curtailing the fertility of the handicapped, disadvantaged, and underprivileged. Additionally, when, in the 1950s, sex manuals briefly shifted the emphasis back to male pleasure and the virtues of domesticity for women, marriage counselors tended to follow this current and place the onus on wives to gratify their husbands' libidinous needs. Yet this trend proved to be temporary: no matter how traditionalist their intentions and rhetoric, pro-sterilization marriage counselors contributed to the "discourse of discontent" among women during the 1950s, setting the stage for what many called the "sexual revolution" of the 1960s.[43]

Alan Guttmacher

The presence of Dickinson, Popenoe, Mudd, Laidlaw, and the Stones was a huge asset to Birthright in its fledgling years. Yet perhaps the most prestigious addition to Birthright's ranks in the post–World War II era was Alan Guttmacher (1898–1974), director of obstetrics and gynecology at New York City's Mount Sinai Hospital from 1952 to 1962 (see insert). Born a rabbi's son in Baltimore, and sometimes mistaken for his identical twin Manfred, a psychiatrist, Alan Guttmacher "was as respectable a rebel as any doctor could be." In the 1920s, he trained at the Johns Hopkins University Medical School and Hospital, but later in life he was fond of remarking that he had learned more from "a decade of Monday-night beer drinking with H. L. Mencken and a small group of his intimates in the back room of a mid-town Baltimore Gasthaus" (p. 270).[44]

Guttmacher, after whom New York City's Alan Guttmacher Institute is named, served on the board of directors of the Margaret Sanger Research Bureau and in various posts with Planned Parenthood Federation of America (PPFA), becoming its national president in 1962. A board member of the American Eugenics Society, he joined Birthright in 1946 and in 1952 agreed to chair its newly formed Medical and Scientific Committee, a post he held until 1965.[45] By the time of Sanger's death, in 1966, Guttmacher was the most venerable living birth control proponent in America. As a physician, he, like Dickinson, supplied Birthright with medical credibility at a time when the sterilization movement was desperately attempting to shed its radical image.

Ultimately, Guttmacher would play a pivotal role in the events that led to the 1973 *Roe v. Wade* decision. He claimed his interest in contraception and abortion had been kindled during four years of residency as a medical student in the 1920s at the Johns Hopkins Medical School, where he witnessed several cases of women who died because of botched abortions.[46] However, as late as 1952, Guttmacher opposed abortion, writing that life began at the moment of conception.[47] It was not until 1964, when he organized the Association for the Study of Abortion, that he openly advocated reform of America's state abortion laws. By the end of the 1960s, he backed complete repeal (p. 368).[44]

In the meantime, Guttmacher was a fervent supporter of sterilization for what he called "poorly motivated people."[48] Like so many other birth control proponents prior to the 1960s, he knew that "contraceptive technology had not advanced since the perfection of the spring-loaded diaphragm in the 1920s" (p. 294).[11] He also shared the widespread belief throughout the birth control movement that there were countless people around the world who, due to ignorance, poverty, or "poor motivation," did not utilize contraception the way they should. According to Guttmacher, these people were chiefly to blame for the fact that "millions of children [were] being brought into being and reared in an atmosphere of moral and economic irresponsibility." As an example of the type of parent he had in mind, he cited the case of an unmarried woman from Philadelphia "on relief all her life" who had "added 11 illegitimate children in twelve years to the community burdens." "In New York [City] nearly half the babies in the metropolitan area are born to families on welfare," Guttmacher added. The best way of breaking the cycle of underclass poverty was to offer voluntary sterilization services to precisely those men and women who were a "burden" on society. Guttmacher was convinced that, were such services available, poor men and women across America and around the world would eagerly undergo sterilizations, an ideal means for exercising "their right for a better life, for liberty and the pursuit of happiness."

Yet there is no mistaking his equally deep belief that they *ought* to be sterilized for the good of society. Publicly, he rejected "compulsory prevention of pregnancy," but he left unanswered the question of who decides which pregnancies are "unwanted."[49] Like so many of his peers in the birth control movement, he harbored the "assumption that un-planned means unwanted," what one critic labeled "a false view of self-determination."[50]

In the 1950s, Guttmacher's ward at Mount Sinai became a center for female sterilization. His willingness to surgically terminate the fertility of the typical "ward patient living in the slums who attends our clinics" was so well known that Guttmacher's "law from Mount Sinai" quickly became legendary. Guttmacher's "law" said that he agreed to sterilize any woman who gave birth to a sixth child on his ward and who requested the op-eration. If a woman was thirty to thirty-five years old, it had to be her fifth living child; if she was thirty-five or older, it had to be her fourth child.[48] Guttmacher largely rejected eugenic rationales for sterilization, empha-sizing instead what he called "socioeconomic" factors. Nine percent of the women who had children on his "ward service" were sterilized, in contrast to only 0.3% of the privately paying female patients. As Guttmacher admitted, "the smaller the pocketbook, the larger the family and the better the chance to have one's sterilization request honored."[51]

One of Guttmacher's most significant contributions to the sterilization movement was his 1959 article in the pulp magazine *True Story*, titled "Surgical Birth Control." That *True Story* agreed to publish "Surgical Birth Control," and that Guttmacher declined to use the word "steriliza-tion" in the title, illustrates the stigma that still surrounded sterilization as late as 1960. Yet by publishing in a magazine with such a wide, lowbrow readership (estimated at 5 million), Guttmacher was clearly trying to re-move this stigma and popularize the notion that sterilization was a per-fectly acceptable form of birth control.[52]

Once a luminary of the family-planning movement, Guttmacher is now a shadowy figure from birth control's past.[53] Yet while alive he was a well-known figure who frequently made headlines in the 1960s as the na-tion's debate over abortion escalated. In hindsight, his involvement in the sterilization movement and his tendency to view the operation as a practical way of reducing America's $4 billion price tag for welfare means he was a product of his time and his historical context. Dickinson may have stressed sterilization's sexual benefits more than Guttmacher, and Gamble's and Olden's justifications of sterilization may have differed somewhat from Guttmacher's, but the Mount Sinai physician was a key member of the sterilization movement during a crucial stage in its evo-lution. In his day, there was no contradiction between sterilizing disad-vantaged patients and being a "rebel" in the struggle to win women their reproductive rights.

Half-wits and Morons

An even bigger rebel, and a more vocal advocate of sterilization than Guttmacher in the post–World War II era, was the Philadelphia-born obstetrician H. Curtis Wood (1903–1984) (see insert). Forgotten soon after he died, Wood is an unjustly overlooked contributor to the crusade to break down public and professional resistance to birth control. Prior to the 1960s, Wood was the foremost spokesperson for the entire sterilization movement. A member of the American Eugenics Society, he joined Birthright in 1943, shortly after he heard a speech about sterilization by Marian Olden. He then spent two years on the group's board of directors and served as its president from 1945 to 1961.[54] Wood continued to be the group's main public figure into the 1970s, appearing as its "medical consultant" on literally hundreds of radio and television programs around the country. When, in 1973, he looked back on his career, he proudly announced that the sterilization movement had "come a long way in thirty-five years."[55]

Wood was a good example of the way in which the sterilization movement routinely attracted activists from the birth control movement. Prior to the 1940s, some birth control advocates, including Dickinson and Margaret Sanger, had endorsed sterilization, especially for poor, uneducated, and mentally challenged women whose health was jeopardized by giving birth to numerous children. Wood's own reason for supporting sterilization dated back to a clinical encounter in 1930. As he told Sanger, he became a convert to birth control when he treated a woman who was gravely ill because of a perforated uterus, the result of a botched abortion, her thirteenth. "She told me that she could not properly feed the five children she had and therefore had resorted to the only means she knew of limiting her fertility," Wood recounted. With this experience seared in his memory, he went on to serve as president of the Pennsylvania Planned Parenthood Federation, until he realized that sterilization was "the more practical solution to the overall problem." It was Wood's fervent hope that PPFA would "some day welcome sterilization as an important plank in their platform." When that occurred, in the 1960s, no one deserved more credit than H. Curtis Wood.[56]

Wood, like Dickinson and many others in the sterilization movement, believed that, year after year, America's overall intelligence level was dropping because "the more intelligent" social groups were practicing birth control while the "ignorant" and "irresponsible" classes were not, leading to a "dysgenic" difference in birth rates between the two categories of people.[57] Yet in the late 1940s Wood also believed that trying to reduce this fertility gap through existing state sterilization laws was becoming increasingly impractical. In state after state, officials encountered more and more difficulties trying to arrange for the sterilization of mentally retarded or mentally ill patients. Much depended on the cooperation of physicians, judges, social workers, and families, and if consensus among all interested parties was weak, an application for sterilization could be held up for months in a frustrating maze of bureaucracy and red tape.[58] For men who voluntarily sought a vasectomy, the problem was aggravated by the fact that the formal procedure demanded by a state sterilization law made such requests public and hence embarrassing.[59]

To get around state sterilization laws, Wood instead wanted obstetricians "to be more sterilization minded." Specifically, he wanted them to perform more postpartum tubal ligations. To Wood, society was full of "half wits and morons" who lived undetected and supposedly produced large numbers of children for whom they could not care adequately. Trying to educate politicians to pass the necessary state laws took too much time, according to Wood, and the laws that were enacted were often toothless or too heavily safeguarded.[60] Over the next two decades and beyond, Wood traveled indefatigably back and forth across the country as the sterilization movement's most visible face. He spoke at hospitals and to numerous medical societies in an effort to make physicians more "sterilization minded." In the history of family planning, no single person has done more to spread the message that human beings have a right to choose sterilization as a means of contraception, yet it never seemed to occur to Wood that doctors who talked their pregnant patients into sterilization could be doing anything wrong.[61]

Naturally, Wood was thrilled that Margaret Sanger endorsed sterilization of people with mental disabilities. For years Sanger had been on record as supporting negative eugenic measures aimed at curbing the fertility of the "unfit" classes, but defenders argue that Sanger had sided with the eugenics movement merely as a rhetorical tactic to enlist support for her chief goal of enabling women to separate sex from reproduction. However, her interest in negative eugenics was genuine and lasted virtually to the end of her life. Even in a day and age when such theories were rapidly going out of fashion, she spoke out in favor of mass sterilization of the "feeble-minded and unfit." In a 1950 speech read to PPFA in New York City by her son Grant, Sanger lamented the high costs of welfare programs and proposed that the federal government offer lifetime pensions to couples with "defective heredity" who agreed to undergo sterilization. She also called on PPFA to promote programs offering a "bonus" or "incentive" to accept sterilization. In letters and other speeches in the 1950s, she confirmed that her faith in "eugenic principles" as the basis for "constructing a decent civilization" was unflagging. A top priority was tackling "the unbalanced birth rate which certainly exists in this country [the United States] as well as most of the English-speaking countries." The best way to rectify this fertility imbalance was sterilization, according to Sanger.[62]

Given these pro-sterilization statements, it was natural that Sanger later agreed to be a sponsor of Birthright. In a 1962 promotional letter, she endorsed the group as "the *only* organization to my knowledge supporting and providing voluntary sterilization for those men and women who request it when other birth control methods failed or proved inapplicable."[63] By then, however, the value of Sanger's support was dubious. In her final years, Sanger was "drug dependent, obsessed with her appearance, hungry for flattery . . . a parody of the woman she had once been" (pp. 373–374).[11] Nonetheless, Wood understandably saw in Sanger a more famous version of himself: a single-minded individual dedicated to "enabling the thinking public to better grasp the worldwide significance of this much misunderstood subject."[64] Wood conceded that his "inability to conform along medical lines" meant that "many of my fellow doctors think I am a bit 'cracked.'" That Sanger early in her career had faced many of the same prejudices made Wood all the more determined to voice his "rather radical ideas."[65]

However, Wood's admiration of iconoclasm did not extend to Marian Olden. Sparks between Wood and Marian Olden began flying almost the moment he joined Birthright, in 1943. Like virtually everyone in the sterilization movement, Wood strongly opposed the Catholic Church's involvement in birth control public policy. However, he tended to agree with the sterilization advocate who told Olden, "[W]e should not stir up doubts about [the Catholic] church and its wisdom. . . . It does us no good to raise the feeling that we are attacking any church, no matter if what we say is really true. . . . To ignore them and their machinations is the wiser procedure."[66] Another sterilization supporter claimed that if Olden were more "diplomatic . . . the opposition of the Catholics will cease, if not give us some positive help."[67] Wood was convinced that in the long run, the best course of action was to build bridges with the medical profession, not hurl invectives against Catholic teaching. Wood concluded that Birthright's difficulties were caused more by Olden's continued affiliation with the group than any Catholic opposition.

The last straw for Wood and Birthright's executive committee was Clarence Gamble's departure. No sooner had Gamble's affiliation with Birthright been terminated than Birthright's executive committee had second thoughts about originally backing Olden. Many had joined the sterilization movement "from a sense of broad interest in the movement and obligation to keep it going, but with little or no enthusiasm for the experience of sitting through a meeting" with Olden presiding.[68] Wood frankly told her that "everyone on the executive committee" thought the movement would progress more "if you did not come to the meetings at all."[69] Olden was accused of chasing influential people from the movement, including wealthy benefactors and foundations. Yet the bottom line was that Birthright's leadership and staff "could not continue working [for the movement] if Mrs. Olden were to be continued in the organization."[70] In June, 1948, Birthright's executive committee voted to sever any "formal connection on a salary basis" between Olden and the organization.[71]

Olden's fate at the hands of Birthright's executive committee was partly due to her lack of social skills, yet it was also due to the tensions along gender lines that lurked below the surface of the sterilization movement. As happened in both the birth control and euthanasia movements, the men in the movement normally were professionals who preferred to dictate policy and delegate secretarial work to women. Women such as Olden who showed independence and tried to exert control over strategy often faced resistance from their male counterparts. In the words of one male family planner, "women workers" in the movement were "too emotionally concerned . . . and too little equipped with the experience, techniques and skill to do an objective job." Margaret Sanger told a female coworker in PPFA, "Go ahead, darling, get kicked around—you will never get kicked upstairs."[72] Olden put it another way: "If there is a hard unpopular job to be done, one that is very uncertain of success, a woman is allowed to do it. But once it is certain that it is going to endure and become an important organization then she no longer 'has the qualifications needed.' "[73]

The severing of ties between Birthright and Olden signaled that the sterilization movement had reached a crossroads as the 1950s dawned. Publicly, its leaders expressed optimism that they were about to turn a corner in their struggle to gain respectability and increase the sterilization rate. Yet in the shadow of World War II, America's moral and political conservatism appeared as formidable as ever. Sterilization advocates knew they still had to wage a steep uphill battle to win the approval of the

medical profession and the American public. They faced the task of en-
listing the support of such birth control groups as PPFA, who were wary
about open association with the seemingly more radical Birthright. Last,
but not least, as the 1950s would demonstrate, the Roman Catholic
Church was at the height of its cultural and political power in twentieth-
century America. The prospects for an abrupt change in the nation's
mores and behavior regarding sex and reproduction looked as dim as
ever.

Notes

1. William Ray Vanessendelft, interview with Marian Olden, April 1976, *A
   History of the Association for Voluntary Sterilization, 1935–1964*. University of
   Minnesota: unpublished doctoral dissertation, 1978, p. 69.
2. Marian Olden, "Birthright, Inc.–Its Roots, Fruits, and Objectives," AVS,
   Box 2, folder 8.
3. Ellsworth Huntington, the president of the American Eugenics Society,
   commended Gosney for his dedication to making sterilization "gradually
   accepted as a necessary measure for preserving the health of the community."
   Ellsworth Huntington to Gosney, October 7, 1940, Gosney Papers, 6.20.
   Cited in Kline W. *Building a Better Race: Gender, Sexuality and Eugenics from the
   Turn of the Century to the Baby Boom*. Berkeley and Los Angeles: University of
   California Press, 2001, pp. 80–81.
4. Winfred Overholser to Olden, September 2, 1942, AVS, Box 1, folder 3.
5. Marian Olden to Sheldon Glueck, November 6, 1947, AVS, Box 2, folder 14.
6. Vanessendelft WR. *A History of the Association for Voluntary Sterilization, 1935–
   1964*. University of Minnesota: unpublished doctoral dissertation, 1978.
7. Olden M. *Human Betterment Was Our Goal*. Privately published, 1970, pp. 22–
   23. For the public health dimensions of immigration to the United States in
   the early twentieth century, see Kraut AM. *Silent Travelers: Germs, Genes, and
   the "Immigrant Menace."* New York: Basic Books, 1994. For the attitude of U.S.
   and Canadian psychiatrists toward immigrants, see Dowbiggin IR. *Keeping
   America Sane: Eugenics and Psychiatry in the United States and Canada, 1880–1940*.
   Ithaca: Cornell University Press, 1997, pp. 133–231.
8. Marian Olden, "Birthright, Inc.–Its Roots, Fruits, and Objectives," pp. 1, 5.
   See also Olden's statements at the May 11–15, 1944, meeting of the American Association of Mental Deficiency that World War II had killed off the
   best American stock while the worst multiplied on the home front. As a result,
   she predicted that after World War II sterilization would "have greater
   support than it has ever had and we must be ready to direct this impetus in
   order to win the battle on the home front which is essential if we are to realize
   the brave new world we envisage." AVS, Box 11, folder 93.

9. For a partisan account of Draper, see Lynn R. *The Science of Human Diversity: A History of the Pioneer Fund*. Lanham, MD: University Press of America, 2001, pp. 3–19. For a very different interpretation of Draper and the Pioneer Fund, see Kühl S. *The Nazi Connection: Eugenics, American Racism, and German National Socialism*. New York and Oxford: Oxford University Press, 1993, pp. 6, 49, 106; also Kenny MG. Toward a Racial Abyss: Eugenics, Wickcliffe Draper, and the Origins of the Pioneer Fund. *Journal of the History of the Behavioral Sciences*. 2002;38:259–283.

10. Paul Popenoe to Olden, January 20, 1947; Olden to Mrs. Winthrop Bradford, February 12, 1947, AVS, Box 2, folder 14. Draper did donate to Birthright in later years, although his contributions were usually in the range of $500 per year.

11. Reed J. *From Private Vice to Public Virtue: The Birth Control Movement and American Society Since 1830*. New York: Basic, 1978.

12. Schoen J. *"A Great Thing For Poor Folks": Birth Control, Sterilization and Abortion in Public Health and Welfare in the Twentieth Century*. University of North Carolina: unpublished doctoral dissertation, 1995.

13. Clarence Gamble to George Cooper, August 12, 1940, CJG, Box 25, file 433.

14. Reilly P. *The Surgical Solution: A History of Involuntary Sterilization in the United States*. Baltimore and London: the Johns Hopkins University Press, 1991, pp. 133–134; Vanessendelft WR. *A History of the Association for Voluntary Sterilization, 1935–1964*. University of Minnesota: unpublished doctoral dissertation, 1978, pp. 82–83.

15. Vanessendelft WR. *A History of the Association for Voluntary Sterilization, 1935–1964*. University of Minnesota: unpublished doctoral dissertation, 1978, pp. 82–83; Schoen J. *"A Great Thing For Poor Folks": Birth Control, Sterilization and Abortion in Public Health and Welfare in the Twentieth Century*. University of North Carolina: unpublished doctoral dissertation, 1995, pp. 117–118, 119–120n.

16. Clarence Gamble to Robert Latou Dickinson, November 15, 1948, CJG, Box 230, file 3554.

17. Woodside M. *Sterilization in North Carolina: A Sociological and Psychological Study*. Chapel Hill: University of North Carolina Press, 1950, pp. 11, 19.

18. Kline W. *Building a Better Race: Gender, Sexuality and Eugenics from the Turn of the Century to the Baby Boom*. Berkeley and Los Angeles: University of California Press, 2001, pp. 87–88. Kline was quoting from files on sterilization patients in the E. S. Gosney Papers and the Records of the Human Betterment Foundation at the California Institute of Technology Archives, Pasadena, CA.

19. Lydia de Vilbiss to Olden, November 11, 1944, AVS, Box 2, folder 12.

20. Clarence Gamble to Marian Olden, July 14, 1946; Clarence Gamble to Marian Olden, July 23, 1946. CJG, Box 230, file 3551.

21. Clarence Gamble to H. Curtis Wood, April 8, 1947, AVS, Box 2, folder 13; Clarence Gamble to Medora Bass, February 24, 1948, CJG, Box 230, file 3554. One Gamble backer within Birthright said it deserved to be called

"Birthwrong" if it ever parted company with Gamble. Robert Latou Dickinson to H. Curtis Wood, May 19, 1947, AVS, Box 2, folder 14.

22. H. Curtis Wood to Birthright's Board of Directors, April 19, 1947, AVS, Box 2, folder 14. Because of his past disputes, Gamble aroused antagonism in Birthright's potential allies, such as PPFA. Gamble's field projects allegedly cost Birthright too much money to administer. He also irked Birthright's leadership by setting up separate state sterilization organizations in Iowa and North Carolina, calling them Human Betterment Leagues.

23. Jones JJ. *Alfred C. Kinsey: A Public/Private Life*. New York and London: W. W. Norton, 1997, pp. 291, 503–508.

24. Dowbiggin I. *A Merciful End: The Euthanasia Movement in Modern America*. New York and Oxford: Oxford University Press, 2003, pp. 74–76, 77, 81, 85, 138.

25. Eleanor Dwight Jones to Marian Olden, May 28, 1945, AVS, Box 2, folder 12; Mrs. Robert Edwards to Birthright, June 28, 1949, AVS, Box 2, folder 13.

26. Kline W. *Building a Better Race: Gender, Sexuality and Eugenics from the Turn of the Century to the Baby Boom*. Berkeley and Los Angeles: University of California Press, 2001, p. 78.

27. Dickinson to the editor of the *Memphis Mirror*, April 19, 1947, AVS, Box 2, folder 14.

28. Dickinson to Mrs. F. B. Fincke, November 6, 1913, AVS, Box 13, folder 106.

29. Reed J. *From Private Vice to Public Virtue: The Birth Control Movement and American Society Since 1830*. New York: Basic, 1978, p. 185; Kline W. *Building a Better Race: Gender, Sexuality and Eugenics from the Turn of the Century to the Baby Boom*. Berkeley and Los Angeles: University of California Press, 2001, pp. 66–94.

30. Gosney ES, Popenoe P. *Sterilization for Human Betterment*. New York: Macmillan, 1931, p. v.

31. Ladd-Taylor M. Eugenics, sterilization and modern marriage in the USA: The strange career of Paul Popenoe. *Gender and History*. 2001;3:310, 312.

32. Popenoe P. The German sterilization law. *Journal of Heredity*. 1934;24:257–260; Ladd-Taylor M. Eugenics, sterilization and modern marriage in the USA: The strange career of Paul Popenoe. *Gender and History*. 2001;3:307.

33. Quoted in "Statement by Mrs. Ruth Proskauer Smith, Executive Director, Human Betterment Association," September 10, 1962, AVS, Box 36, Ruth Proskauer Smith Correspondence.

34. Laidlaw R, Bass M. *Voluntary Sterilization As It Relates to Mental Health*. Presented at the 16th annual meeting of the World Federation for Mental Health, Amsterdam, July 22–26, 1963, AVS, Box 34, Laidlaw folder.

35. Medora Bass to the editor of the *Herald Tribune*, April 8, 1963, AHC, MSB, Box 2.

36. Medora Bass to Rachel Levine, August 12, 1964, AHC, MSB, Box 2.

37. http://www.upenn.edu/gazette/030990bits.html.

38. Mudd S. "Report of Ad Hoc Committee On Population," September 21, 1970, EM, Carton 11, folder 479.

39. In 1944, Mudd lined up 550 case history interviews for Kinsey, the most anyone had arranged for Kinsey in the six years of his research at the University of Indiana, with the possible exception of Robert Latou Dickinson. Kinsey to Emily Mudd, May 15, 1944, EM, Carton 16, folder 729. For Mudd's lengthy involvement in Masters and Johnson's Reproductive Biology Research Foundation (in 1978 renamed the Masters and Johnson Institute), see EM, Cartons 8–9, folders 429– 469.

40. Broderick CB, Schrader SS. The history of professional marriage and family therapy. In Gurman AS, Kniskern DP (eds.). *Handbook of Family Therapy*. New York: Brunner/Mazel, 1981, pp. 5–35.

41. Proctor RN. *Racial Hygiene: Medicine Under the Nazis*. Cambridge: Harvard University Press, 1988, pp. 136–140.

42. Ladd-Taylor M. Eugenics, sterilization and modern marriage in the USA: The strange career of Paul Popenoe. *Gender and History*. 2001;3:306–307.

43. Moskowitz E. "It's Good to Blow Your Top": Women's magazines and a discourse of discontent. *Journal of Women's History*. 1996;8:67–98.

44. Garrow DJ. *Liberty and Sexuality: The Right to Privacy and the Making of Roe v. Wade*. Berkeley and Los Angeles: University of California Press, 1998, p. 270.

45. Alan Guttmacher, pioneer in family planning. *New York Times*, March 19, 1974.

46. Guttmacher A. Why I favor liberalized abortion. *Reader's Digest*. January 1974, 142–145.

47. See Noonan JT Jr. *A Private Choice: Abortion in America in the 1970s*. New York: Free Press, 1979, p. 37. Cited in Patrick Allitt. *Catholic Intellectuals and Conservative Politics in America, 1950–1985*. Ithaca and London: Cornell University Press, 1993, p. 172.

48. Alan F. Guttmacher, "The Place of Sterilization" (1964), AVS, Box 34, Guttmacher folder.

49. Alan F. Guttmacher, "Memorandum: To Medical and Civil Leaders Concerned With Family and Community Welfare," January 11, 1962, AVS, Box 34, Guttmacher folder.

50. Gordon L. *Woman's Body, Woman's Right: A Social History of Birth Control in America*. New York: Penguin, 1980, p. 403.

51. Guttmacher, "The Place of Sterilization" (1964), AVS, Box 34, Guttmacher folder; AF Guttmacher. The population crisis and the use of world resources. In Mudd S (ed.). *The Population Crisis and the Use of World Resources*. Bloomington, IN: Indiana University Press, 1964, pp. 269, 270; Guttmacher decries archaic U.S. sex-conception laws, *Columbia University Law School News*, November 23, 1960; Guttmacher AF. General remarks on medical aspects of male and female sterilization. In Robitscher J (ed.). *Eugenic Sterilization*. Springfield, IL: Charles C. Thomas, 1973, pp. 55.

52. Guttmacher's "Surgical birth control" had been preceded in print by Donald Cooley's "Vasectomy: The sterilization operation for men," which had

appeared in the August 1956 issue of *True: The Man's Magazine*, another pulp magazine.

53. Curiously, given the several biographies of Margaret Sanger, Guttmacher has yet to find a biographer. His papers are located at Harvard University's Countway Library.

54. Vanessendelft WR. *A History of the Association for Voluntary Sterilization, 1935–1964*. University of Minnesota: unpublished doctoral dissertation, 1978, pp. 99–100, 105. Vanessendelft interviewed Wood in April 1976.

55. H. Curtis Wood, Report of the Medical Consultant, AVS annual meeting, March 28, 1973, AVS, Box 110, 1973 Minutes folder.

56. H. Curtis Wood to Margaret Sanger, October 28, 1950, AVS, Box 4, folder 33.

57. H. Curtis Wood to William Vogt, August 2, 1948, AVS, Box 2, folder 15.

58. For an example of the frustrations of a psychiatrist from Arizona over the state's "obsolete, top-heavy, and impractical" sterilization law, see M. W. Conway to Irene Headley Armes, January 3, 1953, AVS, Box 8, folder 74.

59. Paul E. Stearns to Mildred F. Mayers, June 15, 1956, AVS, Box 91, Returned Questionnaires folder.

60. H. Curtis Wood to Robert Latou Dickinson, November 22, 1948, AVS, Box 2, folder 15.

61. H. Curtis Wood to Irene Headley Armes, November 22, 1948, AVS, Box 2, folder 15. This was also the view of E. S. Gosney, who noted that "voluntary sterilization in private practice is of great value. Many students of the subject are convinced that during the next generation the bulk of sterilizations in the United States will be of the voluntary type." Gosney, quoted in Hogue F. Social eugenics. *Los Angeles Times Sunday Magazine*, March 1, 1936, p. 30.

62. "Sterilization: A Modern Medical Program for Human Health and Welfare," AVS, Box 36, Sanger folder. See also "Addresses by Margaret Sanger" in the same folder. For Sanger's reference to "eugenic principles," see Margaret Sanger to C. P. Blacker, May 19, 1953, CMAC, SA/EUG/Box 22, C.304. For an interpretation of Sanger's 1950 PPFA speech that blames her "tragic regimen of drugs and alcohol" for such "impulsive" statements, see Chesler E. *Woman of Valor: Margaret Sanger and the Birth Control Movement in America*. New York: Simon and Schuster, 1992, pp. 417–418. However, Chesler ignores the fact that Sanger's 1950 comments were not all that different from what she had written in the 1920s, when her health had been much better.

63. Margaret Sanger, April 25, 1962, HBAA promotional letter, CJG, Box 231, folder 3570. Her emphasis.

64. Wood to Margaret Sanger, October 28, 1950, AVS, Box 4, folder 33.

65. H. Curtis Wood to Alan Guttmacher, October 14, 1954, AVS, Box 34, Guttmacher folder.

66. Elsie Wulkop to Olden, May 13, 1946, AVS, Box 2, folder 13.

67. Guy Irving Burch to Olden, January 19, 1946, AVS, Box 2, folder 9.

68. Lowett Dewees to Marian Olden, October 31, 1946, AVS, Box 2, folder 13.

69. H. Curtis Wood to Marian Olden, March 12, 1948, quoted in Vanessendelft WR. *A History of the Association for Voluntary Sterilization, 1935–1964*. University of Minnesota: unpublished doctoral dissertation, 1978, p. 135.

70. H. Curtis Wood to Mr. Coleman-Norton, June 17, 1948, AVS, Box 2, folder 15.

71. Minutes of June 11, 1948, executive committee meeting, AVS, Box 2, folder 15.

72. For Sanger's comment, see Florence Rose, personal notes, May 2–25, 1943, Margaret Sanger Papers, Sophia Smith Collection, Smith College, Northampton, MA. For D. Kenneth Rose's remark, see his "Report with Recommendations to the Board of Directors of the Birth Control Federation of America," May 18, 1939, Clarence James Gamble Papers, Francis Countway Library, Boston, MA, p. 3. For both quotations, see McCann CR. *Birth Control Politics in the United States, 1916–1945*. Ithaca: Cornell University Press, 1994, p. 197.

73. Olden M. *From Birthright, Inc. to Voluntary Sterilization, 1943–1963,* p. 274. A female Birthright member noted Olden's story was an old one: "woman conceives a work, makes a success of it, and some ambitious person takes it away from her." Lydia DeVilbiss to Marian Olden, February 5, 1949, quoted in Vanessendelft WR. *A History of the Association for Voluntary Sterilization, 1935–1964*. University of Minnesota: unpublished doctoral dissertation, 1978, p. 146; Olden M. *Human Betterment Was Our Goal*. Privately published, 1970, p. 263. For similar developments in the euthanasia movement, see Dowbiggin IR. *A Merciful End: The Euthanasia Movement in Modern America*. New York and Oxford: Oxford University Press, 2003, pp. 53–54. For the birth control movement, see Gordon L. *Woman's Body, Woman's Right: A Social History of Birth Control in America*. New York: Penguin, 1980, p. 255; McCann CR. *Birth Control Politics in the United States, 1916–1945*. Ithaca: Cornell University Press, 1994, pp. 197–198.

Chapter 3

The Poverty Bomb

A s the 1950s dawned, the sterilization movement in America faced a grim future. The death of Robert Latou Dickinson, in 1950, was a blow to the movement, but its members remained intent on attracting respected health-care professionals with a view toward greater medical acceptance of sterilization in the coming years. The mainstreaming of Birthright, mirrored in its 1950 name change to the Human Betterment Association of America (HBAA), gave movement members hope that partnerships could be formed with other, less controversial birth control organizations.

However, these hopes crashed to earth in the 1950s as the country's cultural and political climate shifted dramatically. Social pressure to marry and bear children peaked in the postwar years, and a resurgent religiosity swept the United States. The pace of involuntary sterilizations under existing state laws slowed significantly, and hospitals made it more difficult for women to obtain tubal ligations. The dominance of Catholic bioethical teaching, which condemned all forms of artificial contraception, put family-planning proponents on the defensive. By the late 1950s, there were indications that the Catholic Church was beginning to liberalize its overall stance on contentious social issues and church–state relations. In the meantime, however, the birth control movement in general and the sterilization movement in particular faced concerted opposition from Church officials and Catholic laity over the ethics and practice of contraception.

Red Tape and Trouble

If anything gladdened the hearts of sterilization proponents in the immediate post–World War II period, it was the vigorous (if uneven) operation of state sterilization laws around the country. In some states, the number of sterilizations performed under existing laws fell, but in others the rate of sterilization actually climbed in the late 1940s and early 1950s. It was not until the 1960s, when eugenics became "virtually a dirty word in the United States" and concerns over individual civil rights rose sharply, that the functioning of state sterilization laws began slowing for good.[1]

During World War II, with national attention focused on the challenges of defeating Germany and Japan, the number of involuntary U.S. sterilizations plunged. Because of the desperate need of the country's armed forces for medical personnel, surgeons were in short supply on the home front. The few surgeons not serving in the armed forces had busier-than-ever practices, leaving them little time to perform low-priority eugenic sterilizations (pp. 128–129).[2] Yet with the return of peacetime, some state sterilization laws briefly enjoyed new life. After a low of 1,183 sterilizations nationally in 1944, there were three consecutive increases between 1947 and 1950. The total of 1,526 operations in 1950 may have been lower than the usual annual rate for the 1930s, but sterilization statutes were anything but dead letters in the postwar period.[3]

As had been the case before World War II, events in California heavily affected the U.S. sterilization rate after 1945. Prior to the 1950s, California officials had been national leaders in the campaign to sterilize inmates of state institutions. Yet between 1949 and 1952, the number of sterilizations under California's law tumbled from three hundred and eighty-one to thirty-nine, never to revive again. Nothing affected California's totals as much as the retirement of Fred O. Butler, medical superintendent of the Sonoma State Home for the Feeble-Minded. Between 1918 and his 1949 retirement, Butler, Birthright's medical director, was personally responsible for over 5,400 sterilizations.[4]

States such as Virginia, North Carolina, and Georgia helped to pick up some of the slack left by Butler's retirement. In 1944, these states combined for two hundred and eighty-five sterilizations (24% of the nation's total). By comparison, in 1958 they sterilized five hundred and seventy-four patients, or 76% of all recorded operations.[5]

At the local level, the sterilization rate largely depended on the attitude of mental health professionals. When medical superintendents favored the operation, the number of sterilizations performed by surgeons at certain institutions could be relatively high. According to Luther T. Hurley of the Fort Wayne (Indiana) State School, in 1954,

[M]any patients [are] released to the community after sterilization has been performed, and they are showing a satisfactory adjustment. Many women especially marry, and are able to take care of their own households, and lead an adjusted life partly due to the sterilization operation which prevents a family of children to overload them emotionally and economically.

Given such positive opinions about sterilization, it was little surprise that as late as 1955, Hurley arranged for seventy-five (forty-five male and thirty female) operations at his institution.[6] Elsewhere, the pattern was similar. At Oregon's Fairview Home, staff sterilized nine hundred and ninety-nine patients between 1923 and 1949, and in 1953 alone, forty-three inmates were sterilized.[7] At Georgia's enormous, 10,000-bed State Sanatorium at Milledgeville, the largest U.S. mental hospital, two hundred and sixty-four sterilizations of mentally ill patients (eighty-five females and one hundred and seventy-nine males) took place in 1957.[8]

Yet by the mid-1950s, certain trends were unmistakable. In 1942, the U.S. Supreme Court decision in *Skinner v. Oklahoma* invalidated an Oklahoma law that permitted the sterilization of felons after three convictions. *Skinner v. Oklahoma* revealed that the court was concerned that sterilization could lead to human rights abuses. Though it did not overturn the 1927 *Buck v. Bell* ruling, *Skinner v. Oklahoma* sent the clear message that public health officials were on shaky constitutional ground when they ordered sterilizations of inmates of state institutions (pp. 128, 130–131).[2]

Except for a few locales, opposition to the reasoning behind sterilization laws was also mounting in the postwar years among health-care professionals who worked with people with disabilities. As a new generation of medical superintendents took over the management of many of the country's hospitals, doubt steadily grew about both sterilization's usefulness in reducing the incidence of genetic disease and its rehabilitative influence on patients. In the words of an official[9] at the South Dakota State School and Home for the Feeble-Minded, in 1949:

We are discovering that better environment of the progeny of the feeble-minded individuals in South Dakota has been valuable in raising the I.Q.s of said progeny. We are further discovering that the so-called heredity basis of feeblemindedness is becoming smaller, percentagewise, as the years go by.

> Careful history taking and neurological examinations reveal that a huge percentage of our patients are suffering from brain disorders which can only be due to birth injuries, encephalitis, tumors, and various congenital malformations. It appears that sterilization is by no means the answer to the problem.

Outright hostility to sterilization was also rising. In the caustic words of a Connecticut medical superintendent, "[W]hen we sterilize the lower 2 per cent of the height curve—the very short people; when we sterilize the lower 2 per cent of the weight curve—the very thin people; *then* we should sterilize the lower 2 per cent of the intelligence curve—the mental defectives."[10]

Additionally, the rate of sterilization slowed because, in many states, sterilization statutes were so safeguarded that it took months of planning and paperwork to have a patient sterilized. In 1946, a physician from West Virginia[11] complained that

> our sterilization laws . . . are so complicated that it takes about six months to get permission to sterilize any particular patient. . . . I hope that some future legislature soon will modify the laws until we can do sterilizations without going through a lot of red tape and trouble.

In Connecticut, the medical director of the Southbury Training School claimed he had "no difficulty in persuading both the retarded patient or their parents" to have an inmate sterilized, but the law required a diagnosis of "inherited transmissible condition as a prerequisite" for the operation. "This limits [the law's] use considerably," he commented ruefully.[12]

Public opinion about sterilization also fluctuated from state to state. One Indiana doctor lamented that he had been "criticized strongly and in public (newspapers and legal aid society) for merely suggesting sterilization."[13] In some states after the war, scandals broke out when the local press alleged that sterilizations at homes for the retarded led to human rights abuses.[14] By contrast, the "informality" of "therapeutic" sterilizations performed by physicians in regular and teaching hospitals away from the glare of public scrutiny grew more and more attractive to sterilization advocates (pp. 69–70).[15] No wonder that physicians such as H. Curtis Wood thought the best way to increase the sterilization rate was to sidestep the cumbersome bureaucracy of state laws and stimulate both popular demand and medical support for the operation.

Yet the relentless opposition of the Roman Catholic Church also sapped the enthusiasm for state sterilization laws. Efforts in Wyoming and Pennsylvania after World War II to introduce an involuntary sterilization act failed because of Catholic attacks.[16] Where similar laws were already on the statute books, Catholic prelates directed judges to stymie efforts to sterilize the handicapped. In 1953, Pope Pius XII officially condemned eugenic sterilization.[17] As the 1950s wore on, the political and cultural power of the American Church indicated to sterilization advocates that a new rationale had to be found to boost demand for sterilization as a surgical remedy for unwanted pregnancy.

In God We Trust

By the 1950s, a formidable Catholic consensus had crystallized in implacable opposition to eugenics in general and sterilization in particular. Beginning in the 1930s, in the wake of Pius XI's *Castii Connubii*, Catholic condemnation of eugenics became virtually unanimous. Catholic medical ethicists taught that the conjugal act should always be open to the possibility of conception. Sterilization for either men or women was viewed as another form of artificial contraception. The excision of a patient's fallopian tubes was considered to be illicit even if she was suffering from tuberculosis or heart ailments. The intention of the surgeon may have been to save the patient's life, but the "mutilation" of healthy reproductive organs to prevent pregnancy was "never permissible." To Catholic ethicists, the views of people such as Clarence Gamble, who argued that sterilization was indicated in some cases of heart, kidney, or lung weaknesses, were dangerous in a day and age when growing numbers of doctors were inclined to perform "unnecessary surgery." Catholic bioethics regarding sterilization were designed to counter what one theologian called the "mutilating mentality" of some surgeons.[18]

To Church leaders, advocacy of birth control, sterilization, abortion, and legalized euthanasia confirmed the so-called "seamless garment" theory popular in Catholic theological circles. This theory stated that taking a permissive attitude toward birth control would lead to grave injustices. In 1931, the editors of the Catholic journal *Commonweal* warned that improving access to contraceptives "would be a long step on the road toward state clinics for abortion, for compulsory sterilization of those declared unfit by fanatical eugenicists, and the ultimate destruction of human liberty at the hands of an absolute pagan state."[19] In 1936, a Fordham University Jesuit called efforts to sterilize the handicapped "an attempt to make America goose-step with foreign state absolutism."[20] When leading birth control advocates such as Margaret Sanger openly praised eugenic sterilization as part of an overall family-planning agenda, and when the horrors of Nazi medicine became front-page news after World War II, Church leaders felt vindicated.

Catholic ability to predict the crimes of Nazi medicine raised the Church's credibility in the postwar years. For years, practicing physicians had dominated the field of medical ethics, such as it was.[21] But as the twentieth century wore on, Catholics, led by Jesuit priests John C. Ford and Gerald Kelly, built up an impressive body of writings that addressed the myriad clinical situations facing doctors, nurses, patients, and families. Exhibiting "a fierce moral seriousness," Ford, Kelly, and other Catholic theologians grappled with a wide variety of health-related questions that concerned both Catholics and non-Catholics. Should a patient be told she has cancer? (Yes.) Is an alcoholic taking a drink committing a mortal sin? (No.) Kelly was responsible for "the first detailed Catholic code of medical ethics, adopted by hundreds of Catholic hospitals in Canada and the United States," and in 1947 began writing a monthly column aimed at Catholic doctors and hospital administrators. As one critic of the Church ruefully admitted in 1954, "Catholic literature on the morals of medical care is both extensive and painstaking in its technical detail, while Protestant and Jewish literature is practically non-existent." Secular literature on bioethics was similarly nonexistent (pp. 219–220).[22]

Catholic teachings on medical morals did not enjoy wide currency in the 1950s solely because of their coherence and subtlety. The decade in U.S. history witnessed a broad tide of popular religiosity that helped to make the Church "the dominant cultural institution in the country."[23] Evangelical and fundamentalist churches experienced remarkable growth after World War II. Evangelist Billy Graham and the Rev. Norman Vincent Peale spoke to millions over radio and in newspapers and books. The U.S. Congress followed the religious winds by adding the words "under God" to the Pledge of Allegiance and the phrase "in God we trust" to all United States currency. President Dwight D. Eisenhower regularly opened cabinet meetings with a prayer. This "new piety" struck some observers as bland and lacking theological depth, but as a new "civil religion" it bred a suspicion of radical ideas that challenged customary mores.[24]

American Catholicism thrived within this religiously tinged cultural climate, its unity, discipline, and hierarchical structure propelling it to the center of U.S. life. Only a generation earlier, many Protestant Americans had viewed Catholics with a deep distrust, the legacy of the longstanding tension between the two strands of Christianity stretching back to the sixteenth-century Reformation. U.S. anti-Catholicism was also due to the fierce xenophobia of nativist Americans toward Irish and Italian immigrants, who arrived in waves between the 1830s and the 1920s. Yet widespread anti-Catholicism seemed to decline in the post–World War II era, replaced by a diffuse public willingness to follow the Church's lead in setting the policy agenda for the country. Everything from politics and movies to the new medium of television reflected the formidable presence of the Church in daily life. Cardinal Dennis Dougherty had the honor of offering the invocation at both the Democratic and Republican nominating conventions in 1948. Catholics monitored Hollywood films for over two decades, pressuring the studios to eliminate scenes of sex and violence from their movies. On television, Bishop Fulton J. Sheen's *Life Is Worth Living* show was watched by more viewers than comedian Milton Berle's *Texaco Comedy Hour*.[25]

Ballot-box power accounted for much of this trend. Between 1930 and 1960, the Catholic share of the national population grew from 19% to 23%. Catholics tended to cluster in large urban areas, such as Philadelphia, New York, Chicago, and Boston. Brooklyn alone held more than 1 million Catholics in 1930. Urban politicians eager to win Catholic votes courted powerful Catholic prelates such as New York City's Francis Cardinal Spellman.[26] In states such as Connecticut and Massachusetts, the Catholic grip on politics was especially tight. In 1942 and 1948, liberals in Massachusetts failed to win referenda allowing doctors to prescribe and distribute contraceptives to married women, thanks to aggressive Catholic campaigning that linked greater access to birth control to euthanasia, abortion, and sterilization (pp. 229–231).[22] Little wonder that the Protestant *Christian Century* ran an eight-part series in 1944–1945, opening with the question, "Can Catholicism Win America?"[27]

Success in defeating proposed state sterilization bills emboldened Catholics to target sterilizations performed in hospitals. At Catholic hospitals, staff tried to discourage even non-Catholic patients from requesting sterilizations. Catholic prelates and lay groups likewise brought pressure to bear on public hospitals where operations were taking place.[23] One Church tactic was to threaten physicians affiliated with birth control organizations with the loss of their ward privileges at Catholic hospitals.[29] Catholic pressure also forced hospital administrators to establish special boards to monitor the rate of sterilization.[30]

Medical Conservatism

Catholic opposition to sterilization coincided with what Alan Guttmacher called the "caution and conservatism of the medical profession."[31] In the years leading up to World War II, it appeared as if doctors and hospitals were easing restrictions on sterilizations. As the medicalization of pregnancy and childbirth gained momentum, physicians exerted more and more control over the reproductive health of their patients.[32] At the same time, patient demand for sterilization was fairly strong. "We're plagued all the time by women who are having their second or third child and want you to sterilize them," one physician admitted.[33] When a woman patient was poor, uneducated, or African American, the likelihood of postpartum tubal ligation in many hospitals was high. It was also high when the patient was white and affluent and wished to stop having babies (pp. 116–117).[34]

Yet in a postwar cultural and political climate stressing fertility and traditional values, whatever reproductive autonomy women enjoyed before 1945 shrank sharply. To determine whether a woman "deserved" a sterilization, the American College of Obstetricians and Gynecologists adopted a formula based on a woman's age multiplied by the number of children she had. If the product was 120 or more, doctors could operate, but only if a psychiatrist and two physicians approved the surgery. The American College of Surgeons and the American Medical Association cautioned physicians that they should not be "too free with tubal ligations." "Sterilizations of convenience" at teaching hospitals were discouraged. Hospitals and physicians who performed high numbers of sterilizations often received letters from professional medical associations questioning their actions. In response, hospitals began establishing sterilization committees as well as abortion committees to determine who qualified for these procedures. Such committees typically demanded clearcut emotional or physical reasons for sterilization. These policies had a chilling effect on members of the medical profession who might otherwise have considered fulfilling requests from patients for a tubal ligation (pp. 117–118).[34] As Guttmacher complained in 1959, many hospitals that had set up joint abortion and sterilization committees required "the same indications for sterilization as are demanded *by law* for abortion—i.e., to save the life of the mother."[35] By that date, the interwar permissiveness toward sterilization had all but vanished.

Overseas Sterilization

It did not improve the mood of America's sterilization advocates that, as they faced strong domestic opposition in the 1950s, sterilization programs were thriving in other parts of the world, notably Puerto Rico, where, by the 1970s, roughly one-third of all married women had been sterilized. No political jurisdiction in history, before or since, has matched this rate. The origins of this remarkable state of affairs date back to 1898, when Puerto Rico was colonized by the United States. At the turn of the twentieth century, the population of Puerto Rico, consisting of people of Cajun and Spanish ancestry, was overwhelmingly Roman Catholic. In the eyes of many U.S. social scientists, it was also in the midst of rapid population growth, a perception that in 1937 would prompt Island legislators to decriminalize birth control (in fact, the colony's birth rate was modest in comparison with those of other Caribbean and Latin American countries) (p. 14).[36] Public health officials in both Puerto Rico and the United States tended to concur that large families were the chief cause of the abject poverty in which so many Puerto Rican women were mired (p. 203).[34] U.S. Assistant Secretary of Agriculture Rexford Tugwell, who toured Puerto Rico in 1934, claimed that on the Island there were "a dozen children behind every bush, many of them indifferently nourished." Although the Puerto Ricans appeared "happy and light-hearted" about having so many children, he argued that "a recognition on the part of the Islanders themselves must be developed by which they will become conscious of the fact that an improved standard of living . . . is possible only to the extent that a definite check on the increase of population is made" (pp. 33–34).[36]

In the late 1930s, colonial as well as mainland opposition to birth control compelled the federal government to cancel its funding for Puerto Rican family planning, but private philanthropists (notably Clarence Gamble) quickly began supplying financial assistance. Applying the lessons he had learned in North Carolina and elsewhere, Gamble exerted his influence over the development of birth control programs in Puerto Rico, including the 1937 founding of a Eugenics Board. Over the following decades, the Island's Eugenics Board authorized relatively few compulsory sterilizations, but the incidence of elective female sterilization rose sharply.[37] By the mid-1950s, about one-sixth of all married women there had been sterilized (p. 56).[38]

Despite the efforts of contraceptive manufacturers and family planners, countless Puerto Rican women preferred sterilization to spermicidal jelly, condoms, foam powder, diaphragms, and oral contraceptive pills. Additionally, in contrast to medical attitudes on the mainland, physicians in Puerto Rico tended to view sterilization favorably (p. 179).[38] Another reason for sterilization's popularity was that government and private hospitals increasingly offered sterilization as a postpartum procedure. Stories abounded of women from all socioeconomic categories flocking by the thousands to hospitals to deliver their third or fourth children and undergoing sterilization during the same visit. Hospitals that did not offer postpartum tubal ligation reported empty maternity wards (p. 139).[36] Puerto Rican women in New York City, who, like their relatives on the Island, found contraceptive measures to be "highly repugnant or unacceptable," thought little of "disappearing" to Puerto Rico for a week to be "fixed."[39] One estimate said that two to three births per mother had been averted by sterilization in Puerto Rico.[40] Thus, thanks largely to sterilization, the Puerto Rican birth rate fell from one hundred and sixty per 1,000 women aged fifteen to forty-nine in 1940 to one hundred and two in 1970, a harbinger of later events in other parts of the globe (p. 11).[38]

Several aspects of Puerto Rico's sterilization policy caught the attention of mainland sterilization proponents. The persistent opposition of Catholic prelates to sterilization in Puerto Rico was a bitter reminder to HBAA members of the similar battles they were waging in the United States, but the Island's example also demonstrated that victory was possible, especially if they could win physicians' backing. Likewise, Puerto Rico confirmed that when it came to popularizing sterilization, language mattered a great deal: thanks to people calling it "la operación," sterilization was viewed as a mere surgical intervention. This process of medicalization transformed an erstwhile taboo topic into a more neutral, less value-laden subject, paving the way to broad acceptance (p. 141).[36] Yet perhaps the most instructive feature of the sterilization campaign in Puerto Rico for U.S. advocates was how the operation could be justified on the basis of its ability to relieve poverty and combat overpopulation. If (as its defenders claimed) it helped to avert as many as three unwanted births per mother, its potential for easing worldwide overcrowding and slowing the depletion of finite natural resources appeared to be enormous. The sterilization movement would capitalize on this powerful argument in later decades.

Japan was another example of what sterilization advocates could accomplish in the name of family planning and population control. In 1940, Japan enacted a eugenic sterilization law, but by the end of World War II the number of Japanese sterilized under these laws was only four hundred and fifty-four.[41] Unconditional surrender in 1945 ushered in a radically new era in the history of Japanese sterilization. The country was occupied by Allied forces, headed by General Douglas MacArthur and dominated by Americans and U.S. policy analysts. The consensus among the occupiers was that population pressure had caused Japanese militarism and imperialism, and thus they encouraged Japanese legislators to pass laws to reduce the country's fertility rate. When over 4 million repatriates (mostly male) combined with the mass discharge of Japanese soldiers to produce a postwar baby boom, the Japanese Diet enacted the Eugenic Protection Law in 1948. Though the bill's main goal was to "prevent the increase of inferior descendants," it would never have been passed without the mounting concern over the country's "over-population problem." The Eugenic Protection Law permitted both abortion and sterilization in the name of reducing the birth rate, making the bill the world's most permissive abortion legislation. Sterilization could be performed for a long list of conditions and circumstances, including the health of the mother. Between 1949 and 1956, the annual total of Japanese sterilizations rose from 5,356 to 42,662. The combined impact of sterilization and abortion helped to lower Japan's birth rate by 43% between 1947 and 1955.[42]

Yet to sterilization advocates it was not immediately obvious how sterilization policies in defeated, foreign-occupied, and war-ravaged Japan could be applied to postwar America, with its decidedly different political culture and its unprecedented affluence and economic expansion. Sterilization policy in the Scandinavian countries Sweden, Denmark, Norway, and Finland appeared to fit the American experience more closely. Long renowned for offering progressive "cradle to grave" welfare programs designed to redistribute wealth to all classes of society, the Scandinavian countries also implemented policies that led to the sterilization of thousands of citizens. During the interwar period, these nations had passed laws permitting sterilization to prevent hereditary illness, improve the overall health of women, and protect the mentally handicapped from pregnancy. Between 1935 and 1975, almost 63,000 Swedes were legally sterilized, roughly the same number as in the United States, a country with a population about twenty times the size of Sweden's. Over the same time period, Norway, with a population of only 3 million in 1940, sterilized 41,000 of its citizens (pp. 109–110, 178).[43]

Although circumstances often varied from one country to another, Scandinavian sterilization laws were united on the basis of "reform eugenics," the belief that such measures, while they could not dramatically affect the biological quality of the race, could at least benefit society and improve the lives of some men, women, and children. A 1936 Swedish commission stated that "it has earlier been a rather common belief that sterilization among hereditary sick and inferior human beings would result in a strong and rapid improvement of humankind, and erase mental diseases, feeble-mindedness, and other cases of severe inferiority. This belief is not correct." Many individuals were sterilized without proper consent, but the prevalent view was that their weak intelligence warranted the operation. As one leading Swedish policy expert said in 1942, "[S]terilization is such an important operation that the individual should not be allowed to decide the matter for himself. Very many of those who should be sterilized are feeble-minded or mentally ill and are therefore not even able to understand what it is all about, or cannot, at least, judge the reasons." By the 1950s, sterilization policy in Scandinavia had evolved to the stage where the operation was an accepted part of a broad, state-run welfare system designed to improve the health and happiness of all citizens. A "broad consensus" uniting physicians, scientists, women's organizations, and legislators from all parts of the political spectrum backed sterilization laws in Sweden, Finland, Denmark, and Norway, conferring on sterilization a respectability that American advocates could only envy (pp. 106, 115, 262).[43]

The vigor of foreign sterilization programs underscored the challenges facing the sterilization movement. As Robert Latou Dickinson asked rhetorically in 1947, "Can we not learn from the experience of progressive countries like Sweden and Denmark what great benefit to a nation is derived from a sound eugenic program?"[44] In fact, in the late 1950s, HBAA hired a consultant to study Sweden's sterilization program. The consultant's conclusion pointed to the need for America's sterilization movement to alter its strategy. Sterilization in Sweden was "an organic part of a fundamental and comprehensive and far-reaching development of population policy, family policy, and social legislation." The contrast with the United States was stark. There, a "paralysis of the sterilization laws in most states" was becoming evident in the 1950s, due to sterilization being limited to heavily safeguarded, compulsory legislation affecting chiefly institutionalized men and women. The lesson from Sweden was that the scope of sterilization programs had to be widened to affect a greater portion of the population and had to emphasize therapeutic and social rationales, not just eugenic considerations. If sterilization was to become more extensive in American society, it also had to be "closely interwoven with social legislation" based on a "population policy which seeks to encourage parenthood among its best-endowed stocks through such positive measures as the provision of family allowances, better housing, free medical care, advice on the spacing of pregnancies, and so on" (p. 162).[15] In other words, access to sterilization had to be viewed broadly as a key component of a wide-ranging public health and social welfare program. Above all, sterilization policy had to shed its image as punitive and coercive.[45]

Ruth Proskauer Smith

To achieve this goal, sterilization supporters had their work cut out for them. Before the wider acceptance of sterilization could become a reality in America, the sterilization movement had to roll back Roman Catholic influence over social policy. This was the sort of challenge that particularly appealed to New Yorker Ruth Proskauer Smith. Smith, the HBAA's executive director from 1955 to 1964, was an ardent advocate of sterilization as a social welfare measure and a basic human right. She was the archetypal twentieth-century social activist, working tirelessly for the decriminalization of birth control, acceptance of sterilization, and the repeal of America's abortion laws. Besides her work for the HBAA, she was deeply involved in the activities of the Euthanasia Society of America, which sought the legalization of voluntary mercy killing. In 1967, she helped to organize the group that later became the National Abortion Rights Action League (NARAL). In 1970 she served as president and vice-president of the Abortion Rights Association of New York. After *Roe v. Wade* (1973), she threw all her estimable energy into the struggle for the right to die. Still alert and as dedicated as ever in 2000, Smith told an interviewer that when she was ready to die she wanted to be put out of her misery like the aging racehorse Secretariat had been in 1989. Her support for euthanasia, like her support for sterilization, abortion, and birth control, was (in her own words) "all of a piece."[46] At the turn of the twenty-first century, few activists could match her contributions to the cause of American social reform.

Ruth Smith was born in 1907 in Deal, New Jersey, to Alice Naumburg Proskauer, a staunch supporter of human rights, and Joseph Proskauer, a New York Supreme Court justice who wrote Franklin D. Roosevelt's

"Happy Warrior" speech nominating Al Smith as the Democratic Party candidate for president in 1924. Ruth Smith received a master's degree in fine arts from Radcliffe College in 1932. Between 1949 and 1953, she served as executive secretary of the Planned Parenthood League of Massachusetts. From 1953 to 1955, she was the administrator of Alan Guttmacher's contraceptive clinic at Mount Sinai Hospital. Her ties to Guttmacher only strengthened in later years as they struggled together to break down resistance to sterilization and liberalize the country's abortion laws.

Ruth Smith was described as a "lean, soldierly woman [who] had the no-nonsense bearing of a headmistress of a particularly severe turn-of-the-century school for English gentlewomen. Her flinty exterior concealed a heart of steel."[47] These traits stood her in good stead during her years as HBAA's executive director. Back then it was a "mom and pop" organization with a skeleton staff and tiny budget, she reminisced in 2000, but her admiration for H. Curtis Wood and Alan Guttmacher encouraged her to work closely with them to advance the sterilization cause. Ruth Smith was much more willing to defer to physicians Guttmacher and Wood than Marian Olden had ever been. Yet in many other respects Smith carried on the tradition begun by Olden of single-minded and dedicated women activists in the sterilization movement.[46]

Ruth Smith also differed with Marian Olden over heredity as a cause of mental disability. Smith was no adherent of the theory that certain social or racial groups were genetically predisposed to low intelligence. Like Alan Guttmacher, she believed wholeheartedly that all forms of contraception—especially sterilization—should be made available to all women. However, Smith's ardent faith in sterilization led her to advocate public policies that scarcely differed from those Olden favored. Smith thought that poor, uneducated, and seemingly unmotivated families deserved particular attention from family planners. These types of individuals, she argued, contributed most heavily to the incidence of social problems. In a 1959 letter to the *New York Post*, she referred to the drain on "public tax money" of families such as

> one of the cases a court psychiatrist encountered in New York's Children's Court: Both neglectful parents had IQ's under 50, and were themselves so mentally defective and emotionally ill that they could barely keep themselves going, without the responsibility of raising their *12* children. All six children under 16 needed to be placed; four were severe mental defectives and two were emotionally disturbed with dull normal intelligence. All six over 16 were in prison. As you doubtless know it takes $5,500 to keep one man in prison one year.

To Smith, Catholic political intimidation prevented New York City employees from referring such families to community family-planning clinics where, presumably, they would be convinced of the error of their ways. This Catholic obstructionism led her to believe that the root cause of the misery and suffering throughout the world was organized religion.[47] The irony was that while she became a fierce anti-Catholic because of the Church's opposition to euthanasia, sterilization, abortion, and birth control, her father had fought against the anti-Catholic bigotry Al Smith had encountered in his battle for the presidency.

Matters seemed to come to a head in 1959, when the National Conference of Roman Catholic Bishops issued a statement opposing "any public assistance, whether at home or abroad to promote artificial birth control, abortion, or sterilization." President Dwight D. Eisenhower replied that funding for domestic or overseas birth control programs should come from private agencies, not U.S. government sources. Smith was appalled by this position and protested that tax money was "being poured into a bottomless pit here in New York" only to "support . . . quantity production of these many unloved, unwanted, and neglected children," rather than pay for "facilities for education, recreation, and housing for a smaller group with a higher potential." Taxes spent on welfare, in other words, could have been better spent on services for society's fit individuals.[48]

Clearly, Smith believed that sterilization as a birth control method would serve important social goals. Yet she often viewed the popularization of sterilization as a victory for democratic, personal autonomy. Like many U.S. progressives in the post–World War II era, Smith was worried that the Church would use its political clout to impose its value system on non-Catholics, causing a breach in the so-called wall separating church and state. In 1959, Smith, in her capacity as executive director of the HBAA, pressed Roman Catholic Massachusetts senator John F. Kennedy to support "freedom of choice" for people who desired access to contraceptive services. She was overjoyed when Kennedy replied that birth control was a "political" and not a religious issue. But when Smith asked Kennedy if she could make his opinion public as his campaign for the presidency gained steam, Kennedy backed down, citing the "misinterpretations" that might arise from the dissemination of his views on birth control in 1959. To Smith's chagrin, Kennedy was just as silent on the matter even after he became president in 1960. A stellar opportunity for perhaps the most prominent U.S. Catholic to endorse reproductive "freedom of choice" was missed. Only after his assassination, and during the presidency of Lyndon Baines Johnson, would federal policy makers become truly sympathetic toward population control and family planning.[49]

In the meantime, Ruth Smith helped to steer HBAA in the same direction as other groups such as the American Civil Liberties Union and the newly formed Protestants and Other Americans United for the Separation of Church and State. Her fierce opposition to the Catholic Church in matters of public policy was shared by other HBAA members, including Paul Blanshard, the American who most forcefully articulated these concerns during the early Cold War.

Paul Blanshard

For centuries, the Roman Catholic Church has had its share of bitter opponents, but few have enjoyed the media limelight more than Paul Blanshard. Twentieth-century luminaries including Albert Einstein, John Dewey, Bertrand Russell, and Supreme Court justice Hugo Black hailed him for his searing attack on the Church's authority and doctrines. Blanshard (1892–1980), a one-time Congregationalist minister, served as an urban reformer in the La Guardia administration in New York City in the 1930s, and during World War II he was an economic analyst and consultant for the U.S. State Department. He catapulted to national fame in 1949 with the publication of his best-selling *American Freedom and Catholic Power*. Blanshard's book, first serialized in the left-liberal magazine *The Nation* and followed in 1951 by *Communism, Democracy, and Catholic Power*, decried the Roman Catholic Church as a monumental threat to U.S. institutions and American democratic values. Blanshard accused the Church of intolerance, dogmatism, authoritarianism, and the worst form of sectarianism. In *American Freedom and Catholic Power*, he particularly castigated the Church for its official doctrines regarding sex, reproduction, and death. The Church's ethic of celibacy was a policy that "thwarted instincts and suppressed desire," he wrote. Blanshard specifically condemned the Church for frustrating Birthright's efforts to persuade state legislators to pass more eugenic sterilization laws and for directing Catholic judges to prevent such laws from operating when they were on the statute books. "Meanwhile," he asserted, "the feeble-minded who are at large in our population produce future Americans at a much faster rate than normal citizens."[50] Privately, he assured sterilization advocates of his wholehearted support for "eugenic ideals."[51]

Blanshard's thesis was attractive to countless Americans who believed that the genius of America's political system was its pluralism and its "wall of separation between church and state," as Thomas Jefferson had put it in 1801. U.S. liberals, buoyed by the Supreme Court ruling *McCollum v. Board of Education* (1948), interpreted the "wall" theory to mean that no church could impose its dogma on all Americans and that, in the 1948 words of an *Atlantic Monthly* writer, "religious truth is an individual quest."[52] Yet liberals like Blanshard who attacked Catholic doctrine wanted to go even further, and (assuming Catholics weren't thinking for themselves) appealed to Catholics to throw off the Church's authoritarianism. One prominent Unitarian urged Catholicism to reform itself into a form of Christianity "free of all autocratic ecclesiastical control over the mind and conscience of its individual members."[53] For many liberals uneasy about Catholic power, including Paul Blanshard, the first step toward realizing true freedom in America was not the establishment of genuine religious pluralism; it was the democratization of the Church itself, and that could be done only by imposing an entirely different value system on individual Catholics.

Catholics counterattacked, claiming that their appeals to natural-law theory transcended personal choice.[54] Undaunted, sterilization proponents had reason to think their message might resonate with Catholics. Their data indicated that among individual Catholics (especially female laity), the demand for sterilization was high. As long as their records conveyed this information, sterilization advocates backed Blanshard's allegation that democracy's future depended on freeing Catholics from the oppression exerted by their own Church's hierarchy.

Joseph Fletcher

Paul Blanshard's claims that Catholic medical ethics were a grave threat to American democracy and the health of ordinary men and women were music to the ears of clergyman Joseph Fletcher, teacher at the Episcopal Divinity School in Cambridge, Massachusetts. No one, between the 1950s and his death in 1991, tried more to defeat the Catholic ascendancy in bioethics than Fletcher, who ended his career teaching at the University of Virginia Medical School. His celebration of individual choice as the bedrock of a new approach to medical ethics helped to pave the way to a "new morality" that, he wrote, "declares that anything and everything is right or wrong, according to the situation." On close examination, however, Fletcher's "situation ethics" was less about personal choice than about sweeping aside religious objections to birth control methods, including sterilization.

Like so many other individuals who belonged to the sterilization movement, Fletcher is unjustly forgotten in the twenty-first century. Yet, while alive, Fletcher shared with people such as Alan Guttmacher, Robert Latou Dickinson, and Margaret Sanger the ability to grab headlines and deeply influence the evolution of public values regarding life, death, sex, and reproduction. A member of the American Eugenics Society, Fletcher was fond of uttering statements designed to shock conventional opinion, such as his 1973 Nietzschean remark that "the old God is dead." By the "old God," Fletcher meant the God whose "sacralistic inhibitions on human freedom and research" interfered with personal choice.[55] Relentlessly candid and fiercely dedicated to preaching what he believed, Fletcher, by the time he died, had earned the grudging respect of even his most adamant foes.[56]

His attacks on traditional Christian doctrine as "weird and untenable" made him a key founder of the academic discipline of bioethics, while his iconoclastic defense of abortion and legal mercy killing helped to spark debates that were still raging in the early twenty-first century. Fletcher introduced the notion of "situation ethics," the cornerstone of today's biomedical ethics, later codified in his 1979 *Situation Ethics* (which sold a million copies). Fletcher claimed situation ethics started with the question, what is the patient's situation? Since the answer to this question, he reasoned, was different in every case, there were no longer hard-and-fast rules to guide medical conduct. The only consideration that mattered was what suited the patient's situation. The crucial point was an individual's free decision to act in a certain way. Situation ethics sought to "widen freedom" of choice, as well as responsibility. Echoing Paul Blanshard, Fletcher contended that categorical prohibitions against euthanasia, abortion, and sterilization weakened democracy.[57] To his Catholic opponents, fundamental moral principles never changed.[58] To Fletcher, by contrast, there was no such thing as an unchanging ethical principle.

Born in 1905, in Newark, New Jersey, Fletcher, from an early age, was temperamentally and intellectually drawn to radical causes that stressed emancipation from traditional values and institutions. He was an open admirer of Eugene Debs, socialist candidate for the U.S. presidency. Later he joined the campaign to unionize workers in the American South. Involvement in the American Birth Control League led to a close friendship with Margaret Sanger. After World War II, he advocated better relations with the Soviet Union and international control of atomic weapons. This stance on the Soviet Union drew the ire of Senator Joseph McCarthy, who denounced Fletcher as "the Red Churchman." During the 1960s, Fletcher was a staunch supporter of civil rights for African Americans and, alongside some of his seminary students, marched with Martin Luther King Jr. The last two decades of his life were mostly devoted to a leadership role in the nation's right-to-die movement.[59]

To sterilization advocates, the 1954 publication of Fletcher's *Morals and Medicine* by Princeton University Press was a milestone event. *Morals and Medicine* not only defended abortion, euthanasia, birth control, and sterilization but also constituted the first systematic attack on the Catholic hegemony over bioethics. Predictably, Fletcher had trouble publishing the book and blamed his difficulties on "Roman Catholics and many doctors [who] would not agree with my conclusions."[60] Yet even sympathizers such as Alan Guttmacher felt Fletcher's bold foray into medical ethics left a lot to be desired. Given an early draft of the manuscript to referee, Guttmacher[61] wrote that it was

> a poor job and I am certain *no popular* publisher will have anything to do with it. It is verbose, poor style with too many defining parentheses. Furthermore his medical facts are curiously fallacious; I tried to correct many of them. I just feel the whole thing is hopeless.

Yet despite Guttmacher's misgivings, by the 1960s he and the rest of the HBAA were convinced that Fletcher was much more of an asset than a liability to the group. Fletcher's rising notoriety as a clerical bioethicist eager to challenge Catholic norms overshadowed his shaky grasp of medical science.

Thus Fletcher was a natural choice for HBAA president in 1962. He was a nephew of Irene Hadley Armes, Ruth Smith's predecessor as HBAA executive director, serving until her death in 1955. Thanks to his deep interest in reproductive rights and his close friendship with Smith, Fletcher gravitated toward the HBAA in the 1950s and was still active in the group in the mid-1970s, when he chaired its Clergymen's Committee. Fletcher agreed wholeheartedly with HBAA's goals. As he[62] told the press in 1961:

> It is a grave wrong and a cruel offense against personality to allow stunted and defective lives to be procreated when the means to avoid it are available, and Human Betterment is doing what it can to make those means available to married persons who have enough conscience to use them. Sterilization by either surgical or pharmaceutical means is an answer to both

overpopulation and the tragedy of unwanted and congenitally defective births.

As a clergyman, Fletcher was a valuable addition to HBAA ranks, as he was to the several pro-euthanasia groups he supported. Sterilization advocates were intent on convincing the government, the public, foundations, and organized medicine that there was nothing immoral or unethical about the operation. When clergy (especially Catholic theologians) charged that sterilization conflicted with fundamental religious teachings, it was handy to have Fletcher argue otherwise. For example, on April 3, 1963, at the Carnegie Endowment International Center in New York City, HBAA (then the Human Betterment Association for Voluntary Sterilization [HBAVS]) hosted a conference for physicians and clergymen on the question, "Does Voluntary Sterilization Pose an Ethical Problem?" Panelists included Fletcher, Alan Guttmacher, Robert Laidlaw, and Rabbi Balfour Brickner, later Director of Interfaith Activities for the Union of American Hebrew Congregations.[63] Presiding was William Genné, HBAA member and the executive director of the Department of Family Life of the National Council of Churches of Christ. Fletcher emphatically defended sterilization by claiming it enables people to escape "any kind of brute submission to the blind workings of physical nature" and thereby seek "personal self-determination and self-possession" by separating sex from conception.[64] The 1963 conference generated little press coverage, and none of the other speakers quite matched Fletcher's enthusiasm for sterilization. Yet as the 1960s unfolded, Fletcher's characterization of voluntary surgical contraception as a basic individual right and a medically ethical procedure made it easier and easier for the movement to increase the nation's sterilization rate.[65]

The French Plan

Ethical rationales for sterilization such as Fletcher's proved to be useful for the HBAA in the coming years, as did books such as Lee Atwater's *And the Poor Get Children* (1960), which (though paying sterilization little attention) underscored the perception that low-income people found it difficult to practice birth control.[66] Yet in the short term, boosting the number of U.S. sterilizations meant getting counseling, hospital, and surgical services to the people who supposedly needed them the most. This was a stiff task for a movement with severely limited financial resources. The movement's challenge was all the more daunting in a day and age when organized medicine and the public health and welfare systems made it difficult for someone to obtain a sterilization. Thus, when wealthy Philadelphia lawyer Graham French offered the HBAA a startup grant of $10,000 to help subsidize sterilizations for poverty-stricken Americans, the movement's leadership rejoiced. French already knew H. Curtis Wood through their mutual membership in Protestants and Other Americans United for Separation of Church and State, but after he and his wife heard Wood speak in 1956 at a local Planned Parenthood of Pennsylvania meeting about the virtues of sterilization, he contacted HBAA. French and his wife were so impressed with Wood's message—that improved access to sterilization for the poor would cut welfare costs and reduce the size of America's impoverished class—that French was willing to provide loans to those couples who agreed to either vasectomy or tubal ligation. French made it clear that there would be no pressure on these couples to repay the "loans," in effect making them outright gifts.

"We seem destined to become an organization nationally recognized as well as national in name," HBAA's treasurer exulted in 1957.[67] Yet elation over the so-called French Plan quickly ebbed. HBAA was caught flat-footed by French's offer: it lacked the staff and the resources to get the plan off the ground. French made matters more difficult by insisting that none of his donation be used for overhead costs, such as mailing, travel, and telephone. Nor did he agree to pay for legal fees or the extra staff that had to be hired. HBAA had to notify welfare agencies and community service organizations to send them referrals, then connect patients with doctors and obtain ward privileges for surgeons. Events often did not run smoothly. One Baltimore woman, pregnant with her tenth child, wanted her tubes tied right after delivery. Arrangements were made for the delivery and operation to take place at Guttmacher's Mount Sinai ward, but the baby came quickly and had to be delivered on short notice at another hospital that prohibited sterilizations. The tubal ligation had to be postponed until six weeks after delivery.[68]

From 1957 to 1960, HBAA helped to arrange five hundred and eight operations with French's funding. When Guttmacher's article "Surgical Birth Control" was published in *True Story* in 1959, and after noted physician Walter C. Alvarez's nationally syndicated column in favor of sterilization appeared on May 16, 1960, the group's office was flooded with more than 2,500 requests for information on sterilization. Most readers, convinced by Guttmacher that sterilization was a relatively safe, easy, and effective operation that did not diminish sex drive, wanted to know how to find a surgeon to perform the procedure.[69]

Eventually French backed out of helping to fund HBAA's referral service. By 1963, he had decided that HBAA was too poorly run to do the job of arranging sterilizations properly, and he asked that his name be dropped from the organization's letterhead.[70] In the meantime, another sterilization initiative had been launched in rural Virginia at the Fauquier County Hospital, about fifty miles from Washington, D.C. Located in Warrenton, the Fauquier Hospital in 1960 was a small, modern, sixty-three-bed facility that offered a contraceptive program for patients who could not pay their medical bills. The hospital's sterilization service was the brainchild of HBAA board member Alice duPont Mills, whose husband James was on Fauquier's board, as was Dr. H. W. Stinson, who later became HBAA president. It was Mills's money that enabled the hospital to open its contraceptive clinic in the first place.[71]

Beginning in 1960, the Fauquier Hospital staff had been providing information about sterilization to women patients with three or more children who attended the contraceptive clinic, including an offer of a free tubal ligation. By 1963, of two hundred and three medically indigent women patients, sixty-three had been sterilized. About two-thirds of the sterilized patients were African American.[72]

Fauquier's sterilizations, in the words of the *New York Times*, "caused a nationwide uproar." The "uproar" occurred in 1962, when the *Washington Post* reported a tour of the hospital organized by the HBAVS.[73] When the *New York Herald Tribune* and *New York Times* ran the same story off the wire service, a wave of protests followed. A handful of Unitarian pastors endorsed what the hospital was doing, but evangelist Billy Graham condemned sterilization as "a permanent crippling of a vital body function." The president of the Union of American Hebrew Congregations called sterilization, whether voluntary or not, "utterly reprehensible." A senior rabbi of a Reform congregation declared sterilization "a violation of definite moral law." But leading the attack on the hospital's contraceptive clinic was Patrick A. O'Boyle, Washington's Roman Catholic archbishop. In a sermon that worshipers at St. Matthew's Cathedral agreed was the bitterest of his fourteen-year tenure, O'Boyle denounced sterilization as "fundamentally wrong" because it "directly violates a natural right which is so profoundly sacred that it may not be taken away from the individual by the State and may not be voluntarily surrendered to the State by the individual." O'Boyle added that resorting to sterilization as a means of fighting poverty "in the case of many Negroes and not a few whites" would be an abdication of society's moral responsibility to solve its pressing problems through more humane means.[74]

The media also attacked Fauquier's program, questioning how voluntary the sterilizations were and citing the program's "unlimited possibilities for abuse." A Washington, D.C., radio host warned that "coercion can take many subtle forms, and there are always people who believe that they know what is best for someone else and who are prepared to exercise their belief effectively." Catholic and African American journalists accused Fauquier staff of treating blacks like "second-class citizens."[75]

Allegations of racism deeply troubled some HBAA members. Sterilization advocates stressed that of all the Fauquier patients sterilized, only four expressed complaints. They also emphasized the health benefits of the operation for poverty-stricken and chronically ill patients. Yet it was difficult to stifle comments from the hospital's defenders, who confirmed that its sterilization policy was designed to lower welfare costs and save taxpayers money. Similarly, it did not help when the head of Fauquier's staff stated that a major reason behind the sterilization program was that patients were too "ignorant and lazy" to use contraceptives successfully. More eyebrows were raised when it was disclosed that most of the sterilizations were performed shortly after patients had given birth, at a time when they may have been susceptible to pressure. HBAVS executive director Ruth Proskauer Smith worried that Fauquier's practices might be linked to rumors about doctors in America's South routinely tying the tubes of black patients while performing abdominal surgery and getting consent only later. Smith clearly opposed sterilizing patients because of their race, but she was one of many HBAVS members who believed sterilization was a way for underprivileged Americans to have fewer children and break the cycle of welfare dependency, "a hand-up rather than a handout." To Smith, ending poverty, not racism, was the main motive behind the sterilization movement.[76]

Invading Hordes of Unborn

Yet defusing the "poverty bomb" through sterilization meant HBAVS would be continually open to charges of Nazi-like eugenics. This hard lesson was learned again during another privately funded sterilization program, the so-called Hartman Plan. Named after Jesse Hartman (see insert), a New York City industrial real-estate agent, the plan was a pilot project to pay for vasectomies and tubal ligations arranged by the Mountain Maternal Health League of Berea, Kentucky. The Hartman Plan's aim was to strike at "the root of the Appalachian poverty problem" in eastern Kentucky by providing poor families with sterilization, "the most reliable birth control method." Hartman donated $25,000 to HBAVS, a grant to last from June 1 to December 31, 1964, and later donated an additional $10,000. Hartman and HBAVS hoped that the success of the project would encourage the government to ultimately assume the costs of the program itself. Until then, the plan was billed as "the first known partnership between American private philanthropy and government."[77] Yet, like the Fauquier clinic, the Hartman Plan was soon mired in controversy, with at least one radio station calling the plan's organizers a bunch of "Hitlers."[78]

Besides Hartman and Ruth Smith, a key individual involved in the plan was physician Louise Hutchins, mother of four and wife of Berea College president Francis Hutchins. Born to missionary parents in China, Louise Hutchins came to Kentucky in 1939 and ultimately served as board president of the Mountain Maternal Health League, a Planned Parenthood Federation of America affiliate, for nearly fifty years. For thirty-eight years, Hutchins was Berea's only pediatrician, disseminating birth control information and methods to Appalachian families on horseback, by Jeep, on foot, and through the mail. Clarence Gamble had already sponsored a birth control project in the region based on the use of contraceptive jelly. Gamble's funding of the Berea project stopped in 1945, but Hutchins's efforts to end the "baby a year syndrome" that characterized the lives of many Kentucky families continued. In 1963, the Mountain Maternal League began offering prescriptions for the oral contraceptive pill.[79]

Hutchins may have been willing to experiment with different modes of contraception, but she was a fervent backer of sterilization as a family-planning method. As she told Hartman:

> What you have done is far more reaching in breaking the poverty cycle than all the truckloads of food and clothing sent to Appalachia for the Christmas season. . . . We have already proven that our overburdened mothers and fathers desire this help. The next thing is to prove to the powers that be that paying for this surgery is good economics for them.

Hutchins and others involved in the Berea project hoped to capitalize on the fanfare surrounding President Lyndon Baines Johnson's recent call for a "war on poverty." In 1964, Congress, at Johnson's urging, established the Office of Economic Opportunity (OEO), charged with managing an array of programs designed to eliminate poverty. A chief focus of Johnson's "war on poverty" was family planning. Administration officials, including Johnson himself, believed that empowering poor women to avoid unwanted pregnancies would enable the country's underclass to escape the cycle of poverty and would strengthen the family, "the cornerstone of our society," in Johnson's own words.[80]

As the health officer in Kentucky Appalachia declared, "the problem of too many children in needy families lies at the root of the Appalachian poverty problem." While sterilization proponents undoubtedly believed that ending poverty would help the poor themselves, some revealed that they had other goals in mind. "I feel strongly that if the human race is going to protect itself against the invading horde of the yet unborn, it must look to voluntary sterilization as an important measure of defense," exclaimed one HBAVS official. Echoing social-Darwinist theories, Jesse Hartman told the press that "you can't keep up with the building of insane asylums and hospitals and schools. . . . You can't keep up with demands for relief, all caused by the hordes of people unborn. . . . Where is the safety valve? The only hope lies in closing off the demand"—by sterilizing the poor.[81] Louise Hutchins readily admitted that she typically had to raise the subject of birth control with "tired mothers" by asking the question, "Would you like to have a rest?" They (in her opinion) proved to be too ignorant to use conventional methods of birth control or the Pill. Sterilization seemed the only practical solution, and that involved, in most cases, lengthy discussions with patients dispelling misconceptions about the operation and easing anxieties about the costs. Getting husbands to undergo vasectomy meant convincing everyone concerned that the surgery was not castration. Thus, at the clinical level, the differences between talking patients into accepting sterilization and simply providing them with the information on which to base a purely voluntary decision frequently broke down.

In its first year of operation, the Hartman Plan arranged for seventy-six women and thirty-nine men to be sterilized. Ruth Smith noted with relief that the plan's caseload was "almost 100 per cent white."[82] Yet the local public health department ultimately refused to take over the management of Berea's sterilization program, and Hartman's attention shifted much farther south. In May, 1965, Hartman offered the Florida State Department of Public Welfare $25,000 to set up a similar program in Palm Beach and Broward counties, near where Hartman vacationed every winter.

However, the program never went beyond the planning stage. The fact that the poor of these counties were overwhelmingly African American likely doomed the endeavor from the start. As the director of the Broward County Health Department told Ruth Smith, the implication of the Hartman Plan was that "the genes of the poor are not as good for the human race as the genes of the rich."[83] Attitudes such as these indicated that, by the mid-1960s, sterilization advocates had to be very careful in their efforts to end poverty through sterilization when their clients' skin color did not match their own.

Planned Parenthood

HBAA efforts to widen access to sterilization services through the French and Hartman plans and the Faquier Hospital experiment pointed toward the need for closer collaboration with the country's chief family-planning organization, Planned Parenthood Federation of America (PPFA). As Ruth Smith put it in 1959, HBAA "[took] up where Planned Parenthood leaves off."[84] She and HBAA's board believed that sterilization was the ideal form of contraception for (what H. Curtis Wood called) "the relatively unmotivated indigent women who want sex without babies but do not do much about it."[85] To sterilization advocates, PPFA workers should have been informing their clients about sterilization all along. Indeed, over time, HBAA would increasingly rely on PPFA's huge network of centers and clinics across the country to both educate patients about sterilization and refer them to doctors willing to operate. Yet in the short term PPFA balked at working closely with HBAA. Founded by Margaret Sanger as the American Birth Control League (ABCL) in 1921, by 1942 PPFA had adopted its new name (over her bitter protests). The name change mirrored PPFA's keen desire to moderate its radical image so it could win broader popular support, influence public policy, and attract the financial support of major foundations. The drop in the national birthrate in the 1930s to below replacement level for the first time in American history convinced PPFA's leadership that a shift in its central message was expedient. For the time being, PPFA decided to mute Sanger's activist emphasis on spreading contraceptive practice far and wide and to instead stress a "balanced" program of spacing pregnancies that did not necessarily discourage middle-class Americans from having children.[86] The decision to adopt a new name and policy was made all the easier by the fact that by the end of the Depression, Sanger and PPFA had largely parted company. Sanger's feuds with various birth control proponents, including Eleanor Dwight Jones, the equally strong-willed president of the ABCL between 1928 and 1935, had severely tested the patience of many PPFA staff.[87] In later years, as Sanger's interests in population control and the invention of an oral contraceptive mounted, her ties to PPFA grew weaker and weaker. Her visible addictions to alcohol and Demerol over the same period hastened this process.

Sanger's gradual marginalization within the birth control movement in the 1940s was bad news for Birthright/HBAA. She was a stalwart supporter of sterilization as a way to help both society and the individual "underdog," and her continued involvement in PPFA might have led to more cordial relations between it and the sterilization movement. Yet PPFA's new leadership was not only uneasy about Sanger's outspokenness but was also wary about close ties to Birthright. At its December 13, 1945, meeting, PPFA's board of directors ruled that "it is unwise for planned parenthood organizations and organizations promoting sterilization to be associated or join efforts at any point in the educational efforts and promotion of their separate programs."[88] This news dismayed the many PPFA members who also belonged to Birthright, including Eleanor Dwight Jones, who wrote Marian Olden in 1945 that the two organizations "supplement each other. Neither movement can achieve its aim without the other."[89] Yet as long as the Nazi stigma clung to sterilization, and as long as such outspoken people as Marian Olden and Clarence Gamble were part of the sterilization movement, the chances of a formal rapprochement between PPFA and Birthright remained slim.[90]

Nonetheless, in the 1950s, PPFA–Birthright relations began to thaw. The celebration of motherhood and domesticity gathered momentum in the 1950s, and a "baby boom" unfolded. In the United States, almost 77 million babies were born between 1946 and 1964.[91] As the birth rate shot up, interest in birth control also escalated. Research on the oral contraceptive pill was underway and would culminate in the 1960 commercial release of Enovid, the first such pill. Yet in the meantime, the state of birth control technology essentially remained the same as it had been back in the 1920s.[92] All of a sudden, Wood's description of sterilization as "permanent planned parenthood" looked less and less radical to PPFA, and HBAA efforts to forge a "working relationship" between the two groups began to enjoy success.

With Wood, Guttmacher, and Ruth Smith leading the way, talks between HBAA and PPFA became friendlier as the 1950s wore on. In 1950, PPFA issued the following statement about sterilization:

> Although it is believed that the responsibility for national, state and com-
> munity education in the field of sterilization can best be promoted through
> organizations other than Planned Parenthood Federation of America,
> Planned Parenthood affiliates acting in accordance with the laws of their
> states may cooperate with organizations concerned with education in
> the field of sterilization.

In 1952, PPFA was still "not quite ready to walk down the garden path"
with HBAA, in the words of a PPFA official, but to Guttmacher, in 1953,
"integration seemed to be only a matter of time." According to Eleanor
Pillsbury, board member of both PPFA and HBAA and wife of the
Pillsbury flour manufacturer, "the time is coming when Planned Parenthood will have to face up to the facts of sterilization."[93] Adding individuals
such as Abraham Stone, PPFA vice-president, to HBAA's executive committee helped to smooth the process. HBAA hopes also rose following the
1953 news that Mary Steichen Calderone (1904–1999) had become PPFA
medical director.[94] Calderone, described upon her death as the "grande
dame of sex education," was one of several HBAA sex educators and
marriage counselors, along with Robert Laidlaw, Paul Popenoe, Medora
Bass, and Emily Mudd.[95] The daughter of photographer Edward Steichen
and niece of poet Carl Sandburg, Calderone did as much as anyone to
advance the theory that humans are born sexual beings and remain that
way for the rest of their lives, requiring sex education at every stage of life.
A champion of the belief that eroticism is a "norm" and masturbation a
wholesome practice, she co-founded the Sex Information and Education
Council of the United States (SEICUS) in 1964, the same year she convinced the trustees of the American Medical Association that physicians should dispense birth control information to all patients who
needed it.[96]

Calderone met with HBAA officials on numerous occasions between
1954 and 1956. Although she publicly expressed her opposition to sterilization, privately she was "in sympathy with" HBAA's program.[97]
Calderone did her best to ensure that all inquiries about sterilization directed to PPFA should be forwarded immediately to HBAA. In 1957, she
authored a brochure for patients titled *About Sterilization*, which stated that
PPFA "consider[ed] sterilization to be outside our field of interest, but the
doctors and nurses in our centers will be glad to discuss this as well as
medical child spacing, so that you may have an understanding of both."[98]
To HBAA officials, talks with Calderone, legendary for speaking her
mind, were always "friendly."[99]

Gradually, PPFA offices began referring growing numbers of patients to HBAA for sterilization. PPFA preferred to keep its evolving relationship to the sterilization movement quiet until the mid-1960s. Many in PPFA, especially at the state and local levels, believed that it "would injure their cause to accept sterilization in their program." Yet there was persistent, top-down pressure at the board level for friendlier relations with HBAA, often exerted by the many individuals who served on the boards of both groups, as well as other organizations, notably PPFA, HBAA, the American Civil Liberties Union, the Euthanasia Society of America, SEICUS, and (in the 1960s) NARAL.[100] Mary Calderone, despite her reluctance to have PPFA publicly endorse sterilization, agreed to serve on HBAA's Medical and Scientific Committee in 1962. The HBAA's legal counsel was the ACLU's Harriet Pilpel, also PPFA's lawyer. Frances Hand Ferguson, daughter of noted jurist Learned Hand, PPFA president (1953–1956), and longtime HBAA member, repeatedly urged PPFA to endorse sterilization as a form of contraception. In August, 1963, HBAVS headquarters moved to 515 Madison Avenue in New York City, in space adjoining PPFA's national office. Officially, PPFA may have kept HBAA at arm's length throughout the 1950s, uneasy about being associated with a group that advocated sterilization, but a broad philosophic kinship tended to unite the leadership of the two groups. As HBAA increasingly stressed the voluntary side of sterilization after World War II, more and more supporters of birth control, sex education, and marriage counseling saw the operation as just another method of improving the overall quality of life for individual Americans. By removing the fear of pregnancy, sterilization could "[make] life more meaningful in the realm of sex and its part in our lives," in Calderone's words.[101] By 1969, when Planned Parenthood officially recognized sterilization as an acceptable form of birth control and Planned Parenthood affiliates were actually performing vasectomies at their clinics, the lobbying by sterilization supporters within the ranks of Planned Parenthood had finally succeeded in producing a dramatic change in the history of the family-planning movement. More than one sterilization advocate remarked that Margaret Sanger would have wanted it that way.[102]

Thus, by the time John Fitzgerald Kennedy was elected U.S. president, in the fall of 1960, the sterilization movement in America had undergone a wrenching, soul-searching process. The overall goal was to decrease average family size by vastly increasing the nation's sterilization rate, thereby relieving the grinding poverty of so many Americans. The great question was how to do it. A start had been made with Joseph Fletcher's writings on medical ethics. Elite sentiment was gradually viewing sterilization as a human rights issue and less as a eugenic procedure. But who would lead the movement? For years the debate had raged between those who preferred doctors' providing the leadership and those who wanted to follow Margaret Sanger's activist example and win acceptance from a cautious medical profession by first stimulating popular demand. As the 1960s began, it appeared that the doctors under Alan Guttmacher had won. Yet the new, countercultural decade quickly indicated that leadership of the movement was about to shift back into the hands of individuals who had few formal ties to the medical profession. It was about to be taken over once again by activists, propagandists, and social scientists convinced that mass sterilization was an urgently needed public policy. The difference was that in the 1960s, sterilization proponents believed the quantity of births prevented through sterilization was more important than their quality. The new goal was to use sterilization to reduce the overall size of the globe's population. The world was on the verge of a historically unprecedented revolution in reproductive behavior.

Notes

1. Kevles DJ. *In the Name of Eugenics: Genetics and the Uses of Human Heredity*. New York: Knopf, 1985, p. 251.
2. Reilly PR. *The Surgical Solution: A History of Involuntary Sterilization in the United States*. Baltimore and London: The Johns Hopkins University Press, 1991, pp. 128, 129.
3. Reilly PR. *The Surgical Solution: A History of Involuntary Sterilization in the United States*. Baltimore and London: The Johns Hopkins University Press, 1991, p. 135. See also Butler FO. Sterilization in the United States. *American Journal of Mental Deficiency*. 1951;56:360–363.
4. F. O. Butler to Karl M. Bowman, January 11, 1951, AVS, Box 4, folder 34.
5. Reilly PR. *The Surgical Solution: A History of Involuntary Sterilization in the United States*. Baltimore and London: The Johns Hopkins University Press, 1991, pp. 137–138. Iowa's Board of Eugenics, responsible for more than 2,000 sterilizations between 1929 and 1977, approved more than 100 operations per year "during the peak years of the late 1940s and early 1950s." Vogel A. Regulating degeneracy: Eugenic sterilization in Iowa, 1911–1977. *The Annals of Iowa*. 1995;54:120.
6. Luther T. Hurley to HBAA, February 2, 1954, January 3, 1955, AVS, Box 9, folders 76, 77.
7. Irvin B. Hill to HBAA, January 12, 1954, AVS, Box 9, folder 77; Hall IB. Sterilization in Oregon. *American Journal of Mental Deficiency,* 1950;54:399–

403. From 1917 to 1983 Oregon's prison and mental health officials sterilized about 2,500 patients, including 217 sterilizations after 1967. Of the 207 men sterilized at Oregon's State Hospital at Salem in 1918–1941, 141 were castrated, while 30 of the 302 women underwent ovariotomies. See Largent MA. "The greatest curse of the race": Eugenic sterilization in Oregon, 1909–1983. *Oregon Historical Quarterly*. 2002;103:188–209.

8. T. G. Peacock to HBAA, January 10, 1958, AVS, Box 10, folder 84.

9. Report from the State School and Home for the Feeble-Minded, Redfield, South Dakota, January 11, 1949, AVS, Box 7, folder 64.

10. Report of the Manfield Training School, Connecticut, December 29, 1955, AVS, Box 9, folder 83. His emphasis.

11. A. L. Morris to Birthright, March 22, 1946, AVS, Box 7, folder 60.

12. Herman Yannet to Medora Bass, November 3, 1961, AHC, MSB, Box 11.

13. Milton H. Anderson to HBAA, January 8, 1960, AVS, Box 10, folder 88.

14. In 1946, during an election campaign in Minnesota, some politicians charged that residents of the Faribault State Hospital were the victims of wholesale sterilization. After intense media coverage, a grand jury was convened, eventually ruling that the charges were unfounded. Reilly PR. *The Surgical Solution: A History of Involuntary Sterilization in the United States*. Baltimore and London: The Johns Hopkins University Press, 1991, p. 141.

15. Woodside M. *Sterilization in North Carolina: A Sociological and Psychological Study*. Chapel Hill: University of North Carolina Press, 1950, pp. 69–70.

16. E. A. Whitney to Robert Latou Dickinson, April 20, 1946, AVS, Box 2, folder 13.

17. "Pope again denounces sterilization of humans." *New York Herald Tribune*, September 8, 1953.

18. Healy EF. *Medical Ethics*. Chicago: Loyola University Press, 1956, pp. 172–174. For Gamble's side of the debate, see Gamble CJ. Human sterilization. *American Journal of Nursing*. 1951;51:625–626. For Catholic criticism of the "sterilizing mentality" that some physicians seemed to share, see Kelly G. *Medico-Moral Problems*. Dublin: Clonmore and Reynolds, 1955, pp. 48–49.

19. The birth control revolution. *Commonweal*, April 1, 1931, pp. 589–591. Quoted in McGreevy JT. *Catholicism and American Freedom: A History*. New York and London: W. W. Norton, 2003, pp. 223.

20. Father Cox hits proponents of sterilization. *New York Tribune*, January 16, 1936.

21. Rothman DJ. *Strangers at the Bedside: A History of How Law and Bioethics Transformed Medical Decision Making*. New York: Basic Books, 1991, pp. 102.

22. McGreevy JT. *Catholicism and American Freedom: A History*. New York and London: W. W. Norton, 2003.

23. Morris C. *American Catholic: The Saints and Sinners Who Built America's Most Powerful Church*. New York: Vintage, 1998, p. 195.

24. Patterson JT. *America in the Twentieth Century: A History.* Fort Worth: Harcourt, Brace, 1994, pp. 357–358; Allitt P. *Religion in America Since 1945.* New York: Columbia University Press, 2003, pp. 31–33.

25. For Dougherty, see Morris, *American Catholic* (see note 23), pp. 165–195, 224–225; Dolan JP. *The American Catholic Experience: A History from Colonial Times to the Present.* Notre Dame: University of Notre Dame Press, 1992, pp. 384–417; Allitt P. *Religion in America Since 1945.* New York: Columbia University Press, 2003, pp. 8–10.

26. Morris, *American Catholic* (see note 23), pp. 184, 223. For Spellman, see Cooney J. *The American Pope: The Life and Times of Francis Cardinal Spellman.* New York: Times Books, 1984. See also Dolan JP. *The American Catholic Experience: A History from Colonial Times to the Present.* Notre Dame: University of Notre Dame Press, 1992, pp. 191–192.

27. Fey HA. Can Catholicism win America? *Christian Century* (eight-part series), 61–62 (November 29, 1944–January 17, 1945).

28. For an example of such Catholic influence in Michigan, see Mrs. Orlan W. Boston to Marian Olden, October 5, 1946, AVS, Box 11, folder 92.

29. An example of this tactic is the January 8, 1942, letter from Sister Anna Rita to Dr. Armand M. DeRosa, a New Jersey doctor, informing him that "doctors connected with any birth control group or organization shall not be privileged to attend patients" at St. Joseph Hospital in Paterson, New Jersey. As the directors of the Passaic County Planned Parenthood Center noted in 1942, this ruling applied to all Catholic hospitals throughout the state. Mrs. Bertram H. Saunders, et al., "to the friends and subscribers of the Passaic County Planned Parenthood Center," AVS, Box 1, folder 4.

30. In 1953, Catholic pressure also compelled the Welfare and Health Council of New York City to reject the membership bid of the Planned Parenthood Committee of Mothers Health Centers, an affiliate of PPFA. When WHCNYC reversed its decision, fifty-three Catholic agencies resigned in protest. "Catholics quit welfare unit in parenthood controversy." *New York Times,* May 30, 1953.

31. Guttmacher AF. A leading specialist answers questions about birth control. *True Story.* November 1959, p. 154.

32. Leavitt JW. *Brought to Bed: Childbearing in America, 1750–1950.* New York: Oxford University Press, 1986, pp. 169–195.

33. Woodside M. Sterilization and social welfare (n.d.), Papers of the North Carolina Human Betterment League, Series 1, Box 2, file 77, Southern Historical Collection, University of North Carolina, Chapel Hill. Quoted in Schoen J. *Choice and Coercion: Birth Control, Sterilization and Abortion in Public Health and Welfare.* Chapel Hill: University of North Carolina Press, 2005, pp. 118–119.

34. Schoen J. *Choice and Coercion: Birth Control, Sterilization and Abortion in Public Health and Welfare.* Chapel Hill: University of North Carolina Press, 2005.

35. Alan Guttmacher to Joseph Fletcher, November 25, 1959, AVS, Box 33, Fletcher folder. His emphasis.

36. Ramirez de Arellano AB, Seipp C. *Colonialism, Catholicism, and Contraception: A History of Birth Control in Puerto Rico.* Chapel Hill and London: University of North Carolina Press, 1983.

37. According to Clarence Gamble in 1950, the Puerto Rican Eugenics Board had "never met"; the Island's large number of sterilizations were "for health or population purposes rather than to control unsatisfactory heredity." Clarence Gamble to Birthright, January 14, 1950, AVS, Box 2, folder 17.

38. Presser HB. *Sterilization and Fertility Decline in Puerto Rico.* Berkeley: Institute of International Studies, 1973.

39. Minutes of HBAA board meeting, November 16, 1956, AVS, Box 3, Folder 21.

40. Presser HB. Contraceptive sterilization as a grassroots response: A comparative view of the Puerto Rican and United States experience. In Newman SH, Klein ZE (eds.). *Behavioral-Social Aspects of Contraceptive Sterilization.* Lexington, MA, and Toronto: D.C. Heath, 1978, p. 32.

41. Suzuki Z. Geneticists and the eugenics movement in Japan. *Japanese Studies in the History of Science.* 1975;14:157–164; Yoko M. The enactment of Japan's sterilization laws in the 1940s: A prelude to postwar eugenic policy. *Historia Scientiarum.* 1998;8:187–201.

42. Oakley D. American–Japanese interaction in the development of population policy in Japan, 1945–1952. *Population and Development Review.* 1978;4: 617–643; Chandrasekhar S. *Abortion in a Crowded World.* Seattle: University of Washington Press, 1974, p. 113.

43. Broberg G, Roll-Hansen N (eds.). *Eugenics and the Welfare State: Sterilization Policy in Denmark, Sweden, Norway and Finland.* East Lansing: Michigan State University Press, 1996.

44. Robert Latou Dickinson letter to the editor of the *Memphis Mirror,* April 19, 1947, AVS, Box 2, folder 14.

45. Philip Weintraub to Irene Headley Armes, December 1, 1949, August 13, 1950, AVS, Box 2, folders 16, 17. See also Weintraub P. Sterilization in Sweden: Its law and practice. *American Journal of Mental Deficiency.* 1951; 56:364–374.

46. Author's interview with Ruth Proskauer Smith, November 11, 2000, New York City.

47. Nathanson BN, Ostling RN. *Aborting America.* New York: Doubleday, 1979, p. 48.

48. Ruth Proskauer Smith to the Editor of the *New York Post,* December 10, 1959. Her emphasis.

49. Ruth Proskauer Smith to JFK, May 4, 1959; JFK to Smith, June 5, 1959; JFK to Smith, July 1, 1959; Smith to JFK, July 20, 1961. Ruth Proskauer Smith Papers, Schlesinger Library, Radcliffe College, Box 1, folder 2. For the

history of population control and family planning policymaking during the Johnson administration, see Critchlow DT. *Intended Consequences: Birth Control, Abortion and the Federal Government in Modern America.* New York and Oxford: Oxford University Press, 1999, pp. 50–84.

50. Blanshard P. *American Freedom and Catholic Power.* Boston: Beacon, 1950, pp. 151–152. For other references to eugenics, see Chapter 7, "Sex, Birth Control, and Eugenics," pp. 132–155.

51. Paul Blanshard to Irene Headley Armes, October 4, 1951, AVS, Box 40, Blanshard folder. According to marriage counselor and HBAA member Paul Popenoe, in 1951 Blanshard told him he was "going to lay off the Church for a while and devote his time to writing and lecturing on eugenics and population problems. He wanted particularly to talk to me about sterilization . . . ." Popenoe to M. A. Bigelow, December 13, 1951, AHC, Paul Bowman Popenoe Papers, Box 26.

52. Meyer AE. The school, the state and the Church. *Atlantic Monthly.* 182, November 1948, p. 150. Quoted in McGreevy JT. *Catholicism and American Freedom: A History.* New York and London: W. W. Norton, 2003, p. 187.

53. Frederick May Eliot, sermon at the Jefferson Memorial, April 13, 1947, Frederick May Eliot Papers, Harvard Divinity School, folder 24, Box 33. Quoted in McGreevy JT. *Catholicism and American Freedom: A History.* New York and London: W. W. Norton, 2003, p. 184.

54. Kelly G. *Medico-Moral Problems.* Dublin: Clonmore and Reynolds, 1955, pp. 10–11; McGreevy JT. *Catholicism and American Freedom: A History.* New York and London: W. W. Norton, 2003, pp. 231–232.

55. Fletcher J. *To Live and to Die: When, Why, and How.* New York: Springer-Verlag, 1973, p. 296.

56. Neuhaus RJ. All too human. *National Review,* December 2, 1991, p. 45.

57. Fletcher J. *Situation Ethics: The New Morality.* Philadelphia: Westminister Press, 1966, pp. 26–31, 84–124.

58. Kelly G. *Medico-Moral Problems.* Dublin: Clonmore and Reynolds, 1955, p. 3.

59. Dowbiggin IR. *A Merciful End: The Euthanasia Movement in Modern America.* New York and Oxford: Oxford University Press, 2003, pp. 100–104. See also "Dr. Joseph F. Fletcher, 86, dies: Pioneer in field of medical ethics." *New York Times,* October 30, 1991, p. D25.

60. Joseph Fletcher to Irene Headley Armes, January 6, 1953, AVS, Box 33, Fletcher folder.

61. Alan Guttmacher note, January 14, 1953, AVS, Box 33, Fletcher folder. His emphasis.

62. Promotional statement, October 13, 1961, AVS, Box 33, Fletcher folder.

63. On January 22, 1974, Brickner joined other various clergymen at a NARAL rally in New York City to celebrate the first anniversary of the *Roe v. Wade* ruling. See Larry Lader to members of the NARAL board, January 7, 1974. AHC, Medora Bass Collection, Box 11.

64. Proceedings of the HBAVS Conference on the question "Does Voluntary Sterilization Pose An Ethical Problem?" April 3, 1963, AVS, Box 5, folder 44.
65. The redoubtable Harry Emerson Fosdick, Minister Emeritus at the Riverside Church in New York City, echoed Fletcher's comments when he stated his belief that "there is a place for voluntary sterilization programs in our society." See HBAVS, *Statements by Religious Leaders Supporting HBA,* n.d. but likely 1963. See also William Genné to Family Counselors, January 1960, recommending they read Fletcher's "The Clergyman Speaks on Voluntary Sterilization." AHC, MSB, Box 2.
66. Atwater L. *And the Poor Get Children.* Chicago: Quadrangle Books, 1960.
67. "Treasurer's Report," minutes of HBAA's April 17, 1957, board meeting, AVS, Box 3, folder 21.
68. AVS, Box 33, Graham French folder.
69. Mrs. Robert Ferguson and H. Curtis Wood, "At Last a Breakthrough in the Barrier of Prejudice," HBAA pamphlet, December 1960; Ruth Proskauer Smith, "Emergency Memorandum: Office Crisis Caused by New Publicity on Patient Level," May 20, 1960, AVS, Box 69, Goethe folder.
70. Hugh Moore to William Genné, February 12, 1963, HM, Series 2, Box 1, folder 22.
71. "Clinic is backed on sterilization." *New York Times,* September 12, 1962.
72. Gerald Grant, *The Fauquier Hospital Sterilization Study.* The National Conference of Christians and Jews: January 1963. AVS, Box 23, Fauquier Hospital folder.
73. "Fifty indigent mothers sterilized in Fauquier County." *Washington Post,* September 4, 1962.
74. "Clinic is backed on sterilization." *New York Times,* September 12, 1962; "A sterile issue?" *Newsweek,* September 24, 1962, p. 88.
75. "Clinic defended on sterilization." *New York Times,* October 7, 1962.
76. Ruth Smith to Robert Laidlaw, April 16, 1964, AVS, Box 36, Smith folder. See also "$25,000 gift speeds voluntary sterilization program in Appalachia to control poverty bomb." HBAVS News Release, July 7, 1964.
77. "$25,000 gift speeds voluntary sterilization program in Appalachia to control poverty bomb." HBAVS news release, July 7, 1964.
78. A. S. Holmes to WLAP, July 13, 1964, AVS, Box 57, Kentucky Project folder.
79. Mountain Maternal Health League, Planned Parenthood. http://moun tainmaternal.org/_wsn/page4.html.
80. Critchlow DT. *Intended Consequences: Birth Control, Abortion and the Federal Government in Modern America.* New York and Oxford: Oxford University Press, 1999, pp. 51–54.
81. *News* (Pensacola, Florida), August 4, 1964.
82. Ruth Smith to George W. Gore Jr., October 13, 1964, AVS, Box 39, Kentucky Project folder.

83. Paul W. Hughes to Ruth Smith, August 3, 1964, AVS., Box 39, Kentucky Project folder.
84. Ruth Smith to Harry E. Fosdick, April 28, 1959, AVS, Box 41, Fosdick folder.
85. H. Curtis Wood to Medora Bass, February 29, 1968, AHC, MSB, Box 3.
86. Reed J. *From Private Vice to Public Virtue: The Birth Control Movement and American Society Since 1830.* New York: Basic, 1978, pp. 121–122; Kline W. *Building a Better Race: Gender, Sexuality and Eugenics from the Turn of the Century to the Baby Boom.* Berkeley and Los Angeles: University of California Press, 2001, pp. 96–97.
87. "Mrs. F. Robertson Jones dead: Birth control movement leader." *New York Times,* July 31, 1965. For the feud between Jones and Sanger, see McCann C. *Birth Control Politics in the United States, 1916–1945.* Ithaca: Cornell University Press, 1994:177–181. For more on Jones and her involvement in the U.S. euthanasia movement, see Dowbiggin IR. *A Merciful End: The Euthanasia Movement in Modern America.* New York and Oxford: Oxford University Press, 2003, pp. 73–74.
88. Minutes of PPFA Board of Directors' December 13, 1945 meeting, AVS, Box 2, folder 12.
89. Eleanor Dwight Jones to Marian Olden, May 28, 1945, AVS, Box 2, folder 12.
90. H. Curtis Wood to Birthright Directors, April 19, 1947, AVS, Box 2, folder 16.
91. Patterson JT. *Great Expectations: The United States, 1945–1974.* New York: Oxford University Press, 1996, pp. 77, 78, 79; Kline W. *Building a Better Race: Gender, Sexuality and Eugenics from the Turn of the Century to the Baby Boom.* Berkeley and Los Angeles: University of California Press, 2001, pp. 152–153.
92. See Marks LV. *Sexual Chemistry: A History of the Contraceptive Pill.* New Haven and London: Yale University Press, 2001.
93. Mrs. Philip W. Pillsbury to Louise Mills, November 1, 1956, AVS, Box 5, folder 42.
94. "Quotations from Minutes: HBAA and PPFA Relationship," November 23, 1955, AVS, Box 36, Smith folder.
95. Epstein H. "The Grande Dame of Sex Education–Mary Calderone and Sex Information and Education Council of the United States." *The Humanist.* 1999;59(Jan.–Feb.):39–40.
96. "Mary S. Calderone, advocate of sexual education, dies at 94." *New York Times,* October 25, 1999, pp. 52–53. See also Calderone MS. Eroticism as a norm. *The Family Coordinator.* 1974;23:337–341.
97. "Conference with Dr. Mary Calderone," memo of October 25, 1956, AVS, Box 36, Ruth Smith folder.
98. Mary Calderone, "About Sterilization," November 27, 1957, AVS, Box 5, folder 42.

99. "Quotations From Minutes," HBAA and PPFA Relationship, November 23, 1955, AVS, Box 36, Smith folder.

100. As Alan Guttmacher himself acknowledged. See his "The Population Crisis and the Use of World Resources," in Mudd S (ed.), *The Population Crisis and the Use of World Resources.* Bloomington: Indiana University Press, 1964, pp. 268–273. See also H. Curtis Wood's report of the medical director at HBAA's annual meeting, November 13, 1963, AVS, Box 5, folder 43. For many years Wood believed HBAA would progress more rapidly if HBAA were part of PPFA–"there is a significant duplication of supporters and board members in the two groups"–but PPFA is afraid of supporting surgical birth control because it might be "considered too radical, a little less respectable and might lose the financial support of more conservative individuals or foundations."

101. Calderone, Mary Steichen. *Current Biography*, 1967, pp. 53–56.

102. "Abortion and sterilization win support of Planned Parenthood. *New York Times*, November 14, 1968. One PPFA and HBAA member who voiced this sentiment was Medora Bass, whose history with HBAA dated back to the days of Birthright and who served as the group's vice president as late as the 1970s. She also began serving as president of Planned Parenthood of Pennsylvania in 1965 after being on its board since the 1950s. See Bass to Mrs. Cass Canfield, April 22, 1968, AHC, MSB, Box 10, Margaret Sanger Clinic folder. See also "The Most Permanent Birth Control," *Glamour*, March 1981, pp. 236–237, in which the medical director of the Los Angeles PPFA was quoted as saying, "[O]nce you decide that you never want to have a child, or have another child, the safest thing to do is to have a sterilization."

Chapter 4

House on Fire

A s the 1950s wore on, the sterilization movement continued to drift. Revelations about Nazi atrocities created a stigma that hung heavily over the procedure itself. Official support for state sterilization laws was waning rapidly. Medical and religious opposition to sterilization appeared as strong as ever. Public ignorance about surgical birth control seemed pervasive. The nation was in the midst of a baby boom. Mainstream birth control groups such as Planned Parenthood Federation of America (PPFA), though privately supportive, refused to publicly endorse sterilization as a contraceptive method.

Yet the fortunes of the sterilization movement were about to take a new turn. Just when its future looked most bleak, powerful and wealthy Americans, including John D. Rockefeller 3rd, started to warn about the dangers of population growth, notably in developing countries in Asia, Africa, and Latin America. As H. Curtis Wood admitted in 1959, "I do not recall any time when there has been so much discussion of birth control and the world population explosion. I cannot recall a time when so many famous men . . . and prominent U.S. politicians have had their opinions and remarks on these subjects so widely disseminated . . . ."[1] However, activists who sought to cut global fertility rates soon discovered that Third World couples generally disliked using birth control devices such as oral contraceptives and the intrauterine device (IUD). In their search for a reliable means of contraception, many population controllers gradually decided that sterilization was the best of all methods.

To the leaders of Birthright, renamed the Human Betterment Association of America (HBAA) in 1950, the rise of the population control

movement was the best news yet in the group's young history. As dedicated as ever to extolling the virtues of sterilization for the fertile poor and
uneducated classes of society, HBAA could now invoke the specter of
overpopulation to justify the acceptance and expansion of sterilization
services, both domestically and overseas. With the advent of the 1960s,
sterilization proponents saw a whole new horizon opening up for themselves in the field of population control, an opportunity to change the
course of history. What became quickly evident, however, was that no
matter how much they couched their support of sterilization in terms of
population control, many in the movement sounded as if their goals remained firmly rooted in their eugenic past.

William Vogt

The argument that sterilization was a key method of population control
first surfaced in the early 1940s. Prior to World War II, sterilization
proponents often had insisted that sterilization could reduce the rate of
mental disorders as well as boost the national intelligence level, thereby
improving mental and physical health across the generations. Yet in the
1940s, many began asserting that, when it came to birth control, the quantity of human beings mattered as much as their quality. The first prominent American to systematically state the case for population control
through sterilization was William Vogt. Long before media-savvy demographers such as Paul and Anne Ehrlich began warning, in the 1960s, that
overpopulation would lead to mass starvation, Vogt was predicting environmental, political, and social disasters if human breeding was not
dramatically curtailed. Born in 1902 in Mineola, New York, and crippled
with polio in adolescence, Vogt served as consultant on South America
to the U.S. War Department during World War II. In 1951, he became
national director of PPFA, a post he held until 1962, when Alan Guttmacher succeeded him. By then, Vogt was already world famous thanks
to his 1948 runaway best-seller *Road to Survival.* Translated into nine
languages, *Road to Survival* made Vogt one of the most influential opinion-
makers in the post–World War II era.[2]

　　Road to Survival was not just a landmark text in the history of population
control. Like Rachel Carson's *Silent Spring* (1962), *Road to Survival*'s 1948
publication was a major milestone in the history of the U.S. environmentalist movement. Vogt was an ardent conservationist and avid bird-
watcher who drew unsettling conclusions about humans from his study of

bird ecology. *Road to Survival* and Fairfield Osborn's equally disquieting *Our Plundered Planet* (1948) were the first books to draw attention to the unprecedented pressure on natural resources created by the dramatic rise in the earth's population since the eighteenth century. It took all of human history for the world's population to reach the 1 billion mark in the late eighteenth century, but from 1800 to World War II, the size of the human race more than doubled. Predictions as the Cold War began that world population would reach 6 billion by the year 2000 proved to be accurate.

To Vogt and a growing number of social scientists, this situation was a recipe for global catastrophe. "[T]he Day of Judgment is at hand," Vogt predicted darkly (p. 78).[3] He and other demographers turned to Thomas Malthus's 1798 *Essay on the Principle of Population*. Malthus claimed that according to mathematical laws, population tended to outstrip food supply. He then concluded that unless human beings voluntarily limited the size of their families (through abstinence and late marriage), famine and disease would increase the death rate enough to stabilize the ratio between population and food supply. Malthus painted this dismal scenario in order to counter what he thought were the overly optimistic views of eighteenth-century thinkers such as William Godwin and the Marquis de Condorcet, who insisted that population growth was a sign of overall prosperity.[4] Later demographers failed to share Malthus's ethical opposition to artificial contraception and argued that the Malthusian "trap" could be avoided if birth control were practiced widely. Nonetheless, they agreed with Malthus that human breeding was a perpetual menace to civilized society.

To Vogt, events during the twentieth century had proven Malthus right. Modern medicine was "dangerous," Vogt contended, because it saved the lives of millions around the world who might otherwise have perished at the hands of nature. To physicians of the World Health Organization, Vogt asked, "Why are you trying to save the lives of children when you'll just doom them to starvation?"[5] The result of such practices, he asserted, was overcrowded nations whose governments had no alternative but to seek more territory and natural resources for their hungry citizens. Vogt blamed twentieth-century German and Japanese militarism on population growth. According to this line of thinking, both countries turned to war in a desperate attempt to feed their expanding populations. In the post-1945 Cold War standoff between the Soviet Union and the United States, the stakes were as high as possible, Vogt argued. Runaway population growth in India, China, and other developing countries increased international tension because such nations played the two superpowers against each other in their urgent efforts to obtain crucial foreign assistance. The lesson of Hiroshima was that the human race had no time to lose if it wished to escape the annihilation that would result from the Cold War turning "hot" (pp. xiii, 48, 72–73).[3]

Amid the various efforts to defuse international tension in the early Cold War, Vogt maintained that political methods were not enough. He felt the world crisis was so acute that aggressive birth control programs were necessary to prevent the "unchecked spawning" of human beings. He particularly endorsed H. L. Mencken's 1937 proposal to offer people "sterilization bonuses" if they would agree to cease having babies.[6] In a familiar example of the blending of eugenic and population control concerns, Vogt contended that "it would certainly be preferable to pay permanently indigent individuals, many of whom would be physically and psychologically marginal, $50 or $100 rather than [society] support their hordes of offspring that, by both genetic and social inheritance, would tend to perpetuate their fecklessness." Yet to Vogt the eugenic benefits of such incentive programs of sterilization were secondary to the primary goal of reducing overall fertility: *all* human beings were "parasites" on Planet Earth, and their numbers had to be cut quickly and drastically. He preferred that it be done voluntarily, but, like many in his own day, his definition of voluntarism did not rule out offering sterilization incentives to the "psychologically marginal," who, it was widely assumed, could not be counted on to limit the size of their families without such rewards. The bottom line was that the "freebooting, rugged individualist" who had done so much to build modern industrial society was now "the Enemy of the People" (p. 6, 59, 285).[3]

Vogt's support for sterilization made him a natural ally of the HBAA. In the 1950s, Vogt sat on the group's Medical and Scientific Committee and was a key liaison between HBAA and PPFA. One member of HBAA's Board of Directors remarked that as "a great scholar . . . and a great leader," Vogt was a tremendous "catch" for the organization.[7] Vogt's affiliation with PPFA pointed to the warming relations between the sterilization and family-planning movements. His association with HBAA also indicated the evolving symbiotic relationship between the sterilization movement and the emerging population control movement. As H. Curtis Wood confided to Vogt in 1948, he had always wanted to form "a new super organization" called the "American Society for Human Survival" that would combine the "best features of the Planned Parenthood movement, selective sterilization, world population control, and the conservation of natural resources and tie all these items together into one really worthwhile program."[8] At an HBAA meeting in 1950, Wood returned to the same theme: "As long as we concentrate on just the sterilizing angle we will only get limited interest and support by the few intelligent enough to see its importance." If a future organization embracing populationists, conservationists, eugenicists, mental health professionals, and PPFA members like Vogt became a reality, "we might really get somewhere with reasonable speed," Wood predicted.[9]

Hugh Moore

In fact, Wood was twenty years too early. By the late 1960s, HBAA had become such a group, closely identified with activist figures such as Paul Ehrlich (see insert), author of *The Population Bomb* (1968), and the anti-natalist organization Zero Population Growth. Meanwhile, William Vogt's message about the need for global population control was hailed by many as the wave of the future. One notable American who thanked Vogt for "really waking me up" was the millionaire businessman Hugh Moore (1887–1972) (see insert). Moore later became HBAA president and chairman of its executive committee (1964–1969), having been a generous donor to the group since 1949. His second wife, Louise (Wilde) Moore, whom he married in 1947, was a noteworthy sterilization activist in her own right. She also served on HBAA's board of directors (1959–1963) and, after Moore's death, married birth control defender Joseph Van Vleck. Hugh Moore was chiefly responsible for changing the name of the organization, in 1962, to the Human Betterment Association for Voluntary Sterilization (HBAVS), and in 1964 to the Association for Voluntary Sterilization (AVS), mirroring his refusal to hide the fact that group's *raison d'être* was sterilization advocacy. By the time he died, in 1972, few around the world had preached the virtues of sterilization as a method of population control more vocally than Hugh Moore.

Born in Fort Scott, Kansas, Moore's chief claim to fame was his invention of the Dixie Cup, the first sanitary paper drinking vessel. Moore promoted the Dixie Cup as a replacement for the common tin cup found in train stations, hospitals, and other locations. The Dixie Cup made Moore fabulously wealthy. By 1957, when he sold his business to the American Can Company, 40 million people a day were using the Dixie Cup (p. 30).[10]

Yet Moore was not just a businessman. He also had an avid curiosity about a wide range of topics, including socialism, anarchism, and Eastern religions. Unitarianism intrigued him because of its claim to harmonize reason and religion. In the 1930s, as the international situation worsened, his attention steadily shifted to maintaining world peace. A consultant to the State Department at the United Nations Conference in 1945 and an active supporter of the St. Lawrence Seaway, Moore grew increasingly alarmed about the progress communism was making in the developing world after World War II. Reading Vogt's *Road to Survival* converted him body and soul to the theory that population growth was the root cause of international conflict and the spread of communism.[11] In addition to the legalization of euthanasia and the repeal of America's abortion laws, the remaining twenty-five years of his life were devoted to the population control movement, including leadership roles in the Population Reference Bureau, International Planned Parenthood Federation, and the Population Crisis Committee. In 1954, long before Paul Ehrlich made the "population bomb" a household phrase with the title of his 1968 bestseller, Moore coined the term in one of his booklets warning about the dangers of overpopulation. In the words of one HBAA member, Moore gave "International Planned Parenthood the wings to get off the ground."[12] Overall, he "brought a vivid sense of urgency to the [population] movement," another friend testified.[13]

Described as a man who liked to give but not take orders, Moore carved out his own colorful place in the population control movement as a tireless advocate of sterilization. He surrounded himself with like-minded men, running his organizations like petty fiefdoms. This factor, combined with his well-documented low opinion of women, caused friction in the early 1960s as he began his takeover of the HBAA. However, Moore's generosity to the HBAA since the early 1950s and the group's desperate need for funding made it increasingly difficult for officials such as Ruth Proskauer Smith to resist his rising clout within the organization. By 1964, thanks to Moore's influence over HBAA policy, its chief focus was clearly shifting from defusing the "poverty bomb" to defusing the "population bomb." Seeing the handwriting on the wall, Ruth Smith departed as HBAA executive director to pursue her interests in abortion rights activism. Over the next half decade, the group would largely be run by Hugh Moore and his followers.

Moore made it clear that he did not support sterilization because it emancipated individuals; he was mostly uninterested in maternal health or women's reproductive rights.[14] Moreover, as he freely admitted, his focus was "not primarily domestic but rather international–in the hope that through sterilization something might be done to ease the social strains which bring on war."[15]

Yet Moore's comparative lack of interest in domestic or women's issues did not mean that he ignored these causes. His preference for male rather than female sterilization echoed the argument of women's reproductive-rights activists that women should not be saddled with the sole responsibility for birth control.[16] In the years leading up to *Roe v. Wade*, Moore also threw his financial support behind the founding of National Association for the Repeal of Abortion Laws (NARAL) and abortion reform campaigns in Nevada, New York, Michigan, and other states (pp. 150–151).[10] Moore backed the repeal of the country's abortion laws chiefly because he thought abortion was one means for reducing population growth, not because he was a defender of reproductive "choice" for women. Nonetheless, the result was the same. In the pre–*Roe v. Wade* era, when the ultimate success of the abortion rights movement was far from a certainty, activists were grateful for his support.

When, in the 1960s, domestic social issues such as crime, welfare, and pollution became topics of grave concern, Moore tried to capitalize on their links to population control. In 1966, he stirred controversy with his prediction that the population of the United States would exceed 350 million by the end of the century, resulting in "over-crowded cities, polluted air and water, countless unwanted and suffering children, sky-rocketing taxes for welfare! Half of the babies now born in some cities are from indigent families on relief. Need we say more?"[17] In 1968, he paid a New York City firm to develop advertisements that linked overpopulation to urban crime, poverty, and pollution. One ad, titled "Have You Been Mugged Today?," depicted what many believed was a young black man mugging a victim. The ad sparked charges of racism and heated accusations that Moore was blaming the poor and minorities for the "population explosion" and the crime it supposedly caused.[18]

Moore's perfervid support for population control contrasted sharply with the less flamboyant style of John D. Rockefeller 3rd, grandson of oil magnate John D. Rockefeller. John D. Rockefeller 3rd (1906–1978) spent most of his adult life donating his time, energy, and wealth to public charity and social reform, joining groups such as the Child Refugee Committee, the United Service Organizations, and the American Red Cross. Based on prewar travels to Japan and his activities as Special Assistant on Far Eastern Affairs to the Under Secretary of the Navy during World War II, Rockefeller gained a reputation as an expert on the Far East. The overcrowding he observed in Africa and Asia convinced him of the need for a scientific approach to research into the social, economic, and political impact of population growth, as well as the development of effective, inexpensive, convenient, and safe birth control technology.

When the Rockefeller Foundation turned down his proposal of a new population division within the Foundation, Rockefeller, in 1952, went ahead and founded the Population Council, his own organization devoted solely to the population question. Within several years, the Population Council had established an international network of population experts at some of America's most prestigious universities and received substantial grants from the Ford Foundation, the Rockefeller Brothers Fund, Mrs. Alan Scaife, and Cordelia S. May. This growing community of social scientists gradually built up a core body of knowledge and a common mode of professional discourse about demographic issues. At the same time, the Population Council offered its technical assistance to population control programs in a wide range of developing countries.[19]

Although always friendly toward those whose tactics he did not agree with, Rockefeller was careful to distance himself from the outspoken Moore and his admirers in the HBAA and the Population Crisis Committee. "I do have real reservations about becoming involved on the propaganda front," he told Moore.[20] Rockefeller had to take into consideration several factors that dictated a cautious approach to population matters, including his brother Nelson's political ambitions. Rockefeller Foundation officials were also concerned that vigorous population control advocacy might offend the religious and ethical sensibilities of political leaders in countries where the Foundation was already doing philanthropic and public health work. Above all, Rockefeller wanted the Population Council to win the respect of informed opinion-makers rather than "stir up the public," Moore's favorite strategy.[21] Rockefeller also had reservations about sterilization as a contraceptive method, preferring condoms, oral contraceptives, and IUDs. Yet, as he told Moore, "[T]here is no difference between us as to our objectives in relation to population stabilization and family planning. We all agree as to the seriousness of the problem and the need for action more commensurate with its magnitude and urgency. Such differences as we have are entirely as to method and approach."[22]

However, some of the opposition to sterilization within the Population Council melted by the mid-1960s, when it became evident that developing-world women did not like using the IUD, whose manufacture and distribution the Population Council assisted. Bernard Berelson, who became the Population Council's director of communications in 1962, urged Council programs to "persuade a wife or husband to undertake sterilization after the birth of their third or fourth child."[23] In 1968, a Population Council official who had just spent five years in Southeast Asia stated that "85 per cent of the people in that part of the world need nothing but vasectomy."[24] As events in later years would demonstrate, this kind of thinking helped to build bridges between ardent sterilization proponents such as Hugh Moore and more moderate members of the population control movement.

Alvin Kaufman

While Hugh Moore, William Vogt, and John D. Rockefeller 3rd were grabbing most of the headlines as defenders of population control, Canadian businessman Alvin Ratz Kaufman (1885–1979) was working more quietly to promote sterilization as the foremost weapon in the struggle to reduce global fertility rates. Kaufman, nicknamed "Canada's Mr. Birth Control," was the successful owner of the Kaufman Rubber Company, manufacturer of Life Buoy rubber footwear, located in Kitchener, Ontario. Opinionated and abrupt in manner, he reminded some of Clarence Gamble. An HBAA official thought Kaufman "a man of few words and rather impatient of any detail that does not pertain to what he conceives to be the crux of the problem."[25] However, at a time when Canada barely had a birth control movement to speak of, Kaufman blazed a path that other, less single-minded family planning activists gratefully followed. By his death, in 1979, Kaufman had been instrumental in arranging some 10,000 vasectomies and at least four hundred tubal sterilizations (p. 136).[26]

A member of the Eugenics Society of Canada after its formation in 1930, and a longtime HBAA benefactor, Kaufman claimed his interest in sterilization and family planning dated back to 1929, when he received complaints that his laid-off employees tended to have the biggest families. Kaufman sent his company nurse to investigate, and she reported back that living conditions were deplorable among these unemployed workers. "The less intelligence the larger the families, and the more hopeless their condition," Kaufman concluded.[27] Convinced of a link between poverty and family size, he decided to set up clinics in Toronto and the Ontario city of Windsor, across the river from Detroit. In 1933, he established the Parents' Information Bureau (PIB), devoted to providing birth control information to people residing in poor neighborhoods. Kaufman soon reached two further conclusions. The first was that simply opening clinics was not enough. Experience quickly taught him that the people who would most benefit from birth control rarely had the initiative or means to travel to a clinic themselves. Instead, he advocated visits of nurses and social workers to the homes of the destitute and deficient, helping their clients to get the proper medical care.

Experience also soon taught him that even after he made arrangements with local doctors to fit women with the pessary diaphragm, the best available contraceptive method of the time, many women never showed up for their appointments, and of those who did many could not be fitted for a diaphragm, due either to doctors' incompetence or obstetrical conditions. Even when fitted with the device, some women abandoned it. Condoms and contraceptive jelly were not much more effectively adopted. As population control proponents would discover later, to their chagrin, women (notably in developing countries) simply would not do what their doctors or social workers told them. The time and expense of the entire exercise exasperated Kaufman, who eventually concluded that sterilization was the solution. Kaufman was so enamored with sterilization that he offered the "sick room" at his Kitchener factory as a place to perform close to 2,000 operations between 1930 and 1970.[28]

No one could ever accuse Kaufman of being less than brutally honest about his motives for supporting sterilization. He undoubtedly believed that in offering sterilization through his PIB, he was doing underprivileged Ontarians a big favor, time and again claiming his clients expressed no regret over their operations. Yet he was also convinced that "spreading the gospel of birth control to needy people" would help to avert "revolution." As he told H. L. Mencken in 1937,[29]

> We are raising too large a percentage of the dependent classes and I do not blame them if they steal and fight before they starve. I fear that their opportunity will not be so long deferred as some day the Governments are going to lack the cash and perhaps also the patience to keep so many people on relief. Many of these people are not willing to work but I do not criticize them harshly for their lack of ambition when they are the offspring of people no better than themselves.

To Kaufman, the poor and uneducated needed to be sterilized because they were "too ignorant" and "too lazy" to practice other methods of birth control.[30] "Personally," he declared in 1952, in a pessimistic moment, "I think [Canada's 'subnormal' families] ought to be dumped in the lake."[25]

Yet Kaufman's stern single-mindedness was a distinct advantage in a country whose cultural climate was even more resolutely opposed to birth control than the United States. Canada's Criminal Code said nothing about sterilization, and no Canadian physician was ever prosecuted for performing sterilizations, but the Canadian Medical Association advised surgeons against performing them. In the 1950s, provincial medical associations often pressured departments of health to discourage sterilizations in hospitals.

Canadian law prohibited sharing contraceptive information unless the "public good" was served, so Kaufman set out to prove in a court of law that birth control did benefit society. In 1936, Dorothea Palmer, one of his visiting nurses, was arrested for providing contraceptive information and devices to families in a largely French-speaking, Roman Catholic district outside Ottawa, the nation's capital. Kaufman and other members of the Eugenics Society of Canada helped to organize her defense, bringing in expert witnesses who testified that Palmer was indeed serving the "public good" by distributing birth control information. The magistrate concurred and, after a trial lasting twenty-one days spread over a five-month period, Palmer was acquitted on March 17, 1937, bringing to a close the most publicized court case involving Canada's law on birth control (pp. 130–132).[26]

Only in 1969 would the Canadian Criminal Code be amended to make the provision of contraceptives legal. In the meantime, Canada's fledgling birth control movement savored this important victory. One observer claimed the verdict did for the Canadian birth control movement what the 1925 Scopes "Monkey Trial" did for the cause of evolution in America. In 1930, virtually no birth control movement existed in Canada.[31] By World War II, clinics were open in Toronto, Hamilton, and Windsor.[32]

Kaufman resembled many in the sterilization movement who shared his belief that civilization could be saved only by "crash programs to spread simple, cheap methods by the most expedient means."[33] Yet Kaufman was no armchair theorist: his views were conditioned heavily by his own observations and experience in trying to reach those in society whose needs for birth control were seemingly most urgent. Clinics and research that might lead to a breakthrough in contraceptive technology were to him a waste of time and money. His methods may have been crude, and his attitudes toward the poor insensitive, but many of Kaufman's faults were assets in a day and age when few imagined that the battle to win widespread approval for birth control was close to being won.

India

On numerous occasions, HBAA provided Kaufman with the names of U.S. surgeons close to the Canadian border willing to perform sterilizations for his clients. Yet Kaufman's gaze also extended beyond Canada and the United States. Like other wealthy North Americans, including Graham French and Jesse Hartman, Kaufman viewed population growth in India with horror. As French told Ruth Smith in 1959, "What I have seen in the Far East and the people I have talked to in the Far East convinces [sic] me that the ultimate solution is sterilization and that, unless the population is controlled, everything we do for these underprivileged countries is just wasted." Smith agreed, telling French, "[I]t is interesting that the impact on you of the teeming population of the East left you with the same reaction I had—that sterilization is the only solution at this time."[34] Kaufman concurred wholeheartedly.

In 1901, India's population had stood at 250 million, but over the next half-century the population doubled as the expansion of public health services sharply lowered the death rate. Top Indian officials were concerned enough that, in 1935, the National Planning Committee of the Indian National Congress, headed by future prime minister Jawaharlal Nehru, endorsed state-sponsored birth control programs. Later, during the early Cold War, the population spike in India and other developing countries attracted the worried attention of government, academic, and public health officials throughout the industrialized world. They feared that the pressure of numbers on natural resources would create shortages that might lead to political and economic instability. The communist victory in China in 1947 raised additional concerns that demographic trends would so destabilize newly independent India that it, too, might fall to communism. Kingsley Davis, a leading population control advocate, warned that demographic problems in "under-developed countries, especially in areas of non-Western culture, make these nations more vulnerable to Communism."[35]

As the 1950s unfolded, a chorus of concern over the consequences of India's population growth rose to a crescendo, setting in motion a fateful series of events that would lead to Prime Minister Indira Gandhi's forced sterilization program during her government's emergency rule from 1975 to 1977. In that nineteen-month period, approximately 7 million Indians were sterilized, and thousands died of complications stemming from their operations. The backlash to this sterilization program brought down Gandhi's government in 1977, and the memory of its abuses has haunted the Indian family-planning movement ever since.

The event that did more than any other to launch the movement in favor of population control in India through sterilization was the 1952 Third International Conference on Planned Parenthood in Bombay, sponsored by the Family Planning Commission of India. This meeting, the site of the founding of International Planned Parenthood, brought together many of the luminaries from the international birth control movement, including Margaret Sanger, Clarence Gamble, Abraham Stone, C. P. Blacker, and Mrs. Dhanvanti Rama Rau, president of the Family Planning Association of India. Well-wishers for the conference's success included Albert Einstein. Its delegates repeatedly stressed that the country's demographic plight was "desperate" and that concerted efforts at population control were long overdue. Speakers addressed not only the various means for curbing fertility but also the ethical and religious barriers to family planning. Nehru, prime minister from 1947 to his death in 1964, told the conference that his government did not believe that India's grave poverty and social tensions could be solved by population control alone, but he expressed his wish that the entire topic be explored through a "scientific approach" uninhibited by any "preconceptions or convictions" of a religious or ethical nature. He also approved of unspecified family planning "experiments" if they served the "social good."[36] Nehru's words were prophetic. The interest generated in birth control was so great that less than a month after the conference adjourned, the Indian parliament adopted its First Five-Year Plan to reduce the nation's population growth rate. India's campaign of population control was underway.

To members of the sterilization movement, the conference was a huge step toward the acceptance of the operation as a legitimate method of birth control. Sterilization advocates were thrilled when India's First Five-Year Plan clearly stated that "certain health conditions permit the doctor to suggest any chemical, mechanical or biological method of contraception or sterilization." The HBAA's Medora Steedman Bass was as pleased as anyone about the Bombay conference's outcome. In India, she saw signs of genuine hope. The news that eight family planning clinics in Bombay were offering a "free service for voluntary sterilization of poor couples with large families" led her to believe that India was in "the forefront as a leader." She told the attendants of the 1952 Bombay meeting that people of all nations should "build an informed public attitude toward the place of sterilization in family planning and its relation to world population problems." Seeking to improve the "quantity and quality of the children to be born" worldwide, Bass argued that nations should follow the example of Sweden's voluntary sterilization program rather than emphasize coercive policies, but her goal was the same as that of the old-time eugenicists: the "sterilization of the unfit."[37]

In later years, Medora Bass's interest in sterilization tended to focus more on the benefits of the operation for the mentally retarded and less on global population issues. Like others in HBAA, she was a key pioneer in the family-counseling and sex education professions. Yet, as she herself noted, the true "turning point" in her career as a family-planning advocate began at the 1952 Bombay meeting.[38] It was then that she realized that India's demographic problems were the whole world's.

Sripati Chandrasekhar

Medora Bass's 1952 epiphany about sterilization's usefulness in curbing population growth was shared by demographer Sripati Chandrasekhar (1918–2001) (see insert), Indira Gandhi's Minister of Health and Family Planning from 1967 to 1970. No one in the developing world did more than Chandrasekhar to encourage sterilization as a global family-planning method. Born in Rajahmundry, India, Chandrasekhar was elected in 1964 to India's Upper House of Parliament as a member of the National Congress Party representing Madras. Three years later, Indira Gandhi appointed him Union Minister of Health and Family Planning. Both before and after he left politics, in 1970, he hobnobbed with presidents, prime ministers, and popes, relentlessly preaching around the world that India was on the verge of disaster due to her rising population and that sterilization was the best means for averting catastrophe. "Our house is on fire," he starkly declared in 1967, adding that sterilization would be India's "salvation." Radical statements about the need for mass sterilization programs in India made him a welcome figure in global family-planning circles. In 1964 he was awarded the G. J. Watumull Memorial Prize in the field of demography, and in 1972 he was the first recipient of the Margaret Sanger Gold Medal. In 1967, his calls for an incentive program in India to stimulate popular willingness to undergo sterilization drew the praise of Chester Bowles, the U.S. ambassador to India, who told the press that "[i]f Dr. Chandrasekhar's new program is pursued with vision and imagination, there is reason to hope that the obstacles can be overcome and that India's burgeoning population can eventually be brought into balance."[39]

Thanks to his many influential admirers in the United States, Chandrasekhar's message also shaped American public opinion and foreign policy. His effect on U.S. foreign aid for overseas family planning was at no point more evident than during his January 19, 1968, visit to the White House and President Lyndon Baines Johnson. Chandrasekhar had been dispatched by Prime Minister Gandhi to implore the president not to cut U.S. funding for India's family-planning programs. Originally scheduled to last twenty minutes, the meeting lasted for most of the afternoon, as Johnson listened intently to Chandrasekhar's impassioned pleas. Johnson was so impressed with Chandrasekhar that he had him flown to the LBJ Ranch, in Texas, to continue their discussions the following weekend. There at his ranch, LBJ pledged $435 million in loans and credits from the U.S. government.[40]

Yet Chandrasekhar's propagandizing in favor of population control long predated his encounter with LBJ. While attending Madras Presidency College in the 1930s, Chandrasekhar wrote his first paper on India's looming population problems, and, as he recalled, "[F]rom then on I lived and breathed demography."[41] In 1940, he traveled to the United States, earning a Ph.D. in sociology from Columbia University in 1944 with a dissertation on population policy in India. After working for the OSS, he married Ann Downes, an American Quaker from New Jersey, in 1947. Downes was a fervent birth control advocate in her own right, and Chandrasekhar regularly credited her with shaping his theories on population. A stint with UNESCO followed, and in 1950 he founded the Indian Institute for Population Studies. By then he was actively urging the Indian government to set up sterilization clinics throughout the country.[42]

In trying to convince his countrymen that population control was an urgent necessity, Chandrasekhar had his work cut out for him. Between the two world wars, attempts to launch a major birth control campaign in India had fallen far short of success. Support for contraception tended to come from a handful of elite Indian women who worked closely with foreign activists such as Margaret Sanger, Clarence Gamble, and England's Marie Stopes. Yet Sanger, Stopes, Gamble, and other mavericks quickly discovered that their theories about birth control could not overcome the reality of India's hot and humid climate and the everyday living conditions of Indian women. To the disappointment of foreign family-planning advocates, contraceptive jelly suppositories melted in shipment, foam powder clumped, and the oil and cotton needed to make cotton wads (Marie Stopes's favorite method) were frequently unavailable to Indian women.[43]

After World War II, amid mounting international interest in population control, Chandrasekhar and other birth control advocates had reasons to be optimistic. Yet, despite bold declarations from Nehru on down, resistance to family planning in India was fierce. The vast majority of India's population lived in desperate poverty, and children (especially males) were viewed as a hedge against a highly uncertain future.[44] In the cities, acceptance of family limitation was growing, but in the country's villages, where about 80% of the population lived, traditional attitudes flourished. Hinduism did not explicitly condemn artificial birth control, nor was there any Indian law prohibiting sterilization. Yet the teachings of Mahatma Gandhi (1869–1948), India's charismatic nationalist leader, favored abstinence and restraint rather than scientific contraception.[45] Also opposed to birth control were India's Muslims and Roman Catholics. Muslim women observed *purdah*, or their seclusion from public observation, and according to Chandrasekhar were "inaccessible even to women social workers."[46] The nation's Hindus particularly objected to male sterilization because they feared that Muslim men, allowed up to four wives, might be able to outbreed them.[47]

To help break down these formidable barriers, Chandrasekhar turned to Canada's A. R. Kaufman. By the 1950s, Kaufman resembled many other North American birth control advocates in that his focus was gradually shifting toward the developing world, and specifically India. Eager to apply the lessons he had learned about contraception in Canada, Kaufman, in 1955, offered to fund Chandrasekhar's newly founded birth control clinic in Mangadu, a cluster of villages about fifteen miles from the city of Madras. Their collaboration lasted until 1960, punctuated by Kaufman's outbursts of impatience that his money pay immediate dividends. Initially, Kaufman paid for the shipment and distribution of rubber sponges and foam tablets, but both men concurred that vasectomy would "likely prevent more babies per dollar than any other method" of contraception, a line of argument that sterilization advocates would repeatedly employ in later years.[48] To Kaufman, the people of India were "too poor, too ignorant, and too lazy to practice birth control," so he believed that sterilization was "the only answer for perhaps 90 per cent of the population."[49] Chandrasekhar did not disagree, but he cautioned Kaufman that "working in conservative and backward villages is a slow and tedious process. Things cannot and should not be hurried in the villages, for the slightest suspicion may not only hamper the work but undo the propaganda I have been carrying on for a long time in many parts of the country."[50] Indeed, progress was slow, with the vasectomy rate at Chandrasekhar's clinic reaching only five per month in 1957. The disadvantages of clinics were as obvious in rural India as they were back in North America. Social workers and medical staff scheduled operations, but patients often did not show up, because they had to work or did not have transportation, or because their relatives and friends talked them out of the surgery. Nonetheless, Chandrasekhar was "personally convinced that vasectomy is the easiest and the best solution for the rural parts of India."[51]

Kaufman and Chandrasekhar saw their family planning "experiment" as a pilot project that the government ultimately would take over and fund. By the early 1960s, it appeared that their efforts were beginning to pay off. In 1961, the central Indian government, admitting that family-planning policy results over the previous eight years "had not been encouraging," unfurled its Third Five-Year Plan to ease population pressure, earmarking nearly five times the total spent in the first two plans combined. The Indian health minister announced that the national government would provide surgical facilities in state-owned hospitals. The states of Madras, Kerala, and Maharashtra declared their commitment to sterilization as a way of reducing the birth rate.

Yet the nettlesome difference between voluntarism and subtle coercion, vague under the best of circumstances, became increasingly cloudy as India's sterilization campaign built momentum. State officials assured the international community that men and women who underwent sterilization surgery knew fully that the operation meant an end to their reproductive powers. Yet controversy dogged government efforts to encourage men and women to be sterilized. The press reported that in Madras, canvassers, social workers, nurses, and doctors frequently were paid for each man whose sterilization they could arrange. Accusations flew freely that patients were not being told what the operation involved. Madras city employees with three children received a free vasectomy and a cash award for both husband and wife. Other government workers were awarded six days off for such operations. Sterilization proponents such as Chandrasekhar insisted that once individuals were fully briefed, they happily accepted the surgery, but the alacrity with which sterilization programs were administered created plenty of potential for abuse. The fact that the same abuses were occurring regularly fifteen years later testified to the urgency surrounding India's family-planning policies and the impact of "propaganda" spread by opinion makers such as Chandrasekhar. It also indicated that changing the country's mores about fertility would take many years to accomplish.[52]

Brock Chisholm

If the sterilization movement was thrilled to have Chandrasekhar on its side as the 1960s dawned, it was also overjoyed that Canadian psychiatrist Brock Chisholm (1896–1971) (see insert) agreed to speak out in favor of sterilization in the 1960s. Before World War II, Chisholm, a World War I veteran, was a little-known Oakville, Ontario, family doctor with a keen interest in psychiatry. With the coming of the war, however, his knowledge of psychiatry was suddenly in great demand. During the war, he swiftly rose through the ranks of the Canadian army to become its Director of Personnel Selection, Director-General of Medical Services, and finally Deputy Minister of Health in the newly created Department of National Health and Welfare in Ottawa. As *Time* magazine noted, Chisholm was the only psychiatrist in the world between 1939 and 1945 to serve as head of army medical services in any country.[53] A decade of rapid career advancement was capped in 1948 when he was named the first Director-General of the World Health Organization in Geneva, Switzerland. Chisholm held his WHO post until 1952, and in the course of those four years received a rude education in the highly contentious topic of global population politics.

In retrospect, it is astonishing that Chisholm enjoyed so much professional success on the national and international stages, given his propensity to say highly unpopular things. As a friend commented, Chisholm liked to explode "verbal atomic bombs which shatter our complacency."[54] In 1944, he publicly blamed Canadian mothers for spoiling their sons and making them unfit for military life and the emotional strain of combat. This trend in upbringing, Chisholm contended, accounted for the close to 25% rate of mental breakdown in the Canadian armed forces.[55] The next year, he created another firestorm of controversy when he warned Canadian parents that teaching their children to believe in Santa Claus would harm them cognitively and emotionally: the social danger of this form of parenting lay in its capacity to create people who could not think for themselves and thus were "easy meat for demagogues and mob orators."[56] Chisholm's haughty tone triggered protests across Canada, but they never seemed to unduly damage his reputation in medical and government circles.

Chisholm's stint at the WHO, from 1948 to 1952, was similarly fraught with controversy, especially over the issue of population control. By the late 1940s, thanks to projects such as the WHO's malaria control program in India, death rates in the developing world were falling steadily while population was soaring. Some officials at the WHO and the Food and Agriculture Organization of the United Nations began considering how to increase food production and reduce fertility rates. On October 29, 1951, Chisholm announced that the WHO, in an effort to solve the problem created by its own successes, had decided to support a pilot project under the HBAA's Abraham Stone designed to teach the rhythm method of birth control in a single village in India. The very same day, Pope Pius XII issued a statement on the rhythm method, declaring it moral for married couples to exercise their conjugal rights during the sterile period in a women's reproductive cycle, but adding that couples who restricted their conjugal acts to the infertile period were "in contradiction to upright ethical values." In a WHO press conference, Chisholm insisted that the rhythm method did not conflict with the Pope's message, but controversy was already brewing. Stone was urging the formation of a special committee to study the manufacture of "scientific contraceptives" for free distribution to India's needy. A few months later, after a tour of India by Eleanor Roosevelt and others, the press in Delhi reported that the rhythm method would never be effective given India's illiterate population.

Roman Catholic howls of protest descended on Chisholm and the WHO. Stone's presence in the WHO pilot project particularly infuriated Catholics. Stone, a PPFA and HBAA member, was also the director of the Margaret Sanger Research Bureau. By 1952, Sanger's name was a red flag for the countless Catholic spokespeople who opposed the birth control movement. When, in May, 1952, a WHO motion to establish an expert committee to explore and report on the health aspects of the population issue was voted down, Chisholm was furious. A long-standing, visceral opponent of organized religion, Chisholm had always had strained relations with the Catholic Church in Canada, but his foray into the politics of population control made him an inviting target for Church attacks. Called "an affront to all Christians," Chisholm was denounced by Catholic Canadians as a "disgrace" to the nation on the international stage. U.S. diplomats, for their part, called him a "pinko."[57] Little wonder that on November 12, 1952, Chisholm, frustrated and embittered, retired from his WHO post. As he noted in his typically blunt style, the furious debate over population control showed there was "nothing admirable in competing with rabbits."[58]

Figure 1.   Medora Steedman Bass

Figure 2.   Sripati Chandrasekhar

Figure 3.   Homer Calver

Figure 4.   Brock Chisholm

Figure 5.   Joseph E. Davis

Figure 6.　Helen Edey

Figure 7.　Paul Ehrlich

Figure 8. Jesse Hartman

Figure 9. Lawrence Lader

Figure 10. Hugh Moore

Figure 11. John Rague

Figure 12.   Margaret Sanger

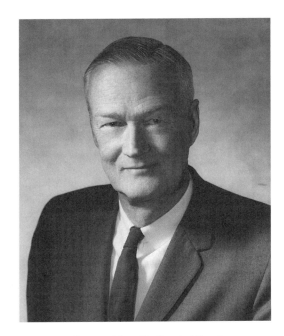

Figure 13.   H. Curtis Wood

Figure 14.   Alan Guttmacher

Leaving the WHO, however, did not mean Chisholm disappeared into quiet retirement. Convinced he had a duty to change opinions in a tense and unstable world, he continued to speak out on global issues, lecturing around the world until his death, in 1971. Population control tended to dominate his concerns. In May, 1956, at New York City's Waldorf-Astoria Hotel, Chisholm gave the keynote address before an audience of eight hundred and fifty at PPFA's annual meeting, calling overpopulation "the world's most pressing problem."[59] In 1962, Chisholm accepted the post of HBAA Honorary President. In 1966, he was named co-chairman (with Margaret Sanger) of the group's International Advisory Committee. Chisholm, like others in the sterilization movement, tended to stress the social and political benefits of family planning. But they also viewed sterilization and other birth control measures as means for realizing the WHO's definition of health as not merely "the absence of illness, but a state of complete physical, mental, and social well-being."[60] HBAA's position was that "education, service and research in the field of voluntary sterilization enhances this 'well-being' for many couples distressed by anxieties and tensions caused by fear of repeated unwanted pregnancies." Chisholm elaborated on this theme when he addressed HBAA members at their annual meeting on February 8, 1962. Repeating the population control movement's article of faith, Chisholm asserted that the "population explosion" was a more dangerous threat than hunger and nuclear war to humanity's survival. Humanity's ability to defuse the population explosion, he complained, was hampered by traditional "prejudices" surrounding birth control. These prejudices had become "incorporated into the religious attitude of considerable numbers of people." The solution, according to Chisholm, lay in humanity liberating itself from these supposedly outdated and "irrelevant" customs. When the human race was able to emancipate itself, Chisholm concluded, it would end "the misery being produced even in the highly-developed countries . . . an enormous amount of misery, poverty, and ill health" due to "the burden of childbearing on women who do not have methods of reducing the incidence of pregnancy." Thus "the responsible and mature person" had to do his or her share to improve this "threatening situation," and

> [s]terilization is, in many types of situations, the most appropriate and effective method of reducing rates of increase in population. Voluntary sterilization, from both the individual and social point of view, is highly reliable, is without aesthetic disadvantages, requires no embarrassing procedures, costs nothing beyond the original operation, and offers no risk to health. Any

objections represent only old prejudices based on long past situations and ancient ignorance.

Complying with the unprecedented demands of the world in the twentieth century, Chisholm contended, would not only help the planet survive; it would also make individuals happier and healthier.[61]

By the early 1960s, the ability of the HBAA to recruit major opinion-makers such as Brock Chisholm and Sripati Chandrasekhar indicated that, slowly but surely, sterilization was becoming a respectable topic in polite company and elite circles. Since World War II, it had been difficult for sterilization proponents to popularize the operation as a method for cutting welfare costs or improving America's gene pool. Advocacy of sterilization struck many Americans as a thinly disguised attempt to punish the poor and racial minorities. In the years after *Brown v. Board of Education*, the 1954 U.S. Supreme Court ruling that racially segregated schools were unconstitutional, and with the growing support for civil rights for African Americans, sympathy for sterilization programs that targeted inner-city neighborhoods or rural communities in Appalachia or the Deep South was in short supply.[62] Catholic opposition to sterilization further hamstrung the efforts of sterilization activists to launch domestic programs. But the mounting international concern over the burgeoning populations of India and other developing countries was steadily making support for sterilization as a population control method fashionable. Resistance to sterilization never quite evaporated, but as the 1960s wore on it became increasingly clear that widespread acceptance of sterilization had finally arrived.

Notes

1. H. Curtis Wood to Clarence Gamble, December 14, 1959, CJG, Box 231, file 3567.
2. "William Vogt," *Current Biography*, 1953, pp. 638–640; "William Vogt, former director of Planned Parenthood, is dead," *New York Times*, July 12, 1968, p. 31.
3. Vogt W. *Road to Survival*. New York: William Sloane Associates, 1948.
4. Malthus TR. *An Essay on the Principle of Population: Text, Sources, and Background Criticism*. Philip Appleman (ed.). New York and London: W. W. Norton, 1976.
5. Frances Hand Ferguson, interview with James W. Reed, June 3, 1974, Family Planning Oral History Project, Schlesinger Library, Radcliffe Institute, Harvard University, Cambridge, MA, p. 37.

6. For Vogt's role in the population control movement, see Critchlow DT. *Intended Consequences: Birth Control, Abortion, and the Federal Government in Modern America.* New York and Oxford: Oxford University Press, 1999, pp. 18–19, 30–31. See also Franks A. *Margaret Sanger's Eugenic Legacy: The Control of Female Fertility.* Jefferson, NC: McFarland and Co., 2005, pp. 55, 132, 163, 208–209. For Mencken's views on sterilization bonuses, see Mencken HL. Utopia by sterilization. *The American Mercury.* 1937;41:405.

7. Frances Hand Ferguson, interview with James W. Reed, June 3, 1974, Family Planning Oral History Project, Schlesinger Library, Radcliffe Institute, Harvard University, Cambridge, MA, p. 37.

8. H. Curtis Wood to William Vogt, August 2, 1948, AVS, Box 2, folder 15.

9. H. Curtis Wood's remarks at December 1, 1950, HBAA meeting, AVS, Box 4, folder 33.

10. Critchlow DT. *Intended Consequences: Birth Control, Abortion, and the Federal Government in Modern America.* New York and Oxford: Oxford University Press, 1999.

11. Donald Critchlow argues that Moore's anticommunism was largely "rhetorical," secondary to his goal of "rall[ying]" American officials to support international family planning." Critchlow DT. *Intended Consequences: Birth Control, Abortion, and the Federal Government in Modern America.* New York and Oxford: Oxford University Press, 1999, p. 16.

12. Quoted in Lader L. *Breeding Ourselves to Death.* New York: Seven Locks Press, 1971, p. 14. See also Critchlow DT. *Intended Consequences: Birth Control, Abortion, and the Federal Government in Modern America.* New York and Oxford: Oxford University Press, 1999, p. 32.

13. Lader L. *Breeding Ourselves to Death.* New York: Seven Locks Press, 1971, p. 11. See also Critchlow DT. *Intended Consequences: Birth Control, Abortion, and the Federal Government in Modern America.* New York and Oxford: Oxford University Press, 1999, p. 33.

14. Hugh Moore Memo, "Re: Chicago Planned Parenthood Letter," July 18, 1960, HM, Series 2, Box 20, folder 11. According to Frances Hand Ferguson, the longtime birth-control activist, Moore's interest in birth control had little to do with the "personal angle." Frances Hand Ferguson, interview with James W. Reed, June 3, 1974, Family Planning Oral History Project, Schlesinger Library, Radcliffe Institute, Harvard University, Cambridge, MA, p. 37.

15. Hugh Moore to Ruth Smith, September 23, 1963, HM, Series 3, Box 15, folder 6.

16. Hugh Moore to Katharine McCormick, March 21, 1961, HM, Series 2, Box 2, folder 8.

17. Hugh Moore, "Dear Friend" letter, November 1966, HM, Series 3, Box 15, folder 7.

18. The advertisement appeared on March 10, 1968, in the *New York Times* and on March 13 in the *Washington Post.* See Critchlow DT. *Intended Consequences: Birth*

Control, Abortion, and the Federal Government in Modern America. New York and Oxford: Oxford University Press, 1999, p. 151.

19. John Sharpless. World population growth, family planning, and American foreign policy. In Critchlow DT (Ed.), *The Politics of Abortion and Birth Control in Historical Perspective.* University Park: Pennsylvania State University Press, 1996, p. 80. See also Critchlow DT. *Intended Consequences: Birth Control, Abortion, and the Federal Government in Modern America.* New York and Oxford: Oxford University Press, 1999, p. 19–25.

20. John D. Rockefeller 3rd to Hugh Moore, June 22, 1965, HM, Series 2, Box 2, folder 18.

21. Hugh Moore to William Draper, May 15, 1961, HM, Series 2, Box 20, folder 21.

22. John D. Rockefeller 3rd to Hugh Moore, January 2, 1968, HM, Series 2, Box 2, folder 18.

23. Bernard Berelson, "Communication Research Program," 25 January 1962, Population Council, Berelson Files, Rockefeller Archives. Quoted in Critchlow DT. *Intended Consequences: Birth Control, Abortion, and the Federal Government in Modern America.* New York and Oxford: Oxford University Press, 1999, p. 29.

24. Homer Calver to Hugh Moore, July 1, 1968, AVS, Box 87, IAVS folder.

25. "Interview Report: between Mr. A. R. Kaufman and Miss I. H. Armes, 22 August 1952," AVS, Box 56, Kaufman folder.

26. Revie L. More than just boots! The eugenic and commercial concerns behind A.R. Kaufman's birth controlling activities. *Canadian Bulletin of Medical History.* 2006;23;119–143.

27. Parents' Information Bureau Bulletin #1, Birth Control Activities and Procedures, June 15, 1933, PIB Papers, University of Waterloo. Quoted in McLaren A, McLaren AT. *The Bedroom and the State: The Changing Practices and Politics of Contraception and Abortion in Canada, 1880–1997.* Oxford and Toronto: Oxford University Press, 1997, p. 105.

28. McLaren A, McLaren AT. *The Bedroom and the State: The Changing Practices and Politics of Contraception and Abortion in Canada, 1880–1997.* Oxford and Toronto: Oxford University Press, 1997, pp. 92–116; Revie L. More than just boots! The eugenic and commercial concerns behind A.R. Kaufman's birth controlling activities. *Canadian Bulletin of Medical History.* 2006;23;129; Angus McLaren, *Our Own Master Race: Eugenics in Canada, 1885-1945.* Toronto: McClelland and Stewart, 1990, pp. 115–117; Reed J. *From Private Vice to Public Virtue: The Birth Control Movement and American Society Since 1830.* New York: Basic, 1978, pp. 218–222.

29. A. R. Kaufman to H. L. Mencken, August 10, 1937, copy in CJG. Quoted in Reed J. *From Private Vice to Public Virtue: The Birth Control Movement and American Society Since 1830.* New York: Basic, 1978, p. 219.

30. A. R. Kaufman to Sripati Chandrasekhar, May 10, 1957, SC, Box 16, folder 53.

31. There was some stirring of interest in birth control in British Columbia in the 1920s but it was "intermittent." McLaren A, McLaren AT. *The Bedroom and the State: The Changing Practices and Politics of Contraception and Abortion in Canada, 1880–1997.* Oxford and Toronto: Oxford University Press, 1997, p. 66. The Canadian Birth Control League was founded in 1931.

32. Matsner EM. The trial of Dorothea Palmer. *Journal of Contraception.* 1937;2:80. Cited in McLaren A, McLaren AT. *The Bedroom and the State: The Changing Practices and Politics of Contraception and Abortion in Canada, 1880–1997.* Oxford and Toronto: Oxford University Press, 1997, p. 92.

33. Reed J. *From Private Vice to Public Virtue: The Birth Control Movement and American Society Since 1830.* New York: Basic, 1978, p. 222.

34. Graham French to Ruth Smith, July 22, 1959; Ruth Smith to Graham French, July 24, 1959, AVS, Box 33, French folder.

35. Davis K. Population and power in the Free World. In Spengler JJ, Duncan OD (eds.). *Population, Theory and Policy.* Glencoe, IL: Free Press, 1956, p. 356.

36. "Birth control not ethically banned for social welfare." *Times of India,* November 25, 1952.

37. Medora S. Bass, "Sterilization from the Lay Volunteer Point of View," paper presented to the Third International Conference on Planned Parenthood, Bombay, November 24–December 1, 1952.

38. See Bass's handwritten comments on Sarah Gamble's December 1973 "Dear Friend" letter on behalf of the Pathfinder Fund, AHC, MSB Box 2.

39. "Steps to check population," *Statesman* (New Delhi), May 28, 1967.

40. "Johnson assures full support to family planning in India. *American Reporter* (New Delhi), February 14, 1968; personal communication, Daniel M. Johnson, December 6, 2005.

41. "Sripati Chandrasekhar, Indian demographer, dies at 83." *New York Times,* June 23, 2001.

42. "Birth control to limit population." *The Times of India,* February 12, 1951.

43. Schoen J. *Choice and Coercion: Birth Control, Sterilization and Abortion in Public Health and Welfare.* Chapel Hill: University of North Carolina Press, 2005, pp. 216–225.

44. As one official of the Pathfinder Fund said, "The crucial difficulty [facing birth controllers] seems to lie in the rural areas [of India]. The cities have a quick appreciation of too many children. Villagers much less so." Martha Willing to Sripati Chandrasekhar, n.d., SC, Box 15, folder 11.

45. Chandrasekhar S. The Hindu view of family planning and abortion. *Population Review.* 1984;28:7–36.

46. Sripati Chandrasekhar to A. R. Kaufman, December 2, 1955, SC, Box 16, folder 52.

47. "Foe of population: Sripati Chandrasekhar." *New York Times,* March 31, 1967.

48. A. R. Kaufman to Sripati Chandrasekhar, November 5, 1959, SC, Box 16, folder 54.

49. A. R. Kaufman to Sripati Chandrasekhar, May 10, 1957, SC, Box 16, folder 53.
50. Sripati Chandrasekhar to A. R. Kaufman, March 15, 1956, SC, Box 16. folder 52.
51. Sripati Chandrasekhar to A. R. Kaufman, June 12, 1957, SC, Box 16, folder 53.
52. "Birth control making little headway." *New York Times*, January 17, 1959; "India adopts sterilization to lower her birth rate." *New York Times*, February 16, 1959; "Sterilization momentum gains in India." *Evening Star*, November 2, 1959; "India to Sterilize 15,000 a month." *San Francisco Examiner*, November 6, 1960.
53. "Notes." *Time*, November 1, 1943, p. 24.
54. "Don't Let Conscience Guide You." n.d., but likely 1949, volume 2, BC.
55. "Mothers' influence seen as bane in Army life by medical director." *Toronto Globe and Mail*, February 12, 1944.
56. Irving A. *Brock Chisholm: Doctor to the World*. Markham, ON: Fitzhenry and Whiteside, 1998, p. 62.
57. For the details of this chapter in Chisholm's career, I have benefited immensely from John Farley's as yet unpublished book manuscript on Chisholm. I thank Professor Farley for allowing me to read it and sharing with me his own thoughts of Chisholm and his accomplishments.
58. Chisholm B. Too many babies. *Weekend Magazine (Victoria Times)*, March 5, 1955.
59. "Chisholm hails recent Catholic initiative on population problems." *Planned Parenthood News*, Summer 1956, pp. 1–2. See also "Speech by Dr. Brock Chisholm," BC, vol. 2.
60. Ruth P. Smith to Chisholm, October 13, 1960, AVS, Box 32, Chisholm File.
61. "Dr. Brock Chisholm warns of population peril." *Human Betterment Association of America News*, Spring 1962, pp. 1–2. The full text of Chisholm's speech, titled "World Health and World Population in the Fateful Sixties," and with his own notes and corrections, is in AVS, Box 32, Chisholm File.
62. Polls showed that even among white Southerners, polled four years before the passage of the 1965 Voting Rights Act, 95% thought that blacks should have the right to vote. Samuel Lubell, *The Hidden Crisis in American Politics*. New York: Norton, 1977, pp. 71, 175. Cited in Heineman KJ. *God Is a Conservative: Religion, Politics, and Morality in Contemporary America*. New York and London: New York University Press, 2005, pp. 15–16.

Chapter 5

A Great Wave

On the evening of October 1, 1969, Hugh Moore, president of the Association for Voluntary Sterilization (AVS), was in a buoyant mood. As he approached the microphone at New York City's Carnegie Endowment Center, he gazed at the overflow audience, which included television host Ed Sullivan; entertainer Arthur Godfrey; feminist author Betty Friedan; and Stanford University biologist Paul Ehrlich, author of the 1968 bestseller *The Population Bomb*. Moore couldn't resist gloating; only "a few years ago," he reminisced, meetings of the board were held "quietly" in a West 58th Street apartment in Manhattan, when

> we were known as the Human Betterment Association, believe it or not. Before that the name had been 'Birth Right!' [sic] These ambiguous terms were adopted because of our not daring to use sterilization, lest we be chased out of town. . . . But one day we decided to canvas[s] our small leadership to find out if they were prepared to call a spade a spade, and by a narrow margin we adopted the name Association for Voluntary Sterilization. We took the big leap. Newspapers gradually began to run our stories on sterilization. It became a topic for popular conversation. Cutting the Fallopian tubes is now a favorite subject at cocktail parties. And a host at a dinner might discuss his vasectomy while carving the roast.

"We have at last arrived," Moore chortled.[1]

Hugh Moore had good reason to celebrate the progress of the sterilization movement by the end of the 1960s. Sterilization, tainted by its links to eugenics, was still a "dirty word" to some in America, and surgical birth control was largely unknown throughout the developing world.[2] Yet in

1966, 64% of Americans polled said they supported voluntary sterilization as a method of birth control. By the early 1970s, a million sterilizations (excluding hysterectomies) were being performed annually in the United States. The number of vasectomy clinics nationwide stood at one hundred and thirty, up from zero just a few years earlier. The federal government was on the verge of approving public funding for domestic and overseas sterilizations. The AVS had forged alliances with groups such as the American Civil Liberties Union (ACLU) and Zero Population Growth (ZPG) in their legal efforts to force hospitals to grant requests for sterilization operations. When added to the improving relations between AVS and the Planned Parenthood Federation of America (PPFA), these partnerships heralded a new era for the sterilization movement. As H. Curtis Wood observed in 1973, the "ground swell" in favor of sterilization that started in the 1950s had become "a great wave."[3]

The Moore Era Begins

What Hugh Moore did not say on the night of October 1, 1969, but what many in his audience knew full well, was that he was a big reason for the turnaround in AVS fortunes. Beginning as modest contributors to the Human Betterment Association of America (HBAA) in the 1950s, Moore and his wife Louise steadily took over the leadership of the group as the 1960s wore on.[4] Their ties to other wealthy donors to population control causes, including the Scaife Family Foundation, the Sunnen Foundation, and the Chichester DuPont Foundation, helped to boost AVS's annual budget by tens of thousands of dollars.[5] The Moores also craftily arranged to get close friends and followers elected to the group's board and advisory committees, while Moore himself became its president. By the end of the 1960s, when Moore decided, for health reasons, to step down as AVS president, the organization was still promoting sterilization as the best overall form of contraception, as it had been doing since the days of Marian Olden. But Moore had also spearheaded a major change in the group's focus. Sterilization as a way of defusing the country's "poverty bomb" gradually had given way to sterilization as a means of defusing the global "population bomb." Thanks to this shift in orientation, the lives of millions of people worldwide would never be the same.

Hugh Moore's ascendancy in the sterilization movement during the 1960s produced a changing of the guard at HBAA. Out the door went the formidable Ruth Proskauer Smith, whose departure brought to a close an era in the history of the sterilization movement. For years she had been a major driving force behind the movement, serving as HBAA executive director since 1955 and often hosting its meetings in her Upper West Side apartment in Manhattan. By the early 1960s, she had taken a decidedly proprietary interest in the organization, and thus watched with dismay as the Moores methodically seized control. Smith particularly fought the change in the organization's name to AVS, preferring to avoid direct references to sterilization. When it became clear that population control was to be the group's new *raison d'être*, she submitted her resignation.

Smith's departure from HBAA was not amicable.[6] On October 29, 1964, its board unanimously accepted her resignation, citing a "failure to arrive at a mutually satisfactory arrangement for the future handling of the greatly increased activities of the Association."[7] In the end, the sterilization movement was simply too small for two such strong-willed individuals as Ruth Smith and Hugh Moore. Moore's contacts with the wealthy and powerful and his proclivity for outspokenness won out.[8]

Free At Last?

Other prominent figures from HBAA's past, including Alan Guttmacher, left less noisily, shifting their energies to the struggle for abortion rights. Guttmacher never ceased believing that sterilization was one of the most effective methods of contraception for the poor. Yet, in 1966, with his time consumed by International Planned Parenthood Federation duties, he resigned from the AVS board of directors.[9] Much had changed since Guttmacher's early days with HBAA. By the mid-1960s, the oral contraceptive pill and the intrauterine device (IUD) were being hailed as major breakthroughs in birth control technology. In 1960, the pharmaceutical giant G.D. Searle and Company had produced the first oral contraceptive pill, dubbed Enovid, and the U.S. Food and Drug Administration (FDA) approved it for use. The product of the dogged encouragement of Margaret Sanger; the collaboration between scientists Gregory Pincus and John Rock; and the financial support of Katherine McCormick, an heir to the International Harvester fortune, the Pill helped to launch a contraceptive revolution in the lives of millions of men and women. Within five years of its FDA approval, over 6 million American women were "on the Pill." By 1968, American women were spending $150 million annually on the Pill, almost as much as Americans spent on all contraceptives in 1958 (p. 236).[10]

Initially, the Pill appeared to be a tectonic turning point in women's history. Helen Gurley Brown, author of the 1962 book *Sex and the Single Girl*, pointed out that prior to the Pill single women had lived with the dread of what pregnancy would do to their reputations. Because rates of sex outside marriage in both Britain and the United States had been increasing since World War II, this was a fear that many women felt deeply. After the Pill, it was possible for single women to enjoy sex for the first time (pp. 203–204).[11] Clare Boothe Luce, the second U.S. female ambassador in history, declared in 1969 that thanks to the Pill, "modern woman is at last free, as a man is free, to dispose of her own body." The Pill produced other results that many women welcomed. Pill use tended to swell women's breasts. "For the first time in my life I have a real bosom," one American woman rejoiced, as C-cup bra sales soared in the United States during the 1960s.[12] Yet the revolution launched by the introduction of the Pill was mostly restricted to the developed world. In 1967, of almost 13 million Pill users worldwide, only 3 million (or 23%) were in developing countries (pp. 233–236, 239).[10]

Though it received less media fanfare than the Pill, the IUD, too, was hailed in the 1960s as a solution to the perennial challenge of birth control. For centuries, people had been inserting objects into women's uteri to either facilitate or prevent conception, exacting a horrendous toll on women's health.[13] In 1909, a German physician began experimenting with a contraceptive device placed entirely in the uterus, making it less likely to provide a path for infection. This device enjoyed the avid support of Robert Latou Dickinson and Clarence Gamble, but for years the medical and public health professions refused to endorse it. Things began to change in the late 1950s, when evidence suggested that substituting plastic for wire would make it easier to insert the device. Upon hearing this news, Guttmacher's interest in the IUD started to mount, as did the Population Council's. In 1962, the Population Council began investing in the clinical testing and statistical evaluation of the IUD, ultimately putting forth $2.5 million. The findings did not remove all doubts about the device's safety, but the sense of urgency surrounding the issue of population control trumped such concerns. In 1962, one doctor admitted at a Population Council conference that IUDs were "horrible things, they produce infection, they are out-moded and not worth using"—but so what, he mused, if a patient did develop an intrauterine infection and had to have her ovaries and fallopian tubes removed? "How serious is that for the particular patient and for the population of the world in general? Not very . . . Perhaps the individual patient is expendable in the general scheme of things, particularly if the infection she acquires is sterilizing but not lethal."[14] As one Population Council member exclaimed in 1964, the IUD "can and will change the history of the world."[15]

Alan Guttmacher cheered the IUD as loudly as anyone. Its contraceptive potential in "huge population groups," as he put it, was enormous.[16] As he told the president of G.D. Searle in 1964[17]:

> IUDs have special application to underdeveloped areas where two things are lacking: one, money, and the other sustained motivation. No contraceptive could be cheaper, and also once the damn thing is in, the patient cannot change her mind. In fact, we can hope she will forget that it is there and perhaps in several months wonder why she has not conceived . . . If Mrs. Astorbilt, or Mrs. Searle or Mrs. Guttmacher gets pregnant while using an IUD, there is quite a stink—the thing is not good and a lot of people will hear about it. However, if you reduce the birth rate of . . . the Korean, Pakistanian or Indian population from 50 to 45 per 1,000 per year to 2, 3, or 5, this becomes an accomplishment to celebrate.

The IUD appeared promising because the "less conscientious" women of "India's swarming throngs" who had the device inserted might forget to remove it even when they desired conception.[18] To Guttmacher, preventing Third World women from having babies was more important than their reproductive right to choose.

Yet ultimately Guttmacher, like many other population control proponents, grew disenchanted with the IUD, sentiments borne out when horrific revelations about the Dalkon Shield surfaced in the early 1970s. The Pathfinder Fund, a Boston-based, nonprofit, population control group launched by Clarence Gamble in 1957, and a leading booster of the IUD, had alone issued 59,000 Dalkon Shields to thirty-five separate family-planning projects in developing countries between 1972 and 1974.[19] Use of the Dalkon Shield, manufactured and marketed by A. H. Robins, caused at least eighteen deaths and over 200,000 cases of miscarriages, hysterectomies, and uterine infections, as well as untold birth defects in the United States, paving the way for a lawsuit filed by over 300,000 women and which led to a $2.5 billion settlement.[20]

Ford Foundation and Population Council studies revealed that in many countries, over half of the women with IUDs stopped using them after less than a year.[21] Indian women in particular tended to dislike the device. By 1967, over a million Indian women had been fitted with IUDs, but the rate of insertions was falling off amid opposition from midwives and complaints of internal bleeding and involuntary expulsions. When financial rewards were offered to women who would accept IUDs, some husbands began removing the devices and sending their wives back for another insertion and bonus, often causing hemorrhages.[22] Indian women were also extremely uncomfortable about male doctors inserting the device.[23]

Similarly, by 1970, when the FDA decreed that high-estrogen birth control pills were unsafe, the original enthusiasm for the Pill was wearing off. As the 1960s unfolded, reports mounted of weight gain, nausea, headaches, depression, ovarian cysts, blood clots, and loss of libido due to Pill use. The 1962 thalidomide crisis over the sedative's link to severe birth defects, and the publication that same year of Rachel Carson's *Silent Spring*, a powerful indictment of the chemical industry, did not help the Pill's fortunes. Such revelations shook the public's faith in the boast of American manufacturers to offer "better living through chemistry." To many women who had intercourse infrequently, taking the Pill daily was "pharmaceutical overkill." Barbara Seaman's *The Doctors' Case Against the Pill* (1969), which vigorously asserted the health risks of the Pill, won her the reputation as the "Ralph Nader of the birth control pill" (pp. 245, 246).[10] One year later, the U.S. Senate held hearings into the safety of the Pill. Wisconsin Democrat Gaylord Nelson, who chaired the hearings, was so impressed with Seaman's book that he asked her to help him decide who should testify (p. 150).[11]

Covered on television, the Nelson hearings were watched by an estimated 87% of women between the ages of twenty-one and forty-five. Little new information surfaced at the hearings, but the event was enough to shake confidence in Pill use. Eighteen percent of Pill-taking women quit during the hearings, and another 23% seriously considered quitting (p. 151).[11] In the wake of the hearings, the FDA ruled that a patient package insert should be adopted in America to warn women of the Pill's potential side effects. Rates of Pill use rebounded in the early 1970s but since then have declined sharply in the United States, the Netherlands, and Australia (though not in Britain). Fears of the Pill's link to cancer, and later to HIV infection, spread widely through U.S. society, with 76% of those polled in 1985 saying they believed there were significant health risks with the Pill. By the 1980s, as bad news about both the Pill and the IUD snowballed, sterilization had become a more common method worldwide than the Pill and IUD combined (pp. 215, 260–265).[11]

The emerging women's health movement also undermined confidence in the Pill. Activists urged women to take medicine "into their own hands" through self-medication and improved public education.[24] In 1971, the

Boston Women's Health Book Collective published *Our Bodies, Ourselves*, a self-help manual that quickly sold 4 million copies in twelve languages. While not condemning the Pill entirely, women's groups objected to "unsafe contraceptives foisted on uninformed women for the profit of the drug and medical industries and for the convenience of men." As one woman wrote to the FDA, "I demand—that as a woman, having the option to take the pill or not, I have all the facts in front of me." The male-dominated medical profession was warned that it had to provide full disclosure for patients and recognize women's "human rights." African American militants joined the chorus, alleging that "the main purpose of the pill is to reduce the number of Negroes in the world." By the early 1970s, the highly publicized controversy swirling around the Pill, covered in depth by such mainstream women's magazines as *Redbook*, *Good Housekeeping*, and *Ladies Home Journal*, had transformed it into a predominantly white, middle-class method of contraception in the United States (pp. 249, 250, 256).[10]

None of this bad press about the Pill escaped Guttmacher's notice. Toward the end of the 1960s, his attention was shifting once again, this time to liberalizing abortion laws as a means of population control and female empowerment. Guttmacher's evolving tolerance toward abortion represented a big change in his attitudes about reproductive health. "I deplore the performance of abortion on virtual demand," he stated in 1959.[25] But by the late 1960s, Guttmacher was front and center within the movement to remove abortion entirely from the criminal code.[26]

Simultaneously, his earlier optimism about reducing population through voluntary birth control was waning, and he mused out loud about the need to "get tough" with men and women (especially in the developing world) whose contraceptive habits were ostensibly poor. Guttmacher's patience with elective birth control policies was wearing thin, and like so many other eminent birth control advocates he was increasingly willing to consider policies that, subtly or not, pressured the poor into submitting to sterilization. "A thousand-rupee [sterilization] bonus would easily solve India's problem in a few years," he told the *New York Times* in 1969.[27]

Thus, near the end of his life Guttmacher was echoing the advice of his one-time poker partner H. L. Mencken: that sterilization bonuses were necessary to curtail the fertility of the poor. To Guttmacher and a growing number of family planning advocates, the world was in the grip of a massive population crisis, and neither the Pill nor the IUD would make enough of a difference in the short term. By his death, in 1974, Guttmacher's interest in sterilization had come full circle since his days as a medical intern in Baltimore. A half-century earlier he had been haunted by the specter of poverty-stricken women on his ward; on his deathbed, the specter that haunted him was the teeming masses of India.

John Rock and Jack Lippes

Guttmacher's sentiments about sterilization drew support from some surprising quarters. In 1968, John Rock and Jack Lippes became AVS board members. Lippes, a gynecologist born in Buffalo, New York, in 1925, was the inventor of the Lippes Loop, an S-shaped IUD that, after its introduction in 1964, quickly became the standard against which all other IUDs were compared. The Population Council funded Lippes's clinical trials of the Loop, viewing it as a "simple, inexpensive, and reliable permanent contraceptive" suited to poor, "unmotivated" women. In 1965, the Population Council launched its campaign to mass-distribute IUDs to developing countries, including India. It also helped India and other nations open their own IUD-making factories.

The Lippes Loop proved to be the most popular IUD in developing countries around the world, excluding communist China. By 1970, over 3 million U.S. women were using IUDs, including the Dalkon Shield. By 1974, 7.5 million women in developing countries had been fitted with IUDs (pp. 265–269).[10] In 1985, Ortho Pharmaceutical Corporation announced that it was ceasing to market the Loop.[28] However, as of the early twenty-first century it was still being manufactured and distributed in countries such as Indonesia.

John Rock (1890–1984) was a Harvard-trained gynecologist who headed the Brookline Reproductive Study Center, in Massachusetts. In the 1950s, Rock joined Gregory Pincus in the scientific testing of progesterone as a contraceptive, and their experiments led to the development of the Pill. A devout Catholic, Rock was the father of five and grandfather of fourteen. On many topics his views were conservative: he opposed the admission of women to the Harvard Medical School, arguing that they were incapable of being good doctors, and before the 1950s his attitudes about fertility tended to be pronatalist.[29] Yet by the time Rock resigned from Harvard, in 1956, his public opinions about family planning had shifted substantially. Just how much they had ultimately changed became evident in 1973, when he told a reporter, "I think it's shocking to see the big family glorified" (p. 353).[15] Rock had come to agree with sex educators and marriage counselors such as Robert Latou Dickinson and

Emily Mudd that the family was doomed unless husbands and wives expressed themselves sexually within marriage—yet full sexual expression within marriage without contraception resulted in too many children. According to Rock, this condemned couples to (what he called) "the sexual martyrdom of which few Americans, including all colors and creeds, are capable." The obvious solution was the medically advised use of birth control. It was the only way to fully satisfy a husband's "coital urge" (pp. 353–354).[15]

Although Margaret Sanger initially opposed the openly Catholic Rock's joining the birth control movement, she quickly changed her mind. "Being a good R.C. and as handsome as a god, he can just get away with anything," Sanger exclaimed (p. 352).[15] Yet it remained debatable whether Rock was indeed a "good R.C." Even before the introduction of the Pill, he had already crossed swords with the Church's hierarchy. Rock always believed that Church officials had no business interfering in the clinical practice of medicine. After being criticized by a priest for performing a hysterectomy, Rock denounced Catholic prelates "who think they know everything." By the end of his life, Rock, who earlier had attended Mass daily, no longer believed in "Heaven and Hell, Rome, all the Church stuff—that's for the solace of the multitude" (p. 217).[10]

Rock's enthusiasm for the Pill never flagged much, but as time went on he grew increasingly alarmed over the specter of population growth and convinced that worldwide sterilization was the best overall method of contraception. In 1969, he warned that a massive famine was "inevitable" within a decade, fretting that there might be "nothing we can do to stop it."[30] So worried was he about humanity's future that he sought funding from Hugh Moore to research the sterilizing effects of a fur-lined jockstrap for men, only to be reminded that in countries such as India, with hot climates, such a device would be highly impractical.[31] In 1967, Rock told a WNBC radio audience that, besides lowering the birth rate, voluntary sterilization would reduce the incidence of abortion.[32] On November 28, 1967, both Rock and Jack Lippes were guest speakers at the AVS-sponsored conference on the role of voluntary sterilization in averting world starvation, held at New York City's Carnegie Endowment International Center. In 1968, Rock and Lippes[33] issued a joint statement that read:

> We believe that in the struggle to control runaway population growth, voluntary sterilization has a vital role to play. There are, of course, other methods: the loop, the pill, etc. We are impressed, however, by the statement of Dr. Sripati Chandrasekhar, India's Minister of State for Family

Planning, who recently said: "Of all methods tried so far in India, only sterilization had yielded significant results."

To Rock, sterilization was likely "the best way to enable many parents to fulfill their duty" to their society and their families.[34] That he and Lippes, discoverers of different, much-ballyhooed birth control methods, believed sterilization achieved "significant results" in densely populated India proved that the prestige of surgical contraception was rising steeply as the 1960s drew to a close.

John Rague

The support from luminaries such as John Rock and Jack Lippes was an encouraging sign for the sterilization movement in the 1960s. However, rhetoric was one thing; concrete achievements were another. By the time John F. Kennedy was sworn in as president, in early 1961, voluntary sterilization was legal in all but three American states, and in those three (Connecticut, Utah, and Kansas) it was permitted for reasons of "medical necessity," a rationale flexible enough to justify operations for a wide range of conditions.[35] Yet many surgeons in the United States and around the world still declined to perform sterilizations. Numerous hospitals refused to approve sterilization operations. The American College of Obstetricians and Gynecologists (ACOG) continued to adhere to an age/parity formula that ruled out many women from obtaining a tubal ligation. The guidelines of the powerful Joint Commission on Accreditation of Hospitals stipulated that "consultation" was necessary before any U.S. hospital could grant a patient's request for sterilization. No private insurance plans would reimburse Americans for the cost of either tubal ligations or vasectomies. Neither the federal government nor any state governments would pay for sterilizations unless they were performed under existing (but increasingly discredited) eugenic statutes. Last, but not least, the U.S. government, despite mounting pressure from the population control movement, was opposed to funding family planning, much less sterilization, as a part of its foreign aid programs.

Yet, in a remarkable turnaround, all these barriers to sterilization had crashed to the ground by the time Gerald R. Ford succeeded Richard Nixon as president on August 9, 1974. In a few short years, the sterilization movement triumphed beyond the wildest dreams of its early leaders.

And if anyone deserved credit for this reversal of fortunes it was John R. Rague, Ruth Proskauer Smith's successor as AVS executive director.

Rague (1917–1981) (see insert), a World War II veteran born in New York City, was one of several Hugh Moore followers who joined the sterilization movement in the 1960s. Like Moore, Rague was a member of the World Federalists, USA, an organization Rague helped to found in 1947 in Montreux, Switzerland. World Federalists described themselves as committed to "a just world order through a strengthened United Nations." The World Federalist movement, still active in the early twenty-first century, seeks the establishment of a world government, including a world parliament, a standing peacekeeping force, and international criminal court. As Rague insisted in 1969, "[T]here can be no peace without world government."[36] The World Federalists typically attracted people convinced of the need for population control, such as Moore and his friend Tom Griessemer, a public relations consultant, AVS board member, and the first secretary-general of the World Federalists. Population controllers believed that their goals were more attainable if broad international organizations such as the United Nations could weaken the power of national governments whose politicians appeared more interested in self-serving and short-term aims than global, long-term needs. In countries such as India, belief systems often conflicted with the agendas of family planners, and World Federalists longed for the day when all the world would share the same values, especially regarding sexuality and reproduction.

Rague was appointed Human Betterment Association for Voluntary Sterilization (HBAVS) associate director on July 30, 1963, and served as AVS executive director from 1964 to 1972, when he was pressured to resign over allegations of conflict of interest relating to his involvement in the fledgling sperm bank industry. Nonetheless, the Rague years were the most dynamic in the group's young history. As Rague observed in 1972, when he joined AVS it enjoyed "tiny" newspaper coverage "and only an occasional bit in an off-beat magazine," such as *True Story*. Yet in 1971 alone, 4,500 articles on sterilization appeared in major newspapers in all fifty states and in reputable magazines such as *Newsweek*, *Time*, *Life*, *Good Housekeeping*, and *Reader's Digest*. AVS speakers appeared in forty-nine states, on four hundred and fifty television and radio programs (including the *Walter Cronkite Show*) on all three major networks. The topic of sterilization cropped up in mainstream 1970s television shows, including *Maude* and *Bridget Loves Bernie*. The producers of the popular program *All in the Family* intended to screen a show in which Archie Bunker's married daughter became pregnant when his son-in-law's vasectomy failed, only to scrap its plans after AVS protests. These and other trends indicated that American public opinion about sterilization had shifted seismically in only a few short years, from widespread disapproval to broad acceptance as a topic of conversation. Nothing less than a "historic sterilization revolution" had occurred, Rague enthused.[37]

A self-described anti-McCarthyite "liberal" and charter member of the National Organization for Women, Rague welcomed the countercultural, more permissive atmosphere of the 1960s. He boasted that he took his fourteen-year-old son to a Playboy club for lunch and hailed the recent emphasis on "rights" in American society. "Women are taking a much stronger role" in society and politics, all of which signaled, he noted approvingly, "the ferment of a complex pluralistic society."[38]

Rague agreed with Hugh Moore that sterilization offered the best hope for "controlling the population explosion."[39] Yet he also believed that sterilization advocacy was consistent with defending the "right of a person to the use of his [sic] own body." As he assured the National Association for the Advancement of Colored People (NAACP) in 1968, AVS opposed compulsory sterilization. Rague stressed that "the right of free choice should not be interdicted by government fiat in a democratic society."[40] That same year, AVS and the ACLU exchanged mailing lists in an effort to gain new members and contributors (AVS added one hundred and fifteen). To Rague, improving access to sterilization was a bona fide progressive reform, freeing individuals from government restrictions and widening civil liberties.

Yet in practice it was difficult to balance this line of reasoning with the task of stimulating interest in sterilization. As one AVS member remarked in 1963, popularizing sterilization could "take place only against the background of interest in population control."[41] This was Rague's strategy when, in 1970, he testified at Gaylord Nelson's U.S. Senate hearings. Forecasting an "ant-hill society" of overcrowding and vast environmental pollution if stringent antipopulation measures were not taken right away, Rague contended that sterilization was a superior method of contraception to the Pill or IUD. When it came to sterilization, "need," "medical know-how," and "public acceptance" were all realities, he told the Senate Committee; "the intellectual and financial commitment from the government is all that is lacking."[42]

These and Rague's other alarmist statements about overpopulation, however, served only to foster impatience with voluntary birth control programs. As Rague himself admitted, concerns over population were bound to "cause all of us to reevaluate some of our traditional positions in regard to freedom in the individual."[43] If he and the AVS were fully aware of the philosophic differences between compulsion and choice in sterilization, they failed to say so. But the grim reality is that such vagueness over the distinction between voluntarism and involuntarism would come back to haunt the sterilization movement in the coming years.

Policy Revolution

In the meantime, any confusion over the exact distinction between coercion and choice was overshadowed by the impressive string of victories enjoyed by the sterilization movement throughout the 1960s. The movement's initial success was the 1961 statement by the American Medical Association (AMA) that sterilization posed no greater danger of civil liability than any other medical and surgical procedure. The AMA stated that until voluntary sterilization was declared illegal by legislation or the courts, it was "largely a matter of individual conscience and principle."[44]

Yet the first big breakthrough occurred in 1964, when Congress established the Office of Economic Opportunity (OEO). The OEO, headed by Sargent Shriver, John F. Kennedy's brother-in-law, enjoyed the full backing of President Lyndon Baines Johnson, who saw it as a major weapon in his war on poverty. Besides the programs administered by the OEO, various programs in the Department of Health, Education and Welfare (HEW) designed to strike at the root causes of poverty were expanded. Although initially the Johnson administration did not name family planning as a key component of the Great Society reforms, in a few short years federal domestic and international agencies began funding family-planning initiatives. In 1965, the U.S. Agency for International Development (USAID) added family planning to its overseas aid program, and HEW followed suit. In 1966, the OEO issued guidelines for family planning programs serving married women with children. Americans under federal jurisdiction, including the families of armed forces personnel and Native Americans, became eligible for the same coverage. To AVS applause, Secretary of Defense Robert McNamara extended such coverage to include sterilizations for armed forces personnel.[45]

In 1967, Congress enacted specific legislation mandating federal family planning. The Foreign Assistance Act earmarked $35 million for

voluntary birth control programs overseas, including voluntary sterilization. As one historian[46] has written:

> The decision to link U.S. foreign-policy objectives with the subsidy of family
> planning and population control was truly exceptional in that it explicitly
> aimed at altering the demographic structure of foreign countries through long-
> term intervention. No nation had ever set in motion a foreign-policy initia-
> tive of such magnitude. Its ultimate goal was no less than to alter the
> basic fertility behavior of the entire Third World! Whether one views this
> goal as idealistic and naive or as arrogant and self-serving, the project
> was truly of herculean proportions.

Additionally, in amending the Social Security Act of 1935, pro-family-
planning Congressmen (such as future president George H. Bush) were
able to insert a section on federal funding for birth control within an
omnibus bill. One impact of the amendments was that federal funds could
be awarded to private organizations such as PPFA. Thanks to lively debate over other aspects of the legislation, "a policy revolution" in federal
family planning went largely unnoticed by birth control critics and the
public alike (p. 80).[47]

As much as anyone, Lyndon Johnson was responsible for this momentous shift in federal family planning policy. Yet such figures as John
D. Rockefeller 3rd and Hugh Moore also played pivotal roles by using
their considerable clout and access to the media to spread the message
throughout Washington, D.C., that population growth had led world
history to a fateful crossroads and urgent steps in fertility reduction were
necessary (pp. 52–53).[47] Evidence of their influence over federal policymaking surfaced in Johnson's 1967 State of the Union address, in which
he declared that "next to the pursuit of peace, the really great challenge of
the human family is the race between food supply and population. . . .
The time for concerted action is here, and we must get on with the job"
(p. 78).[47] When Johnson met personally with Indian Minister of Health
and Family Planning Sripati Chandrasekhar at the White House in January, 1968, the president learned that the concerns of Moore and Rockefeller were shared by some key politicians from densely populated
developing countries.

Yet for Hugh Moore and AVS, this revolution in family planning
policy between 1965 and 1967 did not go far enough. To federal officials,
approving public funding for overseas sterilizations was less controversial
than taxpayer support for domestic sterilizations. In 1965, OEO Director
Shriver issued regulations governing family planning grants through

Community Action Programs to private agencies. Included in this set of restrictions on the forms of family planning advice and assistance such agencies could provide was a ban on funds for either abortions or sterilizations. The ban on funding for sterilizations immediately drew sharp AVS protests. Rague reminded Lyndon Johnson that 64% of Americans polled in September, 1966, had said they approved of voluntary sterilization as a method of birth control. Shriver's proscription of sterilization was "unconstitutional," Rague argued, and he was joined in his protest by the ACLU and the American College of Surgeons. Citing the AMA's 1961 statement that sterilization posed no special legal problems, Rague and the ACLU insisted that Shriver's ban violated the "right of privacy" recently upheld by the U.S. Supreme Court in the 1965 *Griswold v. Connecticut* decision that contraception was legal. To the AVS, Shriver was "foot-dragging" and "discriminating against the poor" by refusing to pay for sterilizations.[48]

Unfortunately for the sterilization movement, vocal groups in U.S. society did not agree that banning federal funding for sterilization amounted to "discriminating against the poor." Shriver enjoyed the support of the Roman Catholic Church, whose American prelates tended to uphold Church teaching that sterilization for contraceptive purposes was "mutilation" and contravened natural law. The Johnson administration, fearing an electoral backlash from U.S. Catholics, tread very carefully when it came to family planning. Pro-family-planning politicians were willing to inch forward with incremental reforms, such as program funds for contraceptives for married women living in two-parent households. Such small-scale reforms generally met the silent approval of liberal Catholic bishops in the National Catholic Welfare Conference and liberal Catholic academics at Georgetown University and the University of Notre Dame. Presidential aide Bill Moyers expressed the hope that Catholic resistance was fading when he remarked that "there is every evidence that even the Pope realizes the times are changing."[49]

Moyers was soon proved wrong about the Pope. Taxpayer support for sterilization eventually began in 1971, but to many Catholic and non-Catholic Americans, such a step was unacceptable. Pope Paul VI's 1968 encyclical *Humanae Vitae*, prohibiting Catholics from using any artificial contraceptives, was criticized by many U.S. Catholics, 68% of whom were resorting to contraceptives in 1970. By the late 1970s, they were using artificial contraceptives with the same frequency as the general population.[50] Nonetheless, *Humanae Vitae* articulated official Church teaching on birth control and specifically condemned "direct sterilization, whether perpetual or temporary, whether of the man or the woman."[51] In the wake of the Pope's firm stand on contraception, AVS searched in vain for prominent Catholics such as John Rock to openly support its agenda.[52]

Numerous African American individuals and groups also attacked sterilization in the 1960s. In the wake of the 1964 Civil Rights Act, countless Americans hoped that race relations were about to enter a new era of harmony. However, the race riots during the summers of 1965 and 1966 dashed many of these hopes. As the decade wound to a close, tensions between the black and white communities escalated and fed suspicions among African Americans about white intentions. Black opposition to family-planning programs had emerged as early as 1962, when Malcolm X, one of the leaders of the Nation of Islam, had alleged that family planning proponents targeted the "colored nations" of the world. As some black militants contended, "birth control is just a plot just as segregation was a plot to keep blacks down."[53] In 1964, African American attacks on birth control prompted a White House official to note that birth control had become "more of a Negro issue than a Catholic one" (p. 70).[47]

African American opposition to overall birth control policy had softened by the early 1970s, when the Congress for Racial Equality and NAACP endorsed family planning. Sterilization advocates celebrated when John L. S. Holloman Jr., former president of the National Medical Association, the largest organization representing African American physicians in the United States, joined the AVS board in 1968. Yet, to the chagrin of John Rague and others in the movement, Holloman remained an exception. In 1968, Roy Wagstaff of the NAACP denounced state-funded sterilization as "Hitlerism."[54] Even fiercer protests erupted in the 1970s, when disturbing news broke about the government-financed sterilizations of African American females on welfare.[55] By the end of the 1970s, the federal government had introduced new guidelines that placed strict limitations on who could be sterilized and when. To the sterilization movement, by contrast, tightening safeguards on access to sterilization services simply punished the deserving poor and other minorities.

No-Baby Sex

Reeling from Catholic and African American opposition, the sterilization movement mobilized in the late 1960s to make sterilization an acceptable option for all Americans. As H. Curtis Wood remarked in 1969, "[T]he one big thing I would like to see AVS accomplish is to put pressure in the right places so *all* women, black and white, rich or poor, are offered *all* methods of fertility control at our hospitals, and public health and welfare institutions."[56] As ever, Wood believed the key to success was overcoming "the ultra conservatism" and "moralistic attitude" of physicians, but others in the movement focused instead on stimulating popular demand for the operation.[57] Convincing men that vasectomies would not result in a "loss of potency" but, at long last, would separate sex from reproduction was one way to increase demand.[58] Such reasoning accorded with cultural currents in existence since the late 1940s, in particular an unprecedented willingness to discuss sex openly. The publicity surrounding the research of Alfred Kinsey and sexologists William Masters and Virginia Johnson, as well as the founding of *Playboy* magazine (1953) and of Mary Calderone's Sex Information and Education Council for the U.S. (SIECUS), in 1966, encouraged public frankness about the sex lives of Americans and strengthened the growing belief that sex was more for pleasure than procreation. Nudity in movies and on stage in productions such as *Hair* (1967) and *Oh! Calcutta!* (1969) became increasingly acceptable. Attitudes toward homosexuality also appeared to be changing in the wake of the 1969 Stonewall Inn gay riots against police in New York City. These and other events steadily eroded the taboos against sex for its own sake, mirroring trends in actual sexual behavior. For example, out-of-wedlock births almost quadrupled between 1940 and 1970, while the incidence of abortion rose in the 1950s.[59] Wood tried to capitalize on these trends when he argued that sterilization was a handy way of having "sex without babies," as he put it. John Rague agreed: "Now that sex and birth control are discussed more openly," he observed approvingly in 1970, "many of the old myths and fears about sterilization have begun to break down."[60]

To Rague and others in the sterilization movement, "women's liberation" also appeared destined to drum up support for sterilization. As women activists demanded full reproductive rights, the movement in favor of liberalizing the nation's abortion laws accelerated swiftly in the late 1960s. Many of the individuals involved in the struggle to decriminalize abortion were also involved in the campaign to win acceptance of sterilization, including Alan Guttmacher, Ruth Proskauer Smith, and journalist Lawrence Lader. Lader (1919–) (see insert), an AVS and ZPG board member and the first chairman of the executive committee of the National Association for Repeal of Abortion Laws (NARAL), was described by Betty Friedan as the "father of abortion rights." He was also the first biographer of Margaret Sanger and the author of *Breeding Ourselves to Death*

(1971).[61] A longtime friend of Hugh Moore, Lader was deeply involved in most of the cutting-edge social reform causes of the late 1960s. He viewed the "surge" in demand for sterilization in the 1960s as "a revolution in public and medical opinion," "one of the most fascinating phenomena of our time." He believed that the rise of the "neo-feminist" movement had been critical in erasing the stigma surrounding sterilization, especially vasectomy, but he also credited the "public information campaign" that AVS had been waging for years.[62]

Caroline Rulon "Lonny" Myers was another example of an activist whose sterilization advocacy combined issues of population, environmentalism, sexual freedom, women's liberation, and reproductive rights. Born in 1922 in Hartford, Connecticut, and a mother of five, Myers became renowned as the foremost U.S. woman physician specializing in vasectomy. She was a member of ZPG, served on NARAL's board, and in 1971 founded, with Episcopalian clergyman Don C. Shaw, Chicago's Midwest Population Center (MPC), which provided contraceptive, abortion referral, and voluntary sterilization services. The Playboy Foundation gave the MPC $6,000 as a start-up grant, and AVS chipped in with a $5,000 loan (paid up by December, 1973). While working earlier in the birth control movement, Myers came to the conclusion that once the "fear of pregnancy" was removed, people could express themselves sexually. As she commented, "[W]e continue to force unwilling women to bear unwanted children because of our punitive attitude toward genital sex. We have so many 'wanted' babies because we teach and reward female sex role stereotypes . . . ." In 1969, she heard Paul Ehrlich speak, and "the urgency hit me": she realized her interests in sex education, birth control, and women's emancipation dovetailed with population concerns. Lauding sterilization as "a safe, permanent method of birth control," Myers devoted the rest of her medical career to vasectomy, performing her first such operation on July 1, 1970. Later that same year, the MPC hosted the First National Conference on Vasectomy, featuring seminars and workshops on "human sexuality with special reference to current sex mores as they relate to the population crisis." Overall, to justify sterilization, the MPC encouraged Americans to affirm "no-baby sex" and explore "the recreational dimension of sexuality."[63]

Other women activists hailed the benefits of sterilization, including Sandra Moseley, founder of the militant feminist group Foresight, which led picketers in front of hospitals and doctors' offices where sterilizations were prohibited.[64] Anselma Dell 'Olio, charter member of NOW and founder and director of the New Feminist Theater, argued in "The

Feminist Case for Vasectomy" that it was a foolproof method for ending patriarchal dominance over women and liberating them from motherhood and the "nuclear family."[65] Men undergoing sterilization allegedly freed women for the first time in history from worries about pregnancy.

Yet indications were that a rising generation of young women was not as enthusiastic about the liberating potential of sterilization as were older women whose backgrounds in the family-planning movement stretched back to the World War II era. Sterilization advocates knew that when they stressed the privacy rights of women who sought tubal ligations, they could count on support from female birth control activists. Yet younger female activists tended to fear the potential for coercion and abuse when sterilization proponents urged that the federal government fund operations for poor and minority women. Surveys in the 1970s would bear out this concern, but in the meantime individuals such as John Rague struggled to convince women's groups that AVS's cause was theirs, too.

Coercion in a Good Cause

If John Rague and AVS found few allies in the women's movement, relations with the increasingly popular environmentalist movement appeared more promising. Conservation of the nation's water, soil, wildlife, vegetation, and minerals had been a consistent concern since the Progressive Era of the early twentieth century. In the wake of World War II, however, worries about the pressure of population on natural resources began to escalate and gripped a significant segment of the environmentalist movement. William Vogt's *Road to Survival* (1948) and Fairfield Osborn's *Our Plundered Planet* (1948) forecasted a grim future for the human race if efforts were not taken to reduce global fertility rates. In her bestselling *Silent Spring* (1962), Rachel Carson blamed the chemical industry for cancer-causing environmental poisoning, but her overall warning that human beings were a threat to the sensitive ecological balance of nature did not differ substantially from either Vogt's or Osborn's (or, for that matter, Hugh Moore's).

Both the Kennedy and Johnson administrations were sympathetic to environmental issues, but environmentalist sentiment spiked abruptly in the late 1960s amid growing media attention to events such as the Santa Barbara oil spill and the Cuyahoga River near Cleveland bursting into flames, both in 1969. Fears about population growth were fanned by such books as *Make Room! Make Room!* (1967) and *Logan's Run* (1967), which described grim, futuristic scenarios of severe overcrowding and increasingly scarce resources. The same theme appeared in Paul Ehrlich's *The Population Bomb*, published in 1968 by the Sierra Club through Ballantine Books. Within two years the book went through thirteen editions. Ehrlich, whose research Hugh Moore helped to fund, borrowed the book title from Moore's pamphlet published a decade and a half earlier. Ehrlich argued that the world faced mass starvation in the next ten years if governments did not commit themselves to zero population growth. Rejecting what he called "sugarcoated solutions," Ehrlich proposed legislation in the form of taxes on families with more than two children, as well as financial incentives for individuals to undergo sterilization. If that struck readers as "coercion," he wrote, it was "coercion in a good cause."[66] Ehrlich practiced what he preached: in 1963 he underwent a vasectomy after the birth of his only child.

Ehrlich's jeremiad and the forebodings of other population-control advocates rapidly reached the highest corridors of power. In 1969, newly elected president Richard M. Nixon declared that the world was "already experiencing a population explosion. . . . We are, in short, in a rush toward a Malthusian nightmare." The time for escaping this nightmare, Nixon warned, was "growing very short."[67]

Nixon's comments and the publication of *The Population Bomb* set the stage for Hugh Moore's 1969 AVS-sponsored conference on conservation and voluntary sterilization. Attendees included Donald J. Zinn of the National Wildlife Federation; Roland C. Clement, vice-president of the National Audubon Society; and Richard H. Goodwin, president of the Conservation and Research Foundation. Ehrlich told the conference that "the first thing that anyone who wishes to consider himself a conservationist should do is stop having children."[68] E. H. Villard, of the Wilderness Society, dubbed the conference a "landmark 'first' " because it was a "blend of conservation and population." As he told John Rague, "[I]t could be a real turning-point. You certainly have our commitment in the Wilderness Society."[69] On April 22, 1970, the first Earth Day was held, with 20 million Americans taking part, including Rague, who manned an AVS booth on New York City's 14th Street, handing out buttons that read "Stop At Two," a reference to populationists' ideal family size. Entertainer and avid conservationist Arthur Godfrey observed that among scientists, "I find, only rarely, any disagreement with the statement that human population is the cause of most, if not all, of our ills."[70]

Rague, himself a member of the Sierra Club, stated in 1968 that "population control and conservation should be working in a new alliance for progress." In 1969, Hugh Moore referred to the "mounting interest on the part of students in the problems of the environment, conservation, and population growth. It seems that many students are getting tired of their Vietnam campaign and are swinging to this new cause—our cause. . . . I am inclined to think that this could turn out to be the most important development in our movement to date."[71] As an AVS member wrote to Hugh Moore in 1970, the sterilization movement was "riding the crest of a big concern about population, with voluntary sterilization getting more popular all the time, helped by the pill scare, Paul Ehrlich, ecology, ZPG, etc."[72]

Concrete ties between AVS and ZPG strengthened the link between sterilization and environmentalism. "Zero population growth" was a phrase first used by demographer Kingsley Davis in 1967 to highlight what goals family planners ostensibly needed to meet in order to address the "strong anxiety over runaway population growth."[73] Renamed Population Connection in 2002, ZPG was founded in 1968 in the wake of the stunning success of Ehrlich's *The Population Bomb*. Shortly after the book appeared, Ehrlich, one of ZPG's founders, made the first of several appearances on Johnny Carson's *Tonight Show*, during which he gave out ZPG's address and telephone number. Subsequently, the group was deluged with phone calls and letters. ZPG endorsed the principle that parenthood was not an inherent right but a privilege conferred by society, whose interests in the 1960s dictated that population growth should be halted. Legendary folk musician Pete Seeger, an early ZPG member, composed the song "We'll All Be A-Doubling" to underscore the organization's message that American couples should "stop at two." Through an advertising blitz featuring posters, magazine advertisements, public service announcements, and bumper stickers that read "Stop Heir Pollution" and "Control Your Local Stork," ZPG caught the public's imagination. By 1972, its membership had leapt to 35,000. A true grassroots organization, ZPG had two hundred and sixty-eight local chapters, where most of its activism took place. Yet in its early years it was anything but diverse: the typical member was white, male, young, and well educated.[74]

Ehrlich, a member of the AVS board of directors, was ZPG's first president, and John Rague served as an advisor to Richard Bowers, a Connecticut lawyer and one of the group's founders. From the outset, AVS and ZPG maintained close relations. ZPG's first meetings were held in AVS office space in Manhattan. Initially, Rague declined to serve on ZPG's board of directors, claiming conflict of interest. Yet by 1972 he was actively involved in both groups. By then, ZPG was no longer interested in simply reducing family size to two children. Rague, Lader, and many in ZPG's national headquarters shared the belief that sterilization was an effective method for achieving "child-free living" for "more than a majority of young people in America (and other parts of Western Civilization)." They fervently hoped that "by 1990, if we try hard, people everywhere on earth by well over a majority will be child-free."[75]

The Stone Wall Breaks

As the 1970s opened, a "child-free" future for most people seemed fanciful. Nonetheless, the swift rise in acceptance of sterilization in the United States in the late 1960s translated into results that advocates could only have dreamt about a decade earlier. In 1968, the *Journal of the American Medical Association* called vasectomy "safe, quick, and legal."[76] The same year, Planned Parenthood–World Population officially included sterilization as part of its overall birth control program.

1970 was a banner year for sterilization. When a reader called for sterilization as the best method for limiting family size, advice columnist Ann Landers replied, "Yes, I'm with you."[77] Most U.S. adults (53% of those polled) expressed approval of vasectomy, including half of all Roman Catholics surveyed.[78] The Ford Foundation announced a grant of $831,000 to support an international training program in simple sterilization techniques at the University of Miami. The American College of Obstetricians and Gynecologists abandoned its age/parity policy and approved female sterilization at the request of a patient, saying consultation was unnecessary. Also in 1970, HEW approved Medicaid payments for sterilization in most states, and in 1971 (at long last, in the eyes of AVS) OEO began funding sterilization operations. The same year, the Joint Commission on Accreditation of Hospitals dropped its requirement of mandatory consultation before performing sterilizations, leaving it up to the medical staff of the various hospitals to decide.[79] By the early 1970s, sterilization proponents knew that some U.S. hospitals continued to force women to submit requests for surgical contraception to special abortion and sterilization committees, but the days of refusing tubal ligation based on the number of children a woman had were steadily coming to an end.[80] In 1971, as he reflected on his long medical career stretching back to the 1920s, Alan Guttmacher remarked that he had "seen the *stone wall* break and fragment in respect to female sterilization."[81]

If barriers to female sterilization tumbled in the 1970s, "Operation Lawsuit" deserved much of the credit. A joint venture mounted by the ACLU, ZPG, and AVS, Operation Lawsuit (1971–1973) was an effort to seek out possible litigants for lawsuits against hospitals that refused to perform sterilization procedures. ACLU and AVS ties harked back to the early 1960s, when both groups had realized they had mutual goals in fighting to liberalize hospital regulations regarding sterilization. On February 6, 1972, the ACLU stated that "the right to practice any birth control procedure by either women or men, including contraception, abortion, *and sterilization,* should be an individual's decision and no compulsion or coercion can be tolerated."[82] ACLU's involvement in Operation Lawsuit conveyed the impression that it, like the legal attempts to repeal state abortion laws, was chiefly dedicated to winning individual reproductive rights. However, the involvement of AVS and ZPG demonstrated that a major aim of Operation Lawsuit was to "stabilize America's population growth."[83]

Prior to 1971, AVS, along with the New York branch of the ACLU, had been trying to bring a test case to court to establish a woman's right to be sterilized and the right of her doctor to perform the operation. Finding women willing to sue posed few problems, as suits were filed in New York City; Salt Lake City; Eugene, Oregon; Tucson; and Highland Park, Michigan. Yet each time they found a case, the hospital in question would agree to do the procedure before a court could rule.[84] Two lawsuits in particular, however, led to decisive court decisions. The first involved Linda McCabe, a twenty-six-year-old mother of four, who in August, 1970, had her request for a sterilization operation turned down by Nassau County Medical Center in Long Island, New York. In December, 1971, the Second Circuit U.S. Court of Appeals in New York ruled that a hospital may be held liable for pain and suffering and violation of constitutional rights caused by its refusal to grant a request for sterilization. In a joint statement, AVS, ZPG, and the ACLU announced that this ruling "creates a huge, new signpost in the direction that hospitals must go if they are to avoid a flood of lawsuits totaling hundreds of millions of dollars within the next few years."[85]

The second noteworthy court case was *Robbie Mae Hathaway v. Worcester City Hospital,* in Massachusetts. Hathaway was a thirty-six-year-old mother of eight who had asked Worcester City Hospital to sterilize her in 1971, but its board had decreed a total ban on such operations. A decision in Hathaway's favor, handed down by the First Circuit U.S. Court of Appeals, led to a U.S. Supreme Court ruling on April 17, 1973, that a total ban on sterilizations violated the equal protection clause of the Fourteenth Amendment of the U.S. Constitution. This ruling, combined with the January 22, 1973, *Roe v. Wade* decision that a woman's constitutionally protected right to privacy included the right to an abortion, effectively ended America's legal battle over sterilization.[86]

Meanwhile, vasectomy clinics like the MPC sprang up across the country. The establishment in 1969 of a vasectomy clinic at PPFA's Margaret Sanger Research Bureau, founded in 1923 in Manhattan, was a milestone, the first such outpatient clinic in U.S. history. AVS donated $30,000 to the Bureau to help set up the vasectomy clinic. Medora Bass (who personally donated $5,000) played a key role in securing Bureau board approval. Psychiatrist and AVS member Helen Edey screened potential vasectomy patients. One year after the clinic's opening, the Bureau was getting fifty to two hundred phone calls and twenty-five to fifty applications a day. "We're booked through May," the Bureau's administrative manager reported in March, 1970.[87] The identification of Sanger's name with a vasectomy clinic may have surprised the public, but to Bass and others in the movement it merely confirmed the historical fact that she had been a longtime proponent of sterilization as a form of contraception.

The sterilization movement received another sizeable boost in 1972, when the *Report of the Commission on Population Growth and the American Future* was issued. The Commission had been established in 1969, at President Richard Nixon's urging and to the delight of population control advocates such as John D. Rockefeller 3rd. At the time, the entire population control movement appeared united, but as the work of the Commission unfolded, divisions that would bulk increasingly large in the 1970s quickly became evident. Commission member Paul Cornely, an African American professor from Howard University, openly complained that the Commission did not have enough "minority input." He and Commission member Grace Martinez, the first Hispanic woman to graduate from the University of Notre Dame law school, also protested the Commission's pro-abortion stance.

Yet another problem for the Commission was that by the time its report was published, the nation's fertility rate was falling and had reached its lowest level since 1820. The "baby boom" of the 1950s was fast becoming the "baby bust" of the 1970s. The perception that the globe faced a population crisis was beginning to falter.[88]

Seeking reelection, Nixon distanced himself from the report and its endorsement of legalized abortion, expanded sex education, and contraceptive services to minors. Rockefeller and his allies were bitter. Nonetheless, sterilization proponents rejoiced when, "[i]n order to permit free-dom of choice," the Commission urged that all "administrative restrictions on access to voluntary contraceptive sterilization be eliminated so that the decision be made solely by physician and patient." The Commission also recommended that "national hospital and medical associations, and their state chapters, promote the removal of existing restrictions." In fact, by 1972 these "restrictions on access" were steadily vanishing anyway, but the AVS board, vividly remembering how history was full of surprising twists and turns, hailed the Commission's conclusions.[89]

Thus, by the early 1970s, the movement's message that "child-free living" through sterilization was desirable was seeping gradually into the consciousness of many young Americans. Among the countless letters written to AVS seeking advice about sterilization were statements from college-age Americans who never wanted children. Young people in America were staying single longer and having children later or not at all.[90] The success of Operation Lawsuit reinforced the message that sterilization was a normal medical procedure, access to which no American ought to be denied. Operation Lawsuit also signaled that the efforts of AVS over the previous decades were about to be rewarded. Indeed, in May, 1972, AVS, for the first time, received a grant from USAID to conduct an international conference on voluntary sterilization and help developing countries establish sterilization services throughout the world. Thanks to this landmark event and other similar developments, the group looked to be entering a new era of respectability. Its victories on legal and political fronts enabled it to switch its focus from activism and public education to medical research and overseas programs. In Lawrence Lader's words, a seemingly irreversible "revolution in public and medical opinion" had occurred. A new, promising future beckoned for the sterilization movement, a scarcely imaginable prospect only ten years earlier. While no one in the movement thought the struggle was over for good, advocates could be excused for thinking that the sterilization "revolution" was poised to sweep the world. Yet, like all revolutions, this "historic" change refused to unfold according to script.

Notes

1. Memo re: Hugh Moore's remarks at the AVS Conference on "Conservation and Voluntary Sterilization: A New Alliance for Progress," HM, Series 3, Box 15, folder 4.

2. For the lingering perception that sterilization was a "dirty word" as late as 1967 because it "smacks of what happened in Germany under Hitler," see "Sterilization Dirty Word." *The Tulsa Tribune*, February 3, 1967.
3. H. Curtis Wood, "Report of the Medical Consultant," AVS Annual meeting, March 28, 1973, AVS, Box 110, 1973 Minutes folder.
4. In 1953, the Moores donated $100, upping it to $200 in 1956 and $500 in 1958. HM, Series 3, Box 15, folder 6.
5. See AVS, "Largest Contributors," 1964, 1965, 1966, 1967, AHC, MSB Box 20.
6. As one board member wrote her:

> It was a great shock and big surprise to me that some compromise or adjustment was not acceptable to you. I hope when your emotional upset calms down that your hurt feelings will be healed and that you will be willing to renew some of your contacts with us. . . . But we must accept your terms, no matter how we may disagree with them and go on from here as best we can. I am sure you care for the organization too much ever to do or say anything that could hurt our program. We must be loyal to those left in charge and believe strongly enough in the value of voluntary sterilization to continue to do our best for the cause.

Louise Mills to Ruth Smith, October 30, 1964, RPS, Box 1, folder 5.
7. Minutes of October 29 and November 19, 1964, meetings of the AVS board of directors, AVS, Box 22, 1964 Minutes folder.
8. Ruth Smith soon joined the Association for the Study of Abortion, an abortion rights group, where in no time her refusal to compromise led to similar tensions with colleagues.
9. In 1965, Hugh Moore had asked Guttmacher if he minded that Moore appointed another chairman of the Medical and Scientific Committee, "less occupied, who might be in a position to give us the time which I think we need." Hugh Moore to Alan Guttmacher, July 15, 1965, HM, Series 2, Box 1, folder 21. See also Mrs. Dudley Mills to Alan Guttmacher, May 10, 1966, AVS, Box 34, Guttmacher folder.
10. Tone A. *Devices and Desires: A History of Contraceptives in America.* New York: Hill and Wang, 2001. See also Gladwell M. John Rock's Error. *The New Yorker*, March 13, 2000, p. 63.
11. Marks LV. *Sexual Chemistry: A History of the Contraceptive Pill.* New Haven and London: Yale University Press, 2001.
12. Seaman B. *The Doctors' Case Against the Pill: 25th Anniversary Edition.* Alameda: Hunter House, 1995, p. 45. Quoted by A. Tone in *Devices and Desires: A History of Contraceptives in America.* New York: Hill and Wang, 2001, p. 235.
13. For a discussion of the possible health complications of inserting foreign objects into the uterus, see Schoen J. *Choice and Coercion: Birth Control, Sterilization and Abortion in Public Health and Welfare.* Chapel Hill: University of North Carolina Press, 2005, p. 286, n. 10.

14. Hartmann B. *Reproductive Rights and Wrongs: The Global Politics of Population Control*, 2nd ed. Boston: South End Press, 1995, p. 213. Quoted in Franks A. *Margaret Sanger's Eugenic Legacy: The Control of Female Fertility.* Jefferson, NC: McFarland and Co., 2005, p. 225.

15. Reed J. *From Private Vice to Public Virtue: The Birth Control Movement and American Society since 1830.* New York: Basic, 1978.

16. Quoted in Franks A. *Margaret Sanger's Eugenic Legacy: The Control of Female Fertility.* Jefferson, NC: McFarland and Co., 2005, p. 225.

17. Alan Guttmacher to John Searle, December 29, 1964, "Searle and Co. Correspondence from 1964," Planned Parenthood Federation of America Papers, Sophia Smith Collection. Quoted in Tone A. *Devices and Desires: A History of Contraceptives in America.* New York: Hill and Wang, 2001, p. 271.

18. Guttmacher A. *Babies By Choice or By Chance.* Garden City: Doubleday, 1959, pp. 161–162. Quoted in Franks A. *Margaret Sanger's Eugenic Legacy: The Control of Female Fertility.* Jefferson, NC: McFarland and Co., 2005, p. 58.

19. David Landman, Memo re: Dalkon Shield, to the board of directors of the Pathfinder Fund, June 19, 1974, EM, Carton 11, folder 487.

20. Tone A. *Devices and Desires: A History of Contraceptives in America.* New York: Hill and Wang, 2001, pp. 271–283; "Robins warns that its IUD may cause severe complications, including death." *Wall Street Journal,* May 29, 1974.

21. Critchlow DT. *Intended Consequences: Birth Control, Abortion and the Federal Government in Modern America.* New York and Oxford: Oxford University Press, 1999, p. 28. See also William Draper to William S. Gaud, November 30, 1966, AVS, Box 36, Rague folder.

22. " 'Revolution' may shake India." *Honolulu Star-Bulletin and Advertiser,* July 19, 1970.

23. "New leader of India birth fight." *San Francisco Chronicle,* March 21, 1967. See also Chandrasekhar S. How India is tackling her population problem. *Foreign Affairs,* October 1968, p. 142.

24. Rodrigues-Triaz H. The women's health movement: Women take power. In Sidel VW, Sidel R (eds.), *Reforming Medicine: Lessons of the Last Quarter Century.* New York: Pantheon, 1984, pp. 107–126.

25. McGreevy JT. *Catholicism and American Freedom: A History.* New York and London: W. W. Norton, 2003, p. 257. He repeated the same sentiment in 1963. Alan Guttmacher to Lloyd Morain, April 23, 1963, AVS, Box 34, Guttmacher folder.

26. Garrow DJ. *Liberty and Sexuality: The Right to Privacy and the Making of Roe v. Wade.* Berkeley and Los Angeles: University of California Press, 1998, pp. 361, 368.

27. Dempsey D. The fertility goddess vs. the Loop: Dr. Guttmacher is the evangelist of birth control. *New York Times Magazine,* February 9, 1969, p. 83. Cited in Franks A. *Margaret Sanger's Eugenic Legacy: The Control of Female Fertility.* Jefferson, NC: McFarland and Co., 2005, p. 59.

28. The reasons cited were declining profit margins due to the controversy surrounding the Dalkon Shield and the fact that the FDA required companies manufacturing and marketing IUDs to submit a pre-marketing approval application that addressed issues of patient safety. "Ortho stops marketing Lippes Loop: cites economic factors." *Contraceptive Technology Update*. 1985; 11:149–152.

29. As he wrote in 1943, "I hold no brief for those young or even older husbands and wives who for no good reason refuse to bear as many children as they can properly rear and as society can profitably engross." Rock J. The scientific case against rigid legal restrictions on medical birth-control advice. *Clinics*, April 1943, pp. 1598–1602.

30. Dempsey D. The fertility goddess vs. the Loop: Dr. Guttmacher is the evangelist of birth control. *New York Times Magazine*, February 9, 1969, p. 82.

31. John Rock to Hugh Moore, February 9, 1967; Hugh Moore to John Rock, February 15, 1967; John Lattimer to Hugh Moore, February 23, 1967; HM, Series 3, Box 15, folder 7.

32. "Eminent Catholic doctor, John Rock, assails stand of Catholic hierarchy against voluntary sterilization: 'One good solution of abortion problem is voluntary sterilization,' declares Rock." AVS Press Release, June 12, 1967; "Catholic doc would allow sterilization." *New York Daily News*, June 12, 1967.

33. SC, Box 5, folder 14.

34. Quoted by John Rague in Rague to R. T. Ravenholt, February 20, 1968, SC, Box 5, folder 14.

35. Pilpel HF, Zavin T. *Your Marriage and the Law*. New York: Collier, 1964, p. 207.

36. John Rague to Stewart Mott, March 7, 1969, AVS, Box 38, Rague folder.

37. John Rague, "Final Progress Report," October 13, 1972, Association for Voluntary Sterilization.

38. John Rague to R. E. Azoulay, May 5, 1972, AVS, Box 38, Rague correspondence.

39. John Rague to Frances Jane Partridge, October 21, 1968, AVS, Box 38, Rague correspondence.

40. John Rague to Roy L. Wagstaff, October 22, 1968, AVS, Box 38, Rague correspondence.

41. Homer Calver to Mabel Ingalls, October 23, 1963, AVS, Box 87, Homer Calver folder.

42. Testimony of John R. Rague, Executive Director, Association for Voluntary Sterilization, Inc., prepared for the Monopoly Subcommittee, United States Senate Committee on Small Business, on the Subject of Voluntary Contraceptive Sterilization as a Major Method of Birth Control, March 3, 1970.

43. John Rague to H. Curtis Wood, September 27, 1968, AVS, Box 38, Rague correspondence.

44. Pilpel HF. Know your rights about voluntary sterilization. In Lader L (ed.), *Foolproof Birth Control: Male and Female Sterilization*. Boston: Beacon Press, 1972, p. 227.

45. John Rague to Lyndon Baines Johnson, November 11, 1966, AVS, Box 36, Rague correspondence. See also Critchlow DT. *Intended Consequences: Birth Control, Abortion and the Federal Government in Modern America*. New York and Oxford: Oxford University Press, 1999, pp. 51–53.

46. Sharpless J. World population growth, family planning, and American foreign policy. In Critchlow DT (ed.), *The Politics of Abortion and Birth Control in Historical Perspective*. University Park: Pennsylvania State University Press, 1996, p. 72.

47. Critchlow DT. *Intended Consequences: Birth Control, Abortion and the Federal Government in Modern America*. New York and Oxford: Oxford University Press, 1999.

48. Critchlow DT. *Intended Consequences: Birth Control, Abortion and the Federal Government in Modern America*. New York and Oxford: Oxford University Press, 1999, p. 75. John Rague to Lyndon Johnson, November 11, 1966, AVS, Box 36, Rague folder; "Proposed statement by ACLU regarding OEO ban on voluntary sterilization," June 29, 1965, AVS, Box 87, Calver folder; Rague to Harriet Pilpel, June 30, 1965, AVS, Box 87, Calver folder; Rague to William H. Burson, September 30, 1968, AVS, Box 38, Rague Correspondence. See also John de J. Pemberton to Sargent Shriver, March 24, 1966; John de J. Pemberton to Sargent Shriver, July 27, 1966; AVS, Box 47, ACLU folder. "Assail poverty unit on birth control ban." *New York News*, August 1, 1966.

49. Douglass Cater to the President, March 30, 1965, Cater File, Box 66, Lyndon Baines Johnson Library. Cited by Critchlow DT. *Intended Consequences: Birth Control, Abortion and the Federal Government in Modern America*. New York and Oxford: Oxford University Press, 1999, p. 74.

50. Allitt P. *Catholic Intellectuals and Conservative Politics in America, 1950–1985*. Ithaca and London: Cornell University Press, 1993, pp. 173–178; Allitt P. *Religion in America Since 1945*. New York: Columbia University Press, 2003, pp. 107–110. See also Critchlow DT. *Intended Consequences: Birth Control, Abortion and the Federal Government in Modern America*. New York and Oxford: Oxford University Press, 1999, pp. 128–132.

51. See the text of *Humanae Vitae* in *Catholic Mind*. 1968;66:35–48.

52. Westoff CF, Jones EF. The secularization of U.S. Catholic birth control practices. *Family Planning Perspectives*. 1977;9:203–207.

53. "Negro doctors fear birth control genocide." *Los Angeles Times*, September 30, 1968. See also Critchlow DT. *Intended Consequences: Birth Control, Abortion and the Federal Government in Modern America*. New York and Oxford: Oxford University Press, 1999, p. 61.

54. "Sterilization 'Hitlerism,' NAACP leader says." Wilmington *Evening Journal*, October 1, 1968.

55. Kennard G. Sterilization abuse. *Essence*, October 1974, pp. 66–67, 85–86; "How society forces sterilization on the poor." *Boston Globe*, April 26, 1974.

56. H. Curtis Wood to Louise Mills, August 16, 1969, HM, Series 3, Box 15, folder 8. His emphasis.

57. Wood HC. What's holding back voluntary sterilization? *Medical Economics*, October 27, 1969, p. 171.

58. John Rague to Frances Jane Partridge, October 21, 1968, AVS, Box 38, Rague correspondence.

59. Rorabaugh WJ, Critchlow DT, Baker P. *America's Promise: A Concise History of the United States*, Vol. 2 [2 vols.]. Lanham: Rowman and Littlefield, 2004, p. 595.

60. Graham E. Vasectomies increase as concern over "Pill," overpopulation grows. *Wall Street Journal*, Nov. 11, 1970, p. 1.

61. Lader's biography of Sanger was riddled with inaccuracies and enveloped in "clouds of gush," as one of Sanger's friends admitted. Chesler E. *Woman of Valor: Margaret Sanger and the Birth Control Movement in America*. New York: Simon & Schuster, 2992, p. 429.

62. Lader L. Voluntary sterilization: The new birth control. In Lader L (ed.), *Foolproof Birth Control: Male and Female Sterilization*. Boston: Beacon Press, 1972, pp. 1–4.

63. Myers L. Vasectomy in a population control center. In Lader L (ed.), *Foolproof Birth Control: Male and Female Sterilization*. Boston: Beacon Press, 1972, pp. 215–223. See also AVS, Box 46, Midwest Population Center folder.

64. "Sterilization is an answer for many." *New York Times*, January 18, 1971.

65. Dell 'Olio A. The feminist case for vasectomy. In Lader L (ed.), *Foolproof Birth Control: Male and Female Sterilization*. Boston: Beacon Press, 1972, pp. 38–41.

66. Ehrlich PR. *The Population Bomb*. New York: Ballantine Books, 1968, pp. 151–152.

67. Richard M. Nixon, "Special Message to Congress on Problems of Population Growth," July 18, 1969. In *Public Papers of the Presidents of the United States: Richard Nixon, 1969*. Washington DC, 1971, pp. 521–530. Piotrow PT. *World Population Crisis: The United States Response*. New York: Praeger, 1973, pp. 168–170.

68. Paul Ehrlich. "Conservation and Voluntary Sterilization–A New Alliance For Progress," LL, Box 14.

69. E. H. Villard to John Rague, October 9, 1969, AHC, Medora Steedman Bass Collection, Box 3.

70. Arthur Godfrey to Hugh Moore, July 8, 1970, HM, Series 2, Box 17, folder 11.

71. Hugh Moore to Cass Canfield, December 10, 1969, HM, Series 2, Box 1, folder 15.

72. Helen Edey to Hugh Moore, December 29, 1970, HM, Series 3, Box 15, folder 7.

73. Davis K. Population policy: Will current programs succeed? *Science*. 1967;158:730–739.

74. Larry D. Barnett, "Zero Population Growth, Inc.: A Study of a Social Movement" (n.d.): a study of ZPG's membership conducted in September–October 1970 revealed that ZPG was an overwhelmingly white group, males

outnumbered women 2 to 1, California had a disproportionately high share of the membership, 60% called themselves "liberal" (as opposed to "conservative" or "middle of the road"), and 65% were Protestants (Catholics underrepresented and Jews overrepresented); ZPG members drawn from "the younger age brackets" and are "disproportionately highly-educated"; 51% opposed government limitation on the number of children Americans could bear; "ZPG members are in general relatively young and highly-educated." See also Piotrow PT. *World Population Crisis: The United States Response.* New York: Praeger, 1973, pp. 190.

75. Bowers to Wayne Davis, September 2, 1972: [cc. Lader and John Rague], LL, Box 12.

76. Editorial. *Journal of the American Medical Association.* 1968;204:209.

77. "Ann Landers." *Chicago Sun-Times,* June 23, 1970, p. 40. Cited in Simon JL. *The Ultimate Resource.* Princeton: Princeton University Press, 1981, p. 381.

78. "Most adults favor male sterilization." *Los Angeles Times,* September 4, 1970.

79. John D. Porterfield to Joseph E. Davis, May 19, 1972, AVS, Box 50, Joint Commission folder.

80. Edey H. Voluntary sterilization and the medical profession. In Lader L (ed.), *Foolproof Birth Control: Male and Female Sterilization.* Boston: Beacon Press, 1972, pp. 232–235.

81. Guttmacher AF. General remarks on medical aspects of male and female sterilization. In Robitscher J (ed.), *Eugenic Sterilization.* Springfield, IL: Charles C. Thomas, 1973, p. 58. His emphasis.

82. Association for Voluntary Sterilization, *News* (Spring 1972), p. 2. My emphasis.

83. Rague JR. Operation Lawsuit. In Lader L (ed.), *Foolproof Birth Control: Male and Female Sterilization.* Boston: Beacon Press, 1972, p. 241.

84. "Mother of ten sues for sterilization." *New York Times,* February 10, 1971; Reilly PR. *The Surgical Solution: A History of Involuntary Sterilization in the United States.* Baltimore and London: The Johns Hopkins University Press, 1991, pp. 146–147.

85. Association for Voluntary Sterilization, "Landmark ruling by 2nd Circuit Federal Court of Appeals makes hospitals liable for proven damages in arbitrary refusal of sterilization operations for women demanding them." Press release, December 23, 1971.

86. Reilly PR. *The Surgical Solution: A History of Involuntary Sterilization in the United States.* Baltimore and London: The Johns Hopkins University Press, 1991, p. 147. See also "Court Overturns Sterilization Ban," *Worcester Telegram,* March 23, 1973; AVS, Box 111, Hathaway Lawsuit folder.

87. Brody J. More than 100,000 persons a year are reported seeking sterilization as a method of contraception. *New York Times,* March 22, 1970; Dunbar E. For men only: Foolproof birth control. *Look,* March 9, 1971. See also Medora Bass to Mrs. Cass Canfield, April 22, 1968, Bass to Grant Sanger, June 12, 1968, AHC, Medora Steedman Bass Collection, Box 10, Margaret Sanger

Clinic folder. Bass claimed she was only doing what Margaret Sanger, who "was interested in sterilization," would have wanted.

88. Critchlow DT. *Intended Consequences: Birth Control, Abortion and the Federal Government in Modern America*. New York and Oxford: Oxford University Press, 1999, pp. 161–173; Piotrow PT. *World Population Crisis: The United States Response*. New York: Praeger, 1973, p. 190.

89. *Report of Commission on Population Growth and the American Future*, p. 142.

90. Piotrow PT. *World Population Crisis: The United States Response*. New York: Praeger, 1973, p. 190.

Chapter 6

Tarred and Feathered

The 1970s began on a high note for the sterilization movement. Like never before, legal, medical, religious, and cultural barriers to sterilization were crumbling in America and abroad. Studies indicated that a "sterilization explosion" was occurring in the United States, while a growing number of men and women in developing countries were also undergoing sterilization.[1] In 1979, a Gallup poll found that two-thirds of adult Americans approved of voluntary contraceptive sterilization.[2] Birth control in general and sterilization in particular were no longer "dirty words." As H. Curtis Wood exclaimed at the 1972 Association for Voluntary Sterilization (AVS) annual meeting, "We've come a long way, baby."[3]

Yet, at this very moment of success, the sterilization movement faced a fierce backlash from both expected and unexpected quarters. In the 1970s, African American attitudes toward sterilization, never warm, became positively frosty as activists and community leaders joined women's organizations and radical political groups in accusing government, the medical profession, and sterilization advocates of targeting the poor and minorities. Evidence of similar abuses surfaced in India, where the government launched mass sterilization programs in poverty-stricken neighborhoods. The fledgling "right to life" movement likewise constituted a source of opposition that grew more formidable with time. Last, but not least, in 1980, Ronald Reagan, the openly "pro-life" former governor of California (1966–1974), was elected president, jeopardizing funding for AVS and other family-planning groups.

By the early 1980s, these attacks had left AVS reeling. Yet despite these shifts in cultural politics, there was no discounting the major achievements of the sterilization movement. As the century drew to a close, sterilization became the favorite form of contraception for U.S. women, and its use in developing countries also rose sharply, helping to produce a drop in global fertility unlike anything since the Black Death. At the outset of the new millennium, untold men and women around the world had indeed decided to "stop at two," but by doing so they had triggered what some social scientists called a demographic crisis that threatened prosperity and security in the coming twenty-first century.

Fertility Insurance

Prior to the 1970s, the debate over sterilization tended to focus on women, but with the spread of vasectomy clinics in the United States and abroad, the topic of male contraception suddenly became respectable for the first time in history. In the early 1970s, vasectomy centers around the country reported long waiting lists. One 1972 estimate claimed that every year, over 300,000 married American men were having vasectomies, in startling contrast to the modest number of such operations performed annually only a few years earlier. Prominent American men joined Paul Ehrlich in bragging about their own vasectomies, including Jim Bouton, onetime major league pitcher and author of the 1970 best-seller *Ball Four*. Bouton, like activist Abby Hoffman, wore a gold vasectomy lapel pin to highlight his operation.[4] Entertainer Arthur Godfrey informed the men in his audiences that he wanted to "jolly you out of a small section of your vas deferens."[5] Overseas, London's *Sunday Times* declared vasectomy "a patriotic operation," while India organized "massive vasectomy camps" where so-called "world records" for vasectomy operations were set. Public health experts announced that the United States was in the grip of a "vasectomy revolution." Others called it "vasectomania."[6]

This "vasectomania" was a stunning turn of events, given that only a few short years before, opposition to vasectomy was pervasive. Relying on their own surveys of patient satisfaction, sterilization advocates typically discounted the possibility that many women might regret their operations, and thus most research was dedicated to making tubal ligation simpler, safer, and more accessible, rather than reversible. Yet for men reversibility was a key concern. Countless men around the world mistakenly believed vasectomy was the same as castration and thus an end to their manhood, a crucial factor in acceptance in developing countries. For example, in Tunisia, men who had vasectomies were hounded in their own neighborhoods.[7] Family planners lamented that in Latin America, men still subscribed to a "machismo" mentality that equated sexual prowess and fertility.[8] In India, some women opposed vasectomy because they, too, thought it affected male sexual potency.[9] A reversible surgical technique would seemingly help to calm any fears that a vasectomized man was somehow unsexed. If reversibility became a reality, "the word 'sterilization' [could] then be eliminated from the vocabulary of the family planner and population control expert," in the words of AVS president Joseph E. Davis (p. 197) (see insert).[10] According to Davis, sterilization advocates would have a much easier job trying to convince men around the world to submit to the operation if they could be reassured that the procedure was reversible.

The quest for a method of reversible vasectomy had inspired the Rockefeller Foundation, in the 1960s, to invest $75,000 in research at Columbia University's College of Physicians and Surgeons. For its part, AVS had backed the studies of Indian surgeon P. S. Jhaver, whose vas-occlusion clip (the "Jhaver Clip") was touted as a device for reversing vasectomy.[11] Yet by the early 1970s, this and other research had proven to be dead ends. The surgical reversibility of vasectomy still seemed to lie far in the future.

To compensate, AVS threw its support behind sperm banks, where vasectomized customers could have their semen frozen and stored in case they changed their minds about having children and opted for artificial insemination. The sperm bank industry, begun in the 1960s, traced its origins to the late-nineteenth-century efforts of physicians to help infertile couples through insemination by sperm donors. By 1969 there were ten U.S. sperm banks. Idant Corporation, launched in 1971, subsequently opened offices in New York City, Baltimore, Detroit, Chicago, Denver, Dallas, and Los Angeles. It soon became the world's largest sperm bank. The same year, the Repository for Germinal Choice, a sperm bank for Nobel Laureates and other geniuses, was founded near San Diego. By 1990, there were one hundred and thirty-five U.S. sperm banks, representing a multimillion-dollar industry.[12]

To sterilization advocates, sperm banks had the potential to revolutionize the entire family-planning enterprise. As AVS president Joseph Davis announced in 1972, "[T]he combination of frozen semen and vasectomy means that we are rapidly approaching, and in many instances have achieved, in effect, a means of 'reversible vasectomy.'"[13] Sperm banks provided a form of "fertility insurance" for men who might otherwise balk at the prospect of vasectomy. In Davis's view, all nations would benefit, but it was in "developing countries" especially and "from the point of view of world population" that the true impact of sperm banks would be felt (p. 198).[10] Davis's comments confirmed that, as late as the 1970s, population control considerations still loomed large in the minds of sterilization advocates.

Bucking Nature and Society

As the "vasectomy revolution" unfolded in the early 1970s, rates of female sterilization also jumped abruptly. In 1970, an estimated 201,000 tubal sterilizations were performed on U.S. women, but that annual rate had more than doubled by 1975.[14] Between 1973 and 1974 alone, the incidence of female sterilization rose by 40%.[15] By 1976, almost 10% of all married U.S. women of reproductive age had been sterilized for contraceptive purposes (p. 24).[16] By that point in America's history, tubal sterilization had become the third most frequently performed surgical procedure on women aged fifteen to forty-four (following abortion and diagnostic dilation and curettage).[14] The Pill was still the most popular method of birth control among women married less than ten years, but the escalating popularity of sterilization meant that it would shortly become the method of choice for all married couples of reproductive age.[17]

Correspondence between AVS's referral bureau and women seeking sterilization demonstrated that this spike in the incidence of female sterilization was fueled to a large extent by the efforts of family planning clinics and the burgeoning women's health movement to educate women about the operation. Some women reported learning of sterilization by reading the bestselling *Our Bodies, Ourselves*, including one eighteen-year-old who claimed she had "put a lot of thought into [her] decision [to be sterilized] and it is not a spur-of-the-moment one."[18] A New Haven, Connecticut, clinic offering vacuum aspiration abortions on an outpatient basis told AVS that clients "often asked about sterilization procedures."[19] Women frequently blamed their abortions on contraceptive failure. Sterilization offered them a way to be done with contraception for good and avoid abortions entirely. A twenty-six-year-old married woman without children told AVS that she had "tried every method from pills to IUDs and they have all proven inadequate. As a result, I have had two abortions. I do not want anymore . . . I *never* want any children."[20] Others were simply tired of taking the Pill. "I know this 21-day-Pill thing's got to end," wearily remarked another woman who sought a sterilization.[21] A thirty-five-year-old Syracuse, New York, woman, married for eleven years, said she never wanted children but wished to stop taking the Pill because of possible "complications."[22]

Improvements in surgical technique also hastened sterilization's popularity. Prior to the late 1960s, gynecologists had been reluctant to perform tubal sterilization, a major operation that involved anesthesia and a lengthy hospital stay, simply to terminate a woman's fertility. Hence sterilizations had ordinarily occurred postpartum or at the time of cesarean section. But once the laparoscope, a fiberoptic instrument, was introduced in the late 1960s, it swiftly gained wide acceptance. The laparoscope enabled surgeons to see the organs in the pelvic area without the need for a large incision, involving only two pencil-wide punctures in the abdomen and small scars. Such technical improvements in the 1970s meant female sterilization could be performed under local anesthesia and in nonhospital settings. The press lavished coverage on laparoscopy, dubbing it "belly-button surgery." Its popularity helped to slow the escalating incidence of vasectomy, as more and more couples agreed that, in comparison with vasectomy, female sterilization was no longer major surgery.[23] By 1976, 38% of U.S. sterilizations were performed with a laparoscope, compared with only 1% in 1970 (p. 24).[16] Laparoscopy appeared to be a major breakthrough in women's health care. One Baltimore surgeon, claiming to have done 3,000 such operations himself, said he was no "women's libber" but felt he had "liberated more women than Gloria Steinem ever thought of."[24]

Yet, as important as such technical advances were, they do not account entirely for the rates of tubal ligation in the 1970s. Many women requested sterilization for lifestyle reasons, a reflection of the extent to which consumerism and affluence had become decisive factors in the everyday lives of Americans. Since the 1940s, countless Americans, benefiting from the country's unprecedented economic prosperity, had been spending billions on consumer goods. As per capita gross national product (GNP) rose from decade to decade, life expectancy, education levels, labor-saving technology, and disposable income made striking advances. Real personal income doubled between 1940 and 1970, making the United States the richest nation in the world. The gap between rich and poor remained wide, millions continued to live below the poverty line, and the "stagflation" and energy crisis of the 1970s convinced some economists that the country's prosperity boom was finally over, but on average Americans had more money than ever before, and more recreational time to spend it. The quest for personal gratification emerged as a major trend, and in the eyes of many people children increasingly loomed as obstacles to the enjoyment of travel and material goods.[25] A Grinnell College undergraduate explained that she did not "want children because I do not enjoy them nor do I want to ruin the style of life I want to lead. But no matter how I try to explain this . . . I come off sounding like a selfish, pleasure seeking woman."[26] A thirty-one-year-old married and childless woman revealed that she and her husband were "not interested in having a family. We have a comfortable living and enjoy things as they are now."[27] To them, and many others with similar goals, sterilization was an attractive option, even if it meant never having children.

Propaganda about the "population bomb" also affected reproductive choice. Numerous women and their partners were reluctant to bring children into an allegedly overpopulated world. A twenty-two-year-old New York City woman informed AVS she was

> planning not to bear children. I did not plan on becoming a mother even as a child. Now that I am grown there is not a doubt in my mind that I have chosen wisely. It is not that I hate kids. It is simply that there are too many people in the world as it is and I cannot see myself adding to it. I do not believe that my debt to society is to reproduce. By not investing my time in adding to the world's population I will be able to do many more fruitful things.

"I have better things to do than add to the population and motherhood," added a twenty-eight-year-old Cincinnati woman. An eighteen-year-old reasoned that because "the population is getting bigger all the time," sterilization was the right decision for her.[28]

Despite the rising demand for female sterilization, male doctors' attitudes toward the operation were frequently negative. One twenty-nine-year-old woman, married for eleven years, was told by her doctor that choosing to be childless was "bucking nature and society."[29] A twenty-nine-year-old single woman claimed that her doctor had described her request for sterilization as "nonsense," advising her to try a new IUD or reconsider her refusal to use the Pill.[30] Typically, the younger the woman, the more medical opposition she faced. One twenty-year-old without children confided that "many doctors feel that I have not yet 'fulfilled my purpose in life,' and therefore won't help me out."[31] Older women who chose to be child-free understandably resented the fact that numerous physicians tried to talk them out of their decisions. Yet in the 1970s such medical paternalism was steadily declining as physicians grew more and more respectful of patients' wishes.

As these personal stories demonstrated, one of the most striking trends of the 1970s was that some young women with few or no children were opting for sterilization. For years, AVS had promoted sterilization as a form of contraception most suited to women aged thirty-four to forty-nine who had completed their families and, in a day and age of unreliable contraceptive methods, did not want to live with the worry of another pregnancy. Data prior to the 1970s appeared to confirm that the highest rates of sterilization were found among the women in this age cohort. The American College of Obstetricians and Gynecologists' age/parity guidelines, as well as the failure of medical insurance to cover the costs of the operation, helped to account for this trend. Yet in the 1970s, the percentage of single U.S. women and women under twenty-nine who were sterilized surgically began a steady climb. The Centers for Disease Control and Prevention reported that the steepest rise in the U.S. rate of tubal sterilization between 1975 and 1978 was in the fifteen- to twenty-four-year-old age group.[32] This situation generally persisted until the end of the twentieth century. Between 1994 and 1996, the highest rates of sterilization were recorded among women aged twenty-five to thirty-four, the "peak childbearing years" being twenty to twenty-nine.[33] These trends coincided with what family-planning experts in 1981 were calling an "increasing prevalence of childlessness" among both white and nonwhite U.S. women, refuting the conventional wisdom that many women were simply delaying first births.[34] At the end of the century, family planners were struck by "the relatively high rates of sterilization among single women."[35] If sterilization advocates had once believed that tubal ligation would be largely confined to poor, married women with large families of unwanted children, by the 1980s, the data indicated that this was no longer the case.

Hysterilization

As the number of tubal sterilizations surged in the 1970s, a simultaneous decline in the rate of contraceptive hysterectomy took place. For most of the nineteenth century, hysterectomy—the surgical removal of the uterus—had been an experimental form of surgery with predictably high mortality rates. Yet thanks to improvements in asepsis, anesthesia, surgical prowess, hospital care, and laboratory medicine, as well as the availability of powerful antibiotics, by the mid-twentieth century hysterectomy had become a comparatively safe method of treating a range of uterine conditions, including inflammation, prolapse, bleeding, cysts, fibroids, and tumors. However, by the 1960s, popular magazines such as *Reader's Digest, Ladies' Home Journal,* and *Consumer Reports* were reporting grave concerns about the high incidence of hysterectomy, notably in cases where the uterus was free of disease.[36] By that time, the total number of annual hysterectomies in the United States was roughly 450,000 and was climbing steeply. Between 1968 and 1973, the yearly rate of hysterectomy rose by 26%. At a major Los Angeles–area hospital, the total number of hysterectomies jumped by 293% between 1967 and 1970 alone (pp. 1076–1083).[37] In 1971, the question "How come all those hysterectomies?" sparked a lively and contentious debate at the annual meeting of the American College of Obstetricians and Gynecologists.[38] In 1973, 690,000 hysterectomies were performed in the United States, a rate that surpassed that for any other major operation and was double that in England and Wales. The National Center for Health Statistics predicted in 1976 that if trends continued, half the women in the United States would lose their uterus by the age of sixty-five. This prediction never came true, but by the turn of the century 20 million American women had undergone hysterectomies.[39]

A major reason for the elevated incidence of hysterectomy was the attitude of the medical profession. In the 1950s and 1960s, the high costs of the operation made it a lucrative procedure for surgeons to perform, leading to what one critic called "hip pocket hysterectomies."[40] At the time, organized medicine was also in the grip of a "can-do" approach to sickness that conformed to the cardinal beliefs of most twentieth-century physicians that researchers, practitioners, hospitals, and medical schools ought to run their own affairs as they saw fit, and that the more medicine a society received, the healthier it was. This approach applied to even healthy organs. In the words of one U.S. gynecologist in 1969, "[A]fter the last planned pregnancy, the uterus becomes a useless, bleeding, symptom-producing, potentially cancer-bearing organ and therefore should be removed."[41] Studies showed that residents in teaching hospitals were often encouraged to do as many hysterectomies as possible for training purposes. Medical school students quickly learned the surgeon's slogan: "When in doubt, whip it out."[42] As an Atlanta-hospital physician put it in 1976, "Let's face it, if you're a gynecology resident, how are you going into practice if you ain't yanked some utes?"[43] Other studies indicated that surgeons sometimes performed hysterectomies on the "worried well," patients with vague symptoms (such as "pelvic pain syndrome") without any discernible organic pathology, in order to be seen as "doing something therapeutic."[44]

Another factor that caused the incidence of hysterectomy to climb was its growing use as a method of birth control. For years, some hysterectomies had been performed to end fertility, but with the coming of the contraceptive revolution in the 1960s, sterilization by hysterectomy, or "hysterilization," became routine (p. 197).[45] Rumors abounded of husbands buying their wives "birthday hysterectomies" when they wanted no more children (p. 205).[45] Roman Catholics who obeyed Church teaching on tubal sterilization but were satisfied with their family size would often agree to hysterectomy because it could be justified on the basis of non-contraceptive purposes, including uterine pain and anemia due to dysfunctional bleeding. Hysterectomy appeared to many physicians to be "well-suited" as both a contraceptive and therapeutic operation for "socioeconomically deprived" groups in whom dysfunctional uterine bleeding and diseases of the cervix were common.[46]

Yet in the 1970s, a backlash against organized medicine slowed the trend toward more and more hysterectomies. Critics argued that generous doses of medicine, whether in the form of hospitalization, medication, or surgery, were not actually making society any healthier. Congressional attention focused on surgery, notably "unnecessary" hysterectomies. In 1974, a U.S. Senate investigation revealed that over 2.4 million unnecessary operations were performed yearly in America, causing 11,900 deaths and costing $3.9 billion.[47] Expenditures on health as a percentage of GNP climbed steadily in the 1970s, and health economists began urging reforms to the medical fee system. Medical insurance companies, alarmed over the spiraling costs of health coverage, increasingly questioned the customary medical indications for hysterectomy. Women's health groups attacked physicians, insisting on a franker, less authoritarian relationship to their doctors and protesting specific procedures for women, including hysterectomies and radical mastectomies. Women activists demanded more women doctors and sought to demystify organized medicine's claim to special knowledge about female physiology and psychology. By urging women to learn more about their bodies, they hoped to defeat medical paternalism and convince the profession to be more therapeutically cautious (pp. 391–392).[48]

Some doctors protested that the criticism of hysterectomy was an unjustified assault on the "professional freedom for the practicing physician in this country."[49] Yet, in defending the widespread use of hysterectomy, physicians were fighting against a political, economic, and cultural tide that signaled what one historian has called "the end of the mandate" for twentieth-century organized medicine. By the 1980s, the "golden age" of

American medicine, when patients typically and unquestioningly obeyed their doctors' orders, was a thing of the past.[50]

Against this backdrop of criticism directed at organized medicine, the national hysterectomy rate declined between 1975 and 1990. The rate for 1982 was the lowest since 1970. By 1997, the U.S. hysterectomy rate had fallen to 5.6 in every 1,000 women, from 7.5 in 1990.[51] Key variables affecting the drop in the hysterectomy rate included the growing number of female gynecologists entering the profession and reforms to medical education in the last quarter of the century that made aspiring doctors more sensitive to overall patient needs.[52] Moreover, by the 1990s other, less invasive treatment methods were available for conditions that in the past had justified hysterectomy, such as thermal ablation for uterine bleeding. Yet equally significant was the mounting use of vasectomy and tubal ligation, which decreased the likelihood that women patients and their doctors would consider hysterectomy for mainly contraceptive purposes.[53] At the end of the century, hysterectomy remained a popular operation, but better medical training, broader health-consumer education, and a greater variety of surgical options meant that increasing numbers of Americans thought hysterectomy was "surgical overkill" (p. 200).[45]

What was the impact on fertility of all these hysterectomies? In the 1950s and 1960s, when "hysterilization" was often performed, its effect on the nation's declining birthrate was likely significant. Yet after the 1960s, by far the greatest number of hysterectomies were performed on women over the age of thirty-five—that is, on women who in all likelihood were satisfied with their family size. In the early 1990s, the peak hysterectomy rate occurred among women between the ages of forty and forty-four, a statistic that had changed little since the 1960s.[54] By the new millennium, few women were consenting to hysterectomy chiefly to stop having children.

A consequence of this broad campaign against hysterectomy was the mounting acceptance of tubal sterilization. "An elective hysterectomy [for sterilization purposes] is an expensive luxury as compared to a tubal sterilization," one study reported in 1972. When the costs of convalescence and lost income for patients were added to the direct surgical and hospital expenses for the average hysterectomy and the longer recovery time and complication rate, the case for routine elective hysterectomy for sterilization purposes was weak (p. 1082).[37] With the spread of "managed" health care in the 1970s and beyond, and the simultaneous weakening of physician control over therapeutic decision making, the brief heyday of "hysterilization" came to a sudden halt. To a wide range of interested parties, hysterectomy for contraceptive purposes was indeed "surgical overkill."

Murky Distinctions

With growing numbers of young women undergoing tubal ligations, and with federal funds available to pay for the sterilization of low-income women, the question of what exactly distinguished a voluntary from an involuntary sterilization became highly controversial in the 1970s. By that time, disturbing data were emerging that showed that thousands of low-income and minority Americans were being sterilized annually under federal programs and in the absence of government-approved guidelines. Studies reported that U.S. clinics and hospitals that performed sterilizations tended to insist on few requirements before operating. As one 1979 survey showed, in many medical facilities there existed a "bias favoring compulsory sterilization strongly weighted against indigent populations."[55] The era of sterilization under eugenic state laws may have faded into the past, yet the operation itself continued to be performed with troubling regularity on the same types of patients.

If any one incident highlighted the sterilization of low-income and minority people, it was the scandal surrounding the Relf sisters in Alabama: Minnie Lee, age twelve, and Mary Alice, age fourteen. Both African American girls were clients in an antipoverty program administered by the U.S. Department of Health, Education and Welfare (HEW) and staffed by social workers from the federally financed County Community Action Agency in Montgomery, Alabama. On June 13, 1973, two public health nurses arrived at the home of Lonnie Relf, a fifty-six-year-old unemployed and disabled field hand, and his wife, Minnie. The nurses escorted Minnie Lee, Mary Alice, and their mother to the local hospital, where Mrs. Relf, an illiterate welfare mother of four, signed an "X" on a consent form. According to press reports, the next day the girls were operated on, but the girls' lawyer later revealed that only one of the sisters—Minnie Lee—was actually sterilized.[56] Mrs. Relf subsequently insisted that at the time she had not been aware that she had approved a tubal ligation. Whatever the exact circumstances, Minnie Lee was just one of over 16,000 females (and 8,677 men) sterilized at 3,267 clinics around the country in 1972 thanks to federal funding. Even in the 1930s, the rate of eugenic sterilization had never been that high.[57]

The story might never have seen the light of day if it had not been for a Catholic social worker who reported the incident. Shortly thereafter, acting on legal advice, Mr. and Mrs. Relf filed suit against the federal government. When the news of the Relf sisters broke, it sparked a national outcry. Senator Edward Kennedy (D-Massachusetts), who was chairing a U.S. Senate Health Subcommittee investigation into health care and pressing for a bill to tighten controls on government-run medical experimentation, met with the Relfs and arranged to have them testify in Washington, D.C., on July 10, 1973.[58]

Meanwhile, the staff of the Alabama clinic where the Relf sterilization was performed defended the operation. They alleged that Mrs. Relf and the two girls had been briefed as to the exact nature of the operation by two African American nurses. Both girls had been receiving injections of Depo-Provera, a long-lasting, injectable, hormonal contraceptive drug, but its use in welfare patients had been discontinued in February, 1973, because of testimony regarding its health risks at the same Senate hearings chaired by Kennedy. Social workers ruled out birth control pills for the Relf girls because they considered their "mental talents" to be subpar.[59] In fact, Mary Alice, born without a right hand, suffered from a speech impediment and was diagnosed as mentally retarded. Few doubted that the manner of the social workers left much to be desired, but some reporters suspected that initially Mrs. Relf had knowingly consented to sterilization, thinking it best for the girls, yet later denied it when her husband found out, sensing that he, like many African American men, disliked the idea of birth control.[60]

The Relfs' testimony, overshadowed in the summer of 1973 by the Watergate hearings, revealed little solid information, but it did draw attention to the fact that the release and distribution of guidelines that might have prevented this and similar sterilizations had been blocked by the White House. The Nixon administration had drawn up guidelines in 1971, with AVS input, but refused to issue them in an election year for fear of losing Catholic votes.[61] The guidelines were still on government shelves, gathering dust, when public health nurses visited the Relf household.

In the event, Kennedy abruptly closed down the hearings after calling only the Relfs and a single Office of Economic Opportunity physician as witnesses. Black congresswomen Shirley Chisholm and Barbara Jordan, worried that the hearings might degenerate into "a freak show," pressured Kennedy into refusing groups such as Planned Parenthood Federation of America (PPFA) and right-to-life organizations the opportunity to testify.

For his part, Kennedy undoubtedly knew that his bill to control medical experimentation would not have prevented Minnie Lee's sterilization, so there was little more to be gained politically from focusing national attention on what had happened in Montgomery County. In the final analysis, the Relfs' quick visit to Washington left observers with many unanswered questions. As *Newsweek* reported, "[T]he problem was finding out just what the facts [about the Relfs] were."[62]

As far as AVS was concerned, the Relf incident was a public relations disaster. In covering the story, the media repeatedly linked the Relfs to the Tuskegee syphilis experiments, news of which first surfaced in 1972 and similarly sparked national outrage.[63] The Tuskegee experiments had been conducted between 1932 and 1972 by the U.S. Public Health Service. Several hundred African American men, many poor sharecroppers, who suffered from syphilis were denied treatment without their knowledge in order to study the ravages of the disease on black men over long stretches of time.[64] In 1973, media reporting conveyed the message that the Tuskegee and Relf scandals were similarly racist crimes. The Relfs' lawyer reinforced this perception when he remarked that "this is the kind of thing Hitler did."[65]

AVS did its best to distinguish its advocacy of voluntary sterilization from what had happened to the Relfs. In its June 18, 1973, joint statement with the National Welfare and Rights Organization, AVS contended that it opposed "compulsory sterilization." "We are in full agreement with the resolution adopted by the American Civil Liberties Union [ACLU]," AVS stated, that "the whole question of human reproduction should be a matter of voluntary decision with no governmental compulsion"[66]

However, when it came to welfare sterilizations, the ACLU and AVS were not exactly on the same page. While AVS tried desperately to distance itself from the Relf sterilizations, Nial Ruth Cox, an African American, unwed mother from North Carolina, filed legal suit with the ACLU over her sterilization in 1965, when she was eighteen years old. Cox alleged that her mother had been told by welfare officials in North Carolina that unless Nial submitted to the operation, she would lose her benefits. To AVS, the sterilization of Nial Ruth Cox had nothing to do with its concerted efforts over the years to make the operation "freely available to all Americans, regardless of age, number of children, marital status, race, religion, or income."[66] Yet balancing this plea for access with support for sterilization as a method of population control and welfare reform proved to be exceedingly difficult in everyday practice. One AVS member correctly complained that the group's statement on the Relfs' sterilization conflicted with its longtime belief that "there is a lot of irresponsible parenthood in the U.S. on the part of welfare recipients as well as others." Instead, he wanted AVS to go "on record as opposing irresponsible parenthood wherever it occurs."[67] Yet, as later events in the 1970s demonstrated, promoting voluntary sterilization while decrying "irresponsible parenthood" left AVS vulnerable to attacks from both ends of the political spectrum.

The relationship between sterilization and welfare rose to haunt AVS again in 1974, when *Relf v. Weinberger* was heard in federal district court. Judge Gerhard Gesell estimated that since the 1960s, federal programs had paid for the sterilization of between 100,000 and 150,000 low-income American women. Moreover, he stated that "an indefinite number of poor people," including "minors and other incompetents," had been "improperly coerced" into sterilizations when threatened by the loss of their welfare benefits. One South Carolina obstetrician was alleged to have told a maternity ward patient, "Listen here, young lady, this is my tax money paying for this baby, and I'm tired of paying for illegitimate children. If you don't want this [sterilization], find another doctor." In cases such as these, the distinction between family planning and eugenics was "murky," Gesell concluded, a comment that aptly described the dividing line the sterilization movement had unsuccessfully been attempting to navigate for decades.[68]

Less well known, but also indicative of how many U.S. sterilizations were far from elective, was the 1976 class-action court case *Madrigal v. Quilligan*, which pitted ten women of Mexican origin against the obstetricians of the Southern California/Los Angeles County General Hospital. The suit alleged that between 1971 and 1974, hospital staff had pressured the women into postpartum tubal ligations shortly after delivery by caesarean section. The trial, which began in 1978, ended when Judge Jesse Curtis ruled in favor of the defendants, the County Hospital physicians. While conceding that the plaintiffs had suffered "emotional and physical stress," Curtis concluded that the physicians had not been engaged in "conspiratorial action" and that the surgeries had occurred due to "a breakdown in communication between the patients and the doctors."[69]

The County Hospital may have narrowly dodged a punitive settlement in *Madrigal v. Quilligan*, but the evidence unearthed by the trial cast a long shadow over the sterilization movement. The one witness who testified against the doctors recalled that one of them had said that "poor minority women in L.A. County were having too many babies; that it was a strain on society; and that it was good that they be sterilized." Additionally, at County and other hospitals that received HEW funding, women in labor were allegedly browbeaten into sterilizations so that surgeons could practice their craft. According to one 1973 study, obstetricians at County Hospital instructed staff, "Remember everyone you get to get her tubes tied means two tubes for some resident or intern."[70]

Data relating to the sterilization of Native Americans cast an equally gloomy pall over efforts to popularize sterilization in the 1970s. During the heyday of eugenic sterilization, in the 1930s, Native American tribes such as Vermont's Abenakis had been targeted for sterilization, but, far from dying out, this disturbing practice actually thrived in later years.[71] In 1976, the General Accounting Office released data that indicated that 3,406 Native American women in one-third of all Indian Health Services (IHS) districts had been sterilized between 1973 and 1976 without filling out proper consent forms. Other surveys showed that IHS hospital surgeons had been sterilizing Native American women as far back as 1966, with the federal government paying the bills. In 1977, a Native American physician estimated that up to one-quarter of all Indian women of childbearing age had been sterilized, often without informed consent. At a single Oklahoma hospital, one-fourth of all women admitted (for any reason) were sterilized, including all pureblood women of a single tribe. One historian has dubbed the sterilization of Native Americans in the 1960s and 1970s as "effectively genocidal."[72]

Ready to Kill Us

The news of African American and Native American sterilizations, combined with equally troubling details about the sterilization of Puerto Rican women in New York City, inspired physician Helen Rodriguez-Trias to co-found the Committee to End Sterilization Abuse (CESA) in 1974. Born in Manhattan, Rodriguez-Trias (1929–2001) completed her pediatrics residency in 1963 at the University of Puerto Rico and later led a variety of public health reform efforts in the South Bronx, a district with a high concentration of Puerto Ricans and one of the poorest communities in the United States.[73] Having spearheaded the campaign to expose sterilization practices in Puerto Rico, where 35% of all women of reproductive age had been sterilized by 1968, she was equally outraged when she heard similar stories about Puerto Rican and other minority women in New York City (p. 54).[74]

Activists like Rodriguez-Trias had more than anecdotal evidence to support the theory that thousands of American women were being sterilized without proper information, counseling, and consent. Even after HEW belatedly released the ill-fated federal guidelines in 1974, study after study documented that hospitals (especially teaching hospitals) around the country used subtle or not-so-subtle forms of pressure to obtain consent for tubal ligations. The ACLU and Ralph Nader's Health Research Group reported that the majority of U.S. hospitals were either knowingly or unknowingly out of compliance with federal regulations.[75] As the 1970s wound to a close, the number of flagrant abuses was declining, but subtle forms of pressure were still operative, including obtaining consent for sterilization when the patient was in labor or after cesarean section. Rodriguez-Trias and other researchers claimed that between one-third and one-half of sterilized women from minority groups regretted their operations. Birth control groups such as AVS disputed these findings, often using different definitions of what constituted "regret," but by the 1980s it was clear that fully informed consent had indeed been absent in numerous sterilizations (pp. 93–94, 133–135).[74]

Disturbing data such as these sparked a short-lived yet combative movement to fight sterilization abuse, resulting in a conflict that exposed major disagreements among the many interest groups involved in the campaign to widen access to family planning services. To the dismay of many, deep fissures developed among feminists and women's organizations over the sterilization issue. The storm center of the dispute was New York City, where groups like CESA joined other patient-advocacy organizations in urging that restrictions be placed on publicly funded sterilizations of African American and Puerto Rican patients. In 1976, Carter Burden, a New York City councilman, introduced a bill based on guidelines adopted in 1975 by the Health and Hospital Corporation (HHC), the agency responsible for municipal hospitals in New York City. The guidelines called for a thirty-day waiting period between request for sterilization and the actual operation; a prohibition on consent concurrent with child delivery, abortion, or hospitalization for a major procedure; full counseling on all birth control alternatives; and formal assurance that the patient fully understood the permanence of the procedure. The Burden Bill sought to extend the regulations to all New York City private and public health facilities. Yet, as happened during the debates over the HHC guidelines, the 1976–1977 public hearings on the Burden Bill revealed that CESA and its allies faced formidable opposition. Ranged against CESA's coalition were AVS, PPFA, the National Abortion Rights Action League, the American College of Obstetricians and Gynecologists, and some chapters of the National Organization for Women (NOW). "The feminist groups were ready to kill us," one antisterilization activist exclaimed ruefully, because they believed the guidelines patronizingly presupposed that women needed a thirty-day waiting period to make up their minds. For their part, health-care professionals disliked strict guidelines because they felt it was a case of government interfering in the relationship between clinician and patient. Yet the advocates of the HHC regulations, supported by groups like the ACLU and National Black Feminists, were better prepared than their adversaries for the Burden hearings. AVS's associate director confessed that AVS had yet to stake out an official position on the guidelines and requested a delay in the debates, while the integrity of PPFA, "the principal and most effective lobbyist" against the Burden Bill, was suspect because it had recently applied to perform sterilizations at its outpatient clinics. In the end, the Burden Bill passed 38 to 0, with three abstentions.[76]

The scene shifted to Washington, D.C., where, in September, 1977, over one hundred individuals representing fifty organizations met at the National Conference on Sterilization Abuse, organized by the Interreligious Foundation for Community Organization. The delegates were there to convince the federal government to enact similarly stringent safeguards against sterilization abuse, including the controversial thirty-day waiting period and a ban on federal funds to sterilize people younger than twenty-one, mentally incompetent persons of any age, and institutionalized persons of any age.[77] The conference proved to be successful, as HEW bureaucrats, weary from the many attacks they had endured during the 1970s, were relieved to put the issue behind them, even by virtually giving in to groups like CESA. The process of adopting tough sterilization guidelines was facilitated by Joseph Califano, HEW secretary, a Catholic known to be uneasy about sterilization itself. Yet it was not until 1982 that the HHC felt that compliance with the regulations was good enough to no longer require large-sample auditing of hospitals.[78]

AVS reacted to this series of events with dismay. Since the 1973 Relf scandal, it had been apparent to the group's leadership that the coalition that helped to topple barriers to sterilization in the early 1970s was breaking apart. This coalition, consisting of individuals and organizations in favor of birth control, population control, legal abortion, and women's rights, abruptly dissolved when radical feminists and minority activists began protesting the high rates of sterilization among low-income, minority, and immigrant women. One telltale sign that the coalition was unraveling came during the Burden hearings, when NOW's New York chapter defected from the national organization and endorsed the bill. As Burden read the chapter's letter of support into the record, one observer remarked that the AVS and PPFA representatives "writhe[d]" in their seats, moaning "Oh God, those stupid women in NOW." To sterilization advocates, it was mystifying how the same groups could demand that government not interfere in a woman's freedom to obtain an abortion and yet insist that women who requested sterilization should be subject to lengthy waiting periods and extensive counseling. CESA maintained that sterilization and abortion were two very different things and that the potential for abuse was much greater with sterilization, but to AVS, CESA appeared ungrateful, given AVS and PPFA support for the repeal of abortion laws only a few years earlier. Among other things, at stake for AVS and PPFA was their joint program to use a $700,000 fund for out-of-hospital sterilizations. To AVS, the HHC restrictions gravely hampered the effectiveness of such services, to say nothing of their financial operations (pp. 153–154).[79]

The Privilege of Sterilization

To longtime members of the sterilization movement such as Medora Bass, no restriction was more baffling than the prohibition on the sterilization of the mentally retarded. Bass's history with AVS dated back to the days of Birthright in the 1940s. She had been instrumental in launching the French Plan, as well as the vasectomy clinic at the Margaret Sanger Bureau, in 1969. Prior to the 1960s, Bass, like her good friend H. Curtis Wood, had devoted most of her career to advocating sterilization for low-income women, whose poverty she believed to be a result of their low intelligence and high fertility. Yet in the 1960s, as AVS ceased promoting sterilization as a welfare reform and deemphasized hereditarian theories about the causes of mental retardation, Bass began to praise sterilization as a means for the mentally retarded and their parents to enjoy a fuller quality of life. A new era in mental-health-care policy, dominated by the themes of deinstitutionalization, normalization, and community care, had dawned in most of Europe and North America. Custodialism and institutional segregation for the mentally handicapped were considered to be both inhumane and ineffective.[79] Sterilizing the mentally retarded provided relief for parents from the worry of their children becoming pregnant and also benefited the mentally retarded by enabling them to live "normal" lives in the community rather than institutions, and even to marry and express their sexuality.[80] According to Bass, babies born to the mentally retarded were almost all unwanted, and thus the babies' "right . . . to be born to parents who can provide adequate care and discipline" would suffer. Under this form of "involuntary parenthood," no one benefited, including society.[81] For these reasons, sterilization was not so much a matter of choice but a "privilege" that the poor and handicapped ought to be grateful for.[82] How this concept could be squared with the advocacy of voluntary sterilization was a question that evidently did not trouble Medora Bass.

When Bass testified at the 1978 DHEW hearings on proposed sterilization guidelines, she deployed all these arguments, but by then the courts were growing increasingly opposed to the idea of sterilizing the mentally handicapped, even if they and their parents approved. Such legal opinions conflicted with surveys that showed that a sizeable minority of Americans still supported sterilizing those unable to give their full consent.[83] Similarly, half a decade of press reports about sterilization abuse of minors, minorities, and low-income groups had not discouraged millions of Americans in the 1970s from opting for either vasectomy or tubal ligation as a method of family planning. Yet when it came to government-funded sterilizations, the operation was still considered to be a miscarriage of justice. To Bass and many others, misguided interest groups refused to let the sterilization movement bury its eugenic past for good, and the result was that the "deserving" poor and handicapped continued to suffer. Bass, whose involvement in the movement stretched back to the days of Marian Olden and the Sterilization League of New Jersey, could be forgiven for thinking that, despite the passage of years, not much had changed since then.

Cultural Politics

Further unnerving news for AVS was the fact that the controversy over sterilization abuse tended to unite some surprising political bedfellows. Groups like CESA, often derided by opponents as "radicals" and "communist," as well as "minorities who have traditional, long-standing concerns about genocide," found common cause with right-to-life groups on the issue of sterilization.[84] The U.S. pro-life movement had leapt into action soon after the Supreme Court's 1973 *Roe v. Wade* ruling that declared abortion to be a woman's constitutional right. This decision appalled countless Catholics, who swiftly mobilized and threw their weight behind the National Right to Life Committee (NRLC), which by the mid-1970s was politically active on Capitol Hill and in almost every state.[85] According to one pro-choice activist in 1973, "[R]ight to life groups were springing up all over the country"; they were "quite dedicated and mostly Roman Catholic."[86] The cumulative effect of this groundswell of opposition on AVS in particular was to leave the group feeling "tarred and feathered . . . for things for which we are in no way responsible."[87]

The predominantly Catholic nature of the right-to-life movement began to change in the late 1970s as Evangelical Christians joined the crusade. Since the 1920s, Evangelicals, heirs to early-twentieth-century Fundamentalism, had kept their distance from the political realm. Yet, starting in the 1960s, the escalating toleration of abortion, pornography, homosexuality, and the Equal Rights Amendment (ERA) for women steadily drove them back into the political arena. Evangelists such as Jimmy Swaggart, Pat Robertson, and Tammy and Jim Bakker took to the airwaves and forcefully expressed their opposition to all these trends. In 1979, Baptist preacher Jerry Falwell formed the "Moral Majority," a coalition of conservative Southern Protestants and Roman Catholics from around the country, quickly making Falwell a national spokesman for the emerging Christian Right. When Ronald Reagan was elected president in 1980, the right-to-life movement had a powerful ally in the White House; Reagan's election also signaled how, in ten short years, the movement had grown from modest origins into a potent political force and formidable foe of abortion, euthanasia, the ERA, and gay rights. What was once a largely Catholic crusade had broadened, and family-planning organizations that supported abortion rights were squarely in right-to-life activists' crosshairs.[88]

The emerging clout of the right-to-life movement spelled trouble for the sterilization movement. Just when it appeared that the movement had decisively defeated Catholic opposition to sterilization as a form of contraception, it began to face a new realignment of militant political forces united by sharply defined moral visions and based on pragmatic alliances that crossed traditional religious boundaries. By the 1980s, progressivist Protestants, Catholics, Jews, and secularists who supported abortion and euthanasia had more in common with one another culturally and politically than they did with the orthodox members of their own faith traditions (pp. 47, 131–132).[89] At the core of this conflict were a series of what one historian has called "policy brawls" over the very nature of the family (p. 182).[89] Although sterilization never rivaled abortion or euthanasia as an issue that inflamed right-to-life ire, the media coverage of sterilization abuse cases in the 1970s rekindled memories of eugenic sterilization, a policy that most Americans found abhorrent. The perception that sterilization was linked to eugenics made groups like AVS an inviting target for radical and right-to-life attacks. Likewise, when, in the early 1970s, hospitals dismantled their sterilization and abortion committees, it was easy for pro-lifers to link the two issues in the public mind. In other words, as America entered the 1980s, sterilization was one of several "edge-of-life" issues that defined the nation's "culture war" over "fundamentally different moral visions of human life," a conflict that has continued to wrack America's conscience into the twenty-first century.[90] As events would demonstrate, victory in this culture war had very concrete consequences: millions of dollars in government funding now hung in the balance. National policy governing family planning and foreign aid depended on which side of the culture war the occupant of the White House was on.

A Taste for Gimmicry

As sterilization became an "edge-of-life" issue in the midst of the U.S. culture war, outrage over sterilization as a form of state policy helped to topple Prime Minister Indira Gandhi's government in India. The origins of Indian interest in sterilization lay in the post–World War II years, when the country's birth control movement began to stir. Various Indian politicians and officials, bent on rapid modernization and state building after independence in 1947, viewed population growth as a threat to national prosperity, unity, security, and power. At the same time, India's political elites knew that as interest in population control climbed in industrialized countries, foreign aid for economic development would be highly dependant on India's success in reducing its birth rate.[91] In 1952, India became the first country in history to adopt an official population control program. During its first three "Five-Year Plans" (1951–1956, 1956–1961, and 1961–1966), spending on family planning increased from 3 million rupees to 250 million rupees (p. 226).[92]

When a two-year drought struck India, in 1965–1966, creating severe shortages of food, a sense of urgency swept the nation's birth control movement. By the late 1960s, various Indian jurisdictions had experimented with different contraceptive methods, including the IUD and the Pill, but, despite some local successes, demographers were as frustrated as ever. In 1970 alone the nation added 13 million to a population of

554 million.[93] Bureaucratic inertia hamstrung family planners, as did Jamaharlal Nehru's repeated appointments to the Health Ministry of followers of Mohandas K. Gandhi (who opposed artificial contraception). Altering popular attitudes toward fertility turned out to be much more difficult than many family-planning officials had imagined, especially Western aid workers. Indians tended to marry early and believe that children, notably sons, were the best form of old-age insurance. The Hindu religion stipulated that only a son could light a funeral pyre, so stories abounded of couples who kept trying to have sons despite already having large families. Throughout the country's 600,000 villages, countless families believed they could never have too many children.[94] Even though infant mortality rates were falling, a typical villager's sentiment was, "Yes, I have three children now, but will I have three children alive by the time I get old?"[95] Government planners preached that happiness was a two-child family, but couples preferred four.[96] Artificial birth control in general and sterilization in particular drew the ire of prominent figures such as Mother Teresa, the famed nun who worked in the slums of Calcutta helping the destitute and dying.[97] Little wonder that, as one U.S. headline proclaimed in 1968, "Family planning doesn't catch on in India."[98]

At this critical juncture in the history of India's struggle to cut population growth, Sripati Chandrasekhar became Minister of Health and Family Planning under Indira Gandhi. Prior to Chandrasekhar's 1967 elevation to Gandhi's cabinet, various state governments had launched incentive schemes designed to entice Indians to choose sterilization, but officials tended to believe that the total of 3 million operations since 1956 was too small to make much of a dent in the nation's population.[99] Chandrasekhar's appointment was a forceful message to the world that India was preparing to boost that total dramatically. He succeeded Sushila Nayar, who had told the press, "I am not crazy about sterilization" and who urged Indians to follow Mohandas K. Gandhi's advice to practice abstinence or the rhythm method.[100] By contrast, Chandrasekhar arguably was the most outspoken advocate of contraceptive sterilization in the world. Throughout the 1960s, he had been preaching the virtues of vasectomy, calling it the "salvation" of India. He preferred vasectomy to tubal ligation because it was a simpler and less expensive procedure. Linking vasectomy to women's liberation, he praised it as the best way to "pry" India's women "away from their role as breeders." Overall, Chandrasekhar believed mass sterilization was the most effective method for solving India's population woes.[101]

Chandrasekhar benefited from Indira Gandhi's own conviction that drastic steps had to be taken to relieve population pressure on India. Gandhi, who became prime minister in 1966, was not content to wait for industrialization and modernization to reduce fertility rates and thus launched over the next three years "the largest and most vigorous government-sponsored family-planning program in the world." Yet initially she made Chandrasekhar answerable to the Minister of Finance, which restricted Chandrasekhar's ability to put his ideas into practice. His lack of social skills worried her. As an acquaintance reported, Chandrasekhar was "so sure of himself and so carried away by his ideas that he doesn't listen much to other people. . . . Frankly, he doesn't have much tact, and in a touchy program like [family planning], tact is vital." Indeed, Chandrasekhar had barely entered the cabinet before he was in trouble with India's Parliament, having offended Muslims by saying it was all right for them to eat pork and antagonized the Left due to his long and close association with the United States.[100] Later, in 1967, he found himself in hot water again after he denounced traditional Hindu, Muslim, and Roman Catholic teaching on abstinence and revealed that he himself had had a vasectomy after the birth of his third child. Equally unsettling was what one of his aides told the press: "To succeed [at population control] we must catch 45 million men, take them to the nearest hospital and sterilize them. And catch them as fast as we can."[102] Chandrasekhar denied that compulsory sterilization was imminent, but he did state that the first priority of India's family planning agencies was to boost the sterilization rate among slum-dwellers, the rural poor, and low-income groups in general. The implication was that if that did not work, more drastic measures were in store.[103]

Chandrasekhar's lack of "tact" jeopardized his relations with Prime Minister Gandhi. She chastised him for his 1967 interview with *U.S. News and World Report*, in which he accused a succession of Indian ministers of "wast[ing]" many years experimenting with the rhythm method and various contraceptive jellies when they could have been promoting sterilization.[104] Gandhi, afraid of offending India's Catholic minority, similarly berated Chandrasekhar for publicly disagreeing with Catholic doctrine after his audience with Pope Paul VI in 1968.[105] In 1969, she expressed her displeasure over his taste for "gimmicry," referring to publicity stunts such as handing out condoms to newly married couples that "[took] away from the seriousness of our program. It is better to go slow in initiating any move which might cause irritation or invite ridicule," she admonished him.[106] Gandhi, like many Indian politicians, feared the political fallout from being identified publicly as a proponent of family planning.[107] Chandrasekhar, however, defied this political wisdom, and, to no one's surprise and few Indians' dismay, he lost his seat in 1970 and stepped down as a government minister.

Emergency Measures

Chandrasekhar's 1970 departure from government did not silence him. In fact, now that he was a private citizen, Gandhi likely welcomed his continued alarmist statements about India's population, because they justified the increasingly coercive nature of the Indian sterilization program in the early 1970s, especially the spread of the "camp" technique of sterilization (p. 231).[92] Mass sterilization camps dated back to the 1960s in regions such as Maharashtra and Gujerat, thanks chiefly to Chandrasekhar's personal support for using monetary and other rewards to gather large groups of men in one place and perform vasectomies in assembly-line fashion. In the early 1970s, mass vasectomy camps multiplied. Held either in the countryside or in specific towns, and often funded by the U.S. Agency for International Development (USAID), such camps were dubbed family-planning "festivals." Patients and their families, who came from miles around for the ten-minute operation, were entertained by singers and musicians amid tents festooned by colorful banners proclaiming the virtues of family planning. An electric scoreboard flashed out the rising total of vasectomies. The big advantage of a vasectomy camp was that it enabled surgeons to perform large numbers of sterilizations at one time. At a single camp in Ernakulam, a district of Kerala State, 62,913 men were sterilized in a single month in 1971, a "world record in vasectomies performed for a given population group in a given length of time," a Kerala official bragged. The humanitarian group CARE, with funds from USAID, supplied "acceptors" of sterilization with gift kits containing cash, rice, and a saree.[108] An impressed Ford Foundation onlooker observed, "[T]his proves India can do it."[109]

The mass-vasectomy-camp approach faltered in 1973–1974, due not to flagging interest in the policy but to budgetary shortfalls that curtailed the supply of rewards (p. 398).[110] Thus, by 1975 the stage was set for the most notorious sterilization experiment in history, overshadowing anything accomplished anywhere in the name of eugenics. By then, Indian state governments were in the habit of setting sterilization "targets" in the hundreds of thousands, which pressured health officials to dispatch agents or "motivators" into the streets to talk desperately poor urban dwellers into a vasectomy for small cash payments. In practice, this incentive system was little more than a program of bribes offered to desperately poor people without proper information about the nature of the operation. Under such conditions, individual "choice" and informed consent were negligible (p. 395).[110]

Moreover, disturbing reports began surfacing in the media about the sterilization of numerous unmarried teenagers, old men, and members of India's "untouchable" class. In their haste to fulfill their quotas, "motivators" rarely worried whether or not their "acceptors" were capable of impregnating women. All too often, motivators and doctors shared the bulk of the payment, leaving the victims with a pittance.[111] In some localities, sloppy operations had resulted in infections that led to death.[107]

These tales of sterilization took on a powerful veracity when, in July, 1975, Gandhi announced a state of emergency throughout the country. By then India's birth rate was thirty-five per 1,000, far short of the twenty-five that policymakers had hoped it would reach by the mid-1970s. Despite India's having the world's ninth largest industrial economy and being self-sufficient in food production, the country's masses were still mired in appalling poverty and poor health. To Gandhi and many others, the lesson was clear: overpopulation was the root cause of poverty and misery, and mass birth control was the surest way to strike at this cause. "We must now act decisively," she announced in January, 1976, "and bring down the birth rate speedily to prevent the doubling of our population in a mere 28 years. We shall not hesitate to take steps which might be described as drastic."[112]

By "drastic steps," Indira Gandhi had in mind forced sterilization, though the politician in her had doubts about its acceptance by Indians. Her son Sanjay, however, was "all for it," as was Dr. Datta Pai, Bombay's Director of Family Planning. Pai, who, like Chandrasekhar, was a fervent advocate of sterilization, dubbed population growth "people pollution" and, when asked by the media about the government's rounding up childless youths, old men, and men who had already been vasectomized, remarked that "if some excesses [due to forced sterilizations] appear, don't blame me." To him, India was at "war" against population, so "there could be a certain amount of misfiring out of enthusiasm." As Pai admitted, "[T]here has been pressure to show results."[113] Chandrasekhar also lent his voice to the mounting calls for "drastic steps" when, in March, 1976, he declared that it was "time for compulsory sterilization" in India.[114]

Pai, Chandrasekhar, and Sanjay Gandhi may have believed that "enthusiasm" was the reason for abuses, but the more likely factor was the government's elaborate system of incentives and disincentives, all of which constituted a powerful campaign designed to pressure couples to flock to clinics, hospitals, or "camps" for sterilization. "We educate and educate the masses, and we make it worthwhile to them," Pai defiantly told a U.S. reporter, "that's why they come [to get sterilized]." The Indian press, strictly controlled after the national emergency went into effect in June, 1975, published stories advertising the rewards for sterilization, titled "Medical Benefits for Three Kids Only" or "Cut in Jail Term for Sterilization."[115] When districts fell behind in meeting their sterilization quotas, poor urban men of all ages were rounded up by the police and transported to vasectomy camps on the outskirts of India's cities, where they were sterilized. The result was nothing less than a nation mobilized for a "war" on population, in Pai's words. When resistance to sterilization in the form of rioting took place in various localities, resulting in bloodshed and deaths when police intervened, even Prime Minister Gandhi admitted to the Indian Parliament that the violence had caused some fatalities (though she tended to blame troublemakers opposed to her rule, not law enforcement officials).[116]

The riots over Gandhi's sterilization policy were just the tip of the iceberg, because when she and her Congress Party followers were voted out of office, in March, 1977, a major source of voter discontent was widespread displeasure over the government's family-planning programs.[117] Her successor, Morarji Desai, was a self-proclaimed disciple of Mahatma Gandhi's theory of self-control or abstinence as a method of birth control. International and homegrown criticism of Mrs. Gandhi's sterilization policy was fierce, yet the reaction of the international family-planning movement was muted. While few analysts denied that abuses had occurred, the consensus among population experts was that they were the unavoidable consequences of well-intentioned policymakers "pressing the panic button . . . a tragic mistake" for a government trying to solve a problem of enormous dimensions and great urgency. To the birth control establishment, injustices committed in the name of population control were "unnecessary" mistakes to be corrected by better planning and monitoring. According to Pai, the vast majority of sterilizations between 1975 and 1977 in fact had been welcomed by patients.

Despite the political price Gandhi's government paid because of the sterilization program, faith in voluntary sterilization never wavered. By the end of 1979, India's family-planning program, with sterilization as its centerpiece, appeared to be recovering from a near-death experience. In 1981, the newly reelected Indira Gandhi announced that the central government would be spending $1.15 billion on family planning over the next four years.[118] By the early 1980s, incentives in the form of payments and central government bonuses to individual states for meeting sterilization "targets" were back in use, as was a plan (similar to China's) to issue green cards to couples who accepted sterilization after two children, entitling them to priority treatment in health facilities and preferential treatment with regard to jobs and housing.[119]

Still, the timing of India's sterilization scandal could not have been worse for AVS, as it left the impression that the organization was an "uncritical pusher" of coercive sterilization. Under attack from groups on both the right and left of the political spectrum over the new HEW guidelines, sterilization advocates pledged to "work doubly hard to stress the difference between voluntary and coercive sterilization" and to deny any connections to the Indian imbroglio. Some proponents began urging AVS to "get away from the word sterilization" altogether. Forecasting trends that would gather momentum in the 1990s, they instead pushed the group to emphasize the broad "health concerns" linked to family planning, rather than its potential dividends for population control.[120] Yet the damage was done. As a tumultuous decade for the sterilization movement came to a close, more and more events indicated that it had reached yet another watershed in its young history.

Still Number One

Despite the attacks on the sterilization movement in the late 1970s, rays of hope glimmered on the horizon. As government and the courts in the United States imposed strict guidelines on sterilization domestically, overseas access to sterilization was widening swiftly. The Indira Gandhi experiment in mass sterilization may have generated negative publicity for international family planning, but it had not seriously slowed the trend of the late 1970s toward greater acceptance of sterilization in many developing countries. Indeed, as the 1980s dawned, more and more Third World countries were engaged in efforts to use sterilization as a method of population control. Domestically, the topic of sterilization had emerged from the shadows and had cropped up on countless radio and TV shows. The ability of the movement to achieve U.S. welfare reform, environmental conservation, and population control through the popularizing of sterilization may have tapered off, but the enormous potential for such work in developing countries more than made up for these shortfalls. When it came to sterilization, the most popular form of contraception on the planet, AVS was "Number One around the world," the group's executive director proudly declared in 1980.[121]

Thus, had John Rague been alive at the end of the twentieth century, he would hardly have believed his eyes and ears. Back on the first Earth Day in 1970, he had stood shivering on a Manhattan street corner, handing out "Stop at Two" buttons. Could even he have predicted then that within a few short years, a contraceptive revolution the likes of which had never been seen before in human history would have begun to sweep the world, with sterilization playing a leading role? Following in the footsteps of Marian Olden, Clarence Gamble, Margaret Sanger, H. Curtis Wood, Ruth Proskauer Smith, Alan Guttmacher, Sripati Chandrasekhar, and Hugh Moore, by the 1970s, Rague and the AVS had managed to convince the world that sterilization was the best method of family planning and population control. Their prescriptions for expanding women's reproductive rights, alleviating poverty, launching a sexual revolution, defusing the "population bomb," and saving the environment were not only heeded but adopted by lawmakers the world over, to say nothing of key opinion makers such as Bill McKibben. Yet their successes came with a stiff price, causing anxious policy experts in the twenty-first century to ask, "Where have all the babies gone?"

Notes

1. Robert EL. Vasectomy responses. *Family Planning Perspectives.* 1973;5:5–6.
2. Contraceptive sterilization approved by two-thirds of adult Americans, recent Gallup Poll shows. *Family Planning Perspectives.* 1979;11:314–315.
3. H. Curtis Wood, "Voluntary Sterilization: Yesterday, Today and Tomorrow," April 26, 1973, AVS, Box 110, 1972 Board Minutes folder.
4. "Vasectomy after the vogue." *Newsweek.* October 21, 1974.
5. Rogers WC. Beating the drum for vasectomy. *Family Planning Perspectives.* 1972;4:56.
6. Wolfers D, Wolfers H. Comment and controversy: Vasectomania. *Family Planning Perspectives.* 1973;5:196–199. For the letters of H. Curtis Wood and Betty Gonzales of AVS and the Wolfers' reply, see "Letters from readers." *Family Planning Perspectives.* 1974;6:3–5.
7. Johnson JH. Vasectomy: An international appraisal. *Family Planning Perspectives.* 1983;15:47.

8. In the words of *New York Times* columnist James Reston, "the male animal" in Latin America was "worse than the baboon and worships at the cult of virility." The "ignorant male in Latin America" was convinced he is a "dud unless he produces as many children as Bobby Kennedy." Reston J. Santiago: The cult of virility in Latin America. *New York Times*, April 9, 1967.

9. Nag M. Attitudes to vasectomy in West Bengal. *Population Review*. 1966; 10:61–64.

10. Davis JE. Vasectomy: Reversibility and frozen sperm banks. In Lader L (ed.), *Foolproof Birth Control: Male and Female Sterilization*. Boston: Beacon Press, 1972, p. 197.

11. "New birth control device may aid solution of world population explosion with reversible sterilization method: 'Jhaver Clip,' invented by Indian surgeon, may rival 'Loop' and 'Pill.' " AVS press release, September 30, 1968.

12. Daniels CR, Golden J. Procreative compounds: Popular eugenics, artificial insemination and the rise of the American sperm banking industry. *Journal of Social History*. 2004;38:5–27. See also Stern AM. *Eugenic Nation: Faults and Frontiers of Better Breeding in Modern America*. Berkeley and Los Angeles: University of California Press, 2005, p. 214.

13. "AVS fact sheet on sperm banks." AVS *News*, Spring 1972, p. 5.

14. "Contraceptive tubal sterilization rate increases more than twice during the period 1970–1976." *Family Planning Perspectives*. 1979;11:253–255.

15. "1.3 million sterilizations in 1974; rise of 43% over 1973." *Family Planning Perspectives*. 1975;7:274.

16. Wulf D. Female sterilization: A centennial conference. *Family Planning Perspectives*. 1981;13:24.

17. Westoff C, Jones EF. Contraception and sterilization in the United States, 1965–1975. *Family Planning Perspectives*. 1977;9:153–157.

18. GS to Evelyn Bryant, October 6, 1974, AVS, Box 112, 1974 Case Correspondence folder.

19. Julia Karet to Evelyn Bryant, February 23, 1976, AVS, Box 112, 1974 Agencies Correspondence folder.

20. PW to Evelyn Bryant, July 11, 1974, AVS, Box 112, 1974 Case Correspondence folder. Her emphasis.

21. MP to Evelyn Bryant, April 23, September 30, 1974, AVS, Box 112, 1974 Case Correspondence folder.

22. CS to Evelyn Bryant, July 19, 1974, AVS, Box 3, 1974 Case Correspondence folder.

23. "Decline of vasectomy." *Washington Post*, July 5, 1973. See also "Simple sterilization." *Newsweek*, October 8, 1973. Results of several studies among monkeys appeared in the 1970s linking vasectomy and heart and cardiovascular system diseases. Though later researchers failed to confirm such links, the immediate impact was to discourage men from having the surgery.

24. Brody JE. Sterilization: For women an easier way. *New York Times*, March 24, 1976.

25. Patterson JT. *America in the Twentieth Century: A History.* Fort Worth: Harcourt, Brace, 1989, pp. 359–361, 483.
26. SM to Evelyn Bryant, January 30, May 12, 1974, AVS, Box 112, 1974 Case Correspondence folder.
27. JEB to Evelyn Bryant, April 8, 1976, AVS, Box 112, 1976 Case Correspondence folder.
28. NM to Evelyn Bryant, September 28, 1975; SM to Evelyn Bryant, June 9, 1976; GS to Evelyn Bryant, December 8, 1974, AVS, Box 112, 1974 Case Correspondence folder.
29. Evelyn Bryant to EW, April 27, 1976, AVS, Box 112, 1976 Case Correspondence folder.
30. CR to Evelyn Bryant, June 16, 1976, AVS, Box 112, 1976 Case Correspondence folder.
31. SW to Evelyn Bryant, November 12, 1974, AVS, Box 112, 1974 Case Correspondence folder.
32. "Sterilization rates rose most for women 15–24 between 1976 and 1978." *Family Planning Perspectives.* 1981;13:236; Association for Voluntary Sterilization, *News,* January 1982.
33. Mackay AP, Kieke BA Jr, Koonin LM, Beattie K. Tubal sterilization in the United States, 1994–1996. *Family Planning Perspectives.* 2001;33:161–165.
34. "Predict more than two in ten young U.S. women will remain childless." *Family Planning Perspectives.* 1981;13:184.
35. Godecker AL, Thomson E, Bumpass LL. Union status, marital history and female contraceptive sterilization in the United States. *Family Planning Perspectives.* 2001;33:35–41.
36. D'Esopo DA. Hysterectomy when the uterus is grossly normal. *American Journal of Obstetrics and Gynecology.* 1962;83:113–122.
37. Hibbard LT. Sexual sterilization by elective hysterectomy. *American Journal of Obstetrics and Gynecology.* 1972;112:1076–1083.
38. "How come all those hysterectomies?" *Medical World News,* June 11, 1971.
39. Bunker JP. Elective hysterectomy: Pro and con. *New England Journal of Medicine.* 1976;295:264–268.
40. Miller NF. Hysterectomy: Therapeutic necessity or surgical racket. *American Journal of Obstetrics and Gynecology.* 1946;51:808.
41. Wright RC. Hysterectomy: Past, present, and future. *Obstetrics and Gynecology.* 1969;33:562.
42. Konner M. *Becoming a Doctor: A Journey of Initiation in Medical School.* New York: Viking, 1987, p. 103.
43. Young PD. A surfeit of surgery. *Washington Post,* May 30, 1976. Cited in Littlewood TB. *The Politics of Population Control.* Notre Dame and London: University of Notre Dame Press, 1977, p. 126.
44. Roos NP. Hysterectomies in one Canadian province: A new look at risks and benefits. *American Journal of Public Health.* 1984;74:44.

45. Larned D. The epidemic in unnecessary hysterectomy. In Dreifus C (ed.), *Seizing Our Bodies: The Politics of Women's Health*. New York: Random, 1977, p. 197.
46. Langer A, Pelosi M, Hung CT, Devanesan M, Cetrini H, Harrigan JT. Comparison of sterilization by tubal ligation and hysterectomy. *Surgery, Gynecology, and Obstetrics*. 1975;140:235–238.
47. Inlander CB, Levin LS, Weiner E. *Medicine On Trial: The Appalling Story of Medical Ineptitude and the Arrogance That Overlooks It*. New York: Pantheon, 1988, p. 113.
48. Starr P. *The Social Transformation of American Medicine*. New York: Basic, 1982, p. 391–392.
49. Parrott MH. Elective hysterectomy: Discussion. *American Journal of Obstetrics and Gynecology*. 1972;113:533.
50. Starr P. *The Social Transformation of American Medicine*. New York: Basic, 1982, p. 379. See also Burnham JC. American medicine's Golden Age: What happened to it? *Science*. 1982;215:1474–1479.
51. Farquhar CM, Steiner CA. Hysterectomy rates in the United States, 1990–1997. *Obstetrics and Gynecology*. 2002;99:229–234.
52. Bickell NA, Earp JA, Garrett JM, Evans AT. Gynecologists' sex, clinical beliefs, and hysterectomy rates. *American Journal of Public Health*. 1994;84:1649–1652; Carlson KJ, Nichols DH, Schiff I. Indications for hysterectomy. *New England Journal of Medicine*. 1993;328:856–860.
53. Wilcox LS, Koonin LM, Pokras R, Strauss LT, Xia Z, Peterson HB. Hysterectomy in the United States, 1988–1990. *Obstetrics and Gynecology*. 1994;83:554.
54. Kjerulff K, Langenberg P, Guzinski G. The socioeconomic correlates of hysterectomies in the United States. *American Journal of Public Health*. 1993;83:106–108.
55. "Survey finds seven in ten hospitals violate DHEW guidelines on informed consent for sterilization." *Family Planning Perspectives*. 1979;11:366–367. See also "AVS survey reveals clinic vasectomy requirements." *Family Planning Perspectives*. 1976;8:29–30.
56. Philip Reilly, telephone interview with J. J. Levin Jr., Washington DC, January 22, 1983. Reilly PR. *The Surgical Solution: A History of Involuntary Sterilization in the United States*. Baltimore and London: The Johns Hopkins University Press, 1991, pp. 151, 182.
57. "Sterilization in Alabama." *New York Times*, July 12, 1973; Trombley S. *The Right to Reproduce: A History of Coercive Sterilization*. London: Weidenfeld and Nicholson, 1988, pp. 181–184.
58. "Sterilized: Why?" *Time*, July 23, 1973, p. 50.
59. "Clinic defends sterilization of two girls, 12 and 14." *New York Times*, June 28, 1973; "Official links drug ban to two girls' sterilization." *Philadelphia Evening Bulletin*, June 28, 1973.

60. "Bad show on sterilization." *Washington Star News,* July 19, 1973. For more on the ambivalent attitude of minority women toward sterilization and other forms of birth control, see Schoen J. *Choice and Coercion: Birth Control, Sterilization and Abortion in Public Health and Welfare.* Chapel Hill: University of North Carolina Press, 2005.

61. Littlewood TB. *The Politics of Population Control.* Notre Dame and London: University of Notre Dame Press, 1977, pp. 107–132.

62. "A well-meaning act," *Newsweek,* July 16, 1973, p. 26. See also "Sterilization consent not given." *New York Times,* July 11, 1973.

63. Fields C. Blacks major victims of medical experiments. *Boston Globe,* July 17, 1973.

64. Jones JH. *Bad Blood: The Tuskegee Syphilis Experiment.* New York: Free Press, 1993. See also Brandt A. Racism and research: The case of the Tuskegee syphilis study. *Hastings Center Report.* 1978;8:21–29.

65. "A well-meaning act." *Newsweek,* July 16, 1973, p. 26. Georgia State Representative Julian Bond also drew a connection between the Alabama sterilizations and Nazi atrocities. "Sterilizing the poor: Exploring motives and methods." *New York Times,* July 8, 1973.

66. AVS. "Joint Statement Against Forced Sterilization." June 18, 1973.

67. George E. Immerwahr to C. T. Faneuff, August 4, 1973, AVS, Box 43, "Opposition to AVS Policy" folder.

68. Littlewood TB. *The Politics of Population Control.* Notre Dame and London: University of Notre Dame Press, 1977, pp. 109, 128. See also Stern AM. *Eugenic Nation: Faults and Frontiers of Better Breeding in Modern America.* Berkeley and Los Angeles: University of California Press, 2005, p. 202; Franks A. *Margaret Sanger's Eugenic Legacy: The Control of Female Fertility.* Jefferson, NC: McFarland and Co., 2005, pp. 185–186.

69. Stern AM. *Eugenic Nation: Faults and Frontiers of Better Breeding in Modern America.* Berkeley and Los Angeles: University of California Press, 2005, pp. 200, 204–209.

70. Health Research Group. *A Health Research Group Study on Surgical Sterilization: Present Abuses and Proposed Regulations.* Washington, DC: Health Research Group, 1973, p. 7. Quoted in Stern AM. *Eugenic Nation: Faults and Frontiers of Better Breeding in Modern America.* Berkeley and Los Angeles: University of California Press, 2005, p. 204.

71. Gallagher NL. *Breeding Better Vermonters: The Eugenics Project in the Green Mountain State.* Burlington: University Press of New England, 1999; see also Barry E. With unease, Vermont remembers a campaign against "degenerates." *Milwaukee Journal Sentinel,* August 15, 1999.

72. Franks A. *Margaret Sanger's Eugenic Legacy: The Control of Female Fertility.* Jefferson, NC: McFarland and Co., 2005, p. 167; Shapiro T. *Population Control Politics: Women, Sterilization, and Reproductive Choice.* Philadelphia: Temple University Press, 1985, pp. 6, 91–92.

73. Newman L. Helen Rodriguez-Trias. *British Medical Journal.* 2002;324:242.

74. Shapiro T. *Population Control Politics: Women, Sterilization, and Reproductive Choice.* Philadelphia: Temple University Press, 1985, p. 54.

75. "Survey finds seven in 10 hospitals violate DHEW guidelines on informed consent for sterilization." *Family Planning Perspectives.* 1979;11:366–367.

76. Shapiro T. *Population Control Politics: Women, Sterilization, and Reproductive Choice.* Philadelphia: Temple University Press, 1985, pp. 139–140; Trombley S. *The Right to Reproduce: A History of Coercive Sterilization.* London: Weidenfeld and Nicholson, 1988, pp. 185–187.

77. "New regulations governing DHEW sterilization funding now in effect; stress informed consent." *Family Planning Perspectives.* 1979;11:46–47; Reilly PR. *The Surgical Solution: A History of Involuntary Sterilization in the United States.* Baltimore and London: The Johns Hopkins Press, 1991, p. 152.

78. Shapiro T. *Population Control Politics: Women, Sterilization, and Reproductive Choice.* Philadelphia: Temple University Press, 1985, pp. 137, 165; Trombley S. *The Right to Reproduce: A History of Coercive Sterilization.* London: Weidenfeld and Nicholson, 1988, p. 186.

79. Radford JP. Sterilization versus segregation: Control of the "feeble-minded," 1900–1938. *Social Science and Medicine.* 1991;33:449–458.

80. Bass MS. Surgical contraception: A key to normalization and prevention. *Mental Retardation.* 1978;16:399–404.

81. Medora S. Bass to Jeannie Rosoff, August 17, 1973, AHC, MSB Box 3, 1973 correspondence folder.

82. Medora Bass to Rachel Levine, August 12, 1964, AHC, MSB Box 2, 1964 correspondence folder.

83. Whitcraft CJ, Jones JP. A survey of attitudes about sterilization of retardates. *Mental Retardation.* 1974;12:30–33; Reilly PR. *The Surgical Solution: A History of Involuntary Sterilization in the United States.* Baltimore and London: The Johns Hopkins University Press, 1991, pp. 152–57, 161.

84. Minutes of the AVS April 19, 1978, meeting, AVS, Box 110, 1978 Board Minutes folder; Shapiro T. *Population Control Politics: Women, Sterilization, and Reproductive Choice.* Philadelphia: Temple University Press, 1985, p. 157.

85. "Forces against abortion assemble, with optimism." *New York Times,* June 2, 1974.

86. Critchlow DT. *Intended Consequences: Birth Control, Abortion and the Federal Government in Modern America.* New York and Oxford: Oxford University Press, 1999, p. 197; "Abortion under attack." *Newsweek,* June 5, 1978, pp. 36–43.

87. Report of Ira Lubell, AVS executive director, April 16, 1980, AVS, Box 110, 1980 Reports folder.

88. Cassidy K. The right to life movement. In Critchlow DT (ed.), *The Politics of Abortion and Birth Control in Historical Perspective.* University Park: Pennsylvania State University Press, 1996, pp. 128–59; Critchlow DT. *Intended Consequences: Birth Control, Abortion and the Federal Government in Modern America.* New York and Oxford: Oxford University Press, 1999, pp. 202, 208–210.

89. Hunter JD. *Culture Wars: The Struggle to Define America.* New York: Basic, 1991.

90. Hunter JD, Davis JE. Cultural politics at the edge of life. In Critchlow DT (ed.), *The Politics of Abortion and Birth Control in Historical Perspective.* University Park: Pennsylvania State University Press, 1996, p. 106.

91. Chandrasekhar S. How India is tackling her population problem. *Foreign Affairs.* 1968;47:138–150; Edward Pohlman, Central Family Planning Institute, "Large Incentives For 'Group Vasectomies' After Two or Three Children," n.d., SC, Box 61, folder 23.

92. Schoen J. *Choice and Coercion: Birth Control, Sterilization and Abortion in Public Health and Welfare.* Chapel Hill: University of North Carolina Press, 2005.

93. "Population bursting: India pushing birth control." *Washington [DC] Evening Star,* May 28, 1970.

94. Kinsolving L. India trapped by Hinduism. *Staten Island Advance,* September 21, 1970; " 'Revolution' may shake India." *Honolulu Star-Bulletin and Advertiser,* July 19, 1970.

95. "Medical schools to teach family planning, sterilization gains popularity." *Current* (Bombay), September 23, 1967.

96. Ledbetter R. Thirty years of family planning in India. *Asian Survey,* 1984;24:757.

97. "Famed nun in India opposes sterilization." *Los Angeles Times,* May 19, 1974.

98. "Family planning doesn't catch on in India." *Kansas City Times,* January 16, 1968.

99. Officials with the Ford Foundation, which began to fund population control in 1959, contended that these totals were "gross underestimates of actual numbers." Moye W. Freymann to Sripati Chandrasekhar, January 4, 1965, SC, Box 16, folder 39.

100. "Foe of population: Sripati Chandrasekhar." *New York Times,* March 31, 1967.

101. "Sterilization only solution: Dr. Chandrasekhar's analysis." *Hindustan Standard,* April 6, 1962; "A daring plan to emancipate Mom." *San Francisco Chronicle,* January 25, 1965; "Biological emancipation of Indian women: The man who fights for it–Dr. Chandrasekhar." *Current* (Bombay), January 11, 1969; "India, dissatisfied with progress on birth control, plans shift of emphasis." *New York Times,* March 31, 1967.

102. "Behind India's desperate plan." *Daily Express,* July 20, 1967.

103. "Chandrasekhar denies move for compulsory sterilization." *Mail* (Madras), September 21, 1967.

104. "Too many people–Is India facing disaster?" *U.S. News and World Report,* April 3, 1967. Chandrasekhar said India used "the cafeteria approach" to family planning–that is, providing "all the methods known to us which are scientific, which are acceptable, which the women would like, because each case differs from the other."

105. "Pope reiterates birth curb stand." *New York Times,* May 27, 1967.

106. Gandhi to Chandrasekhar, July 19, 1968; Chandrasekhar to Gandhi, July 29, 1968; Gandhi to Chandrasekhar, August 2, 1968; Gandhi to Chandrasekhar, September 30, 1969; SC, Box 16, folder 42.

107. "Officials fiddle while Indians multiply." *Baltimore Sun*, April 26, 1970.

108. Krishnakumar S. Kerala's pioneering experiment in massive vasectomy camps. *Studies in Family Planning*. 1972;3:177, 180.

109. "26,000 sterilized at festival in India." *Los Angeles Times*, July 18, 1971.

110. Vicziany M. Coercion in a soft state: The family-planning program of India. Part one: The myth of voluntarism. *Pacific Affairs*, 1982;55:373–404.

111. "Sterilization: New concession to women." *Hindu* (Madras), May 1, 1967; "Four boys subjected to vasectomy." *Indian Express*, June 9, 1967; "Soulless vasectomy swindle." *Bombay Blitz*, March 9, 1968; "Forced sterilization." *New York Daily News*, February 13, 1970.

112. Ledbetter R. Thirty years of family planning in India. *Asian Survey*. 1984;24:747; "Delhi to penalize couples for not limiting births." *New York Times*, February 26, 1976, pp. 1, 7.

113. Kamm H. India state is leader in forced sterilization. *New York Times*, August 13, 1976, p. A8.

114. "Time for compulsory sterilization." *Indian Express*, March 5, 1976; "Compulsory sterilization." *Deccan Herald*, March 10, 1976.

115. Landman LC. Birth control in India: The carrot and the rod? *Family Planning Perspectives*. 1977;9:101–110.

116. Borders W. Mrs. Gandhi confirms some died in protests over sterilization drive. *New York Times*, October 28, 1976; "Birth control without compulsion." *The Times* (London), March 11, 1977; "The man who defeated Mrs. Gandhi shows distinct distaste for cabinet role." *The Times* (London), April 5, 1977.

117. "India's birth control program may be casualty of election campaign." *New York Times*, March 12, 1977; "Why a village in India voted the way it did." *New York Times*, April 6, 1977.

118. Landman LC. Birth control in India: The carrot and the rod? *Family Planning Perspectives*. 1977;9:101–110; "India's family planning program recovering slowly from setbacks—voluntarism emphasized." *Family Planning Perspectives*. 1979;5:162–163; "Indira Gandhi calls for revitalization of India's family planning program." *Family Planning Perspectives*. 1982;14:149–150.

119. Editorial: Lessons from India. *International Family Planning Perspectives*. 1983;9:1.

120. Minutes of April 20, 1977, September 21, 1977, April 16, 1980 AVS executive meetings, AVS, Box 110, 1980 Board Minutes folder.

121. Report of Ira Lubell, AVS executive director, April 16, 1980, AVS, Box 110, 1980 Reports folder.

Chapter 7

Going Global

As the 1980s dawned, the sterilization movement reached another crossroads in its ongoing struggle to alter global reproductive behavior and fertility rates. After the Association for Voluntary Sterilization (AVS) rebranded itself, in 1984, as the Association for Voluntary Surgical Contraception (AVSC), sterilization advocates for the balance of the twentieth century shifted their official focus away from population and birth control as ends in themselves to women's reproductive health in general, and gradually muted their traditional emphasis on sterilization alone in favor of a broader approach to reproductive health that included post-abortion care, maternal and child health care, HIV/AIDS services, and greater male involvement in family planning. These shifts in orientation have been reflected in AVSC's subsequent name changes, to Access to Voluntary and Safe Contraception International in 1994 and EngenderHealth in 2001. Yet, these and other changes notwithstanding, what remained constant for sterilization proponents was the belief that too many children were being born to the wrong people in the wrong places (p. 26).[1] Thus, although much had changed since the days of Marian Olden and Birthright, at the advent of the twenty-first century, the overall goal of preventing the adverse effects of uncontrolled reproduction for poverty-stricken men and women had not.

Grandiose Plans

A pivotal figure in the shift of the sterilization movement onto the global stage was psychiatrist Helen Edey (1912–1998) (see insert), mother of four children and wife of author and *Time* magazine editor Maitland A. Edey. Born in New York City, Helen Edey was the daughter of manufacturer Morris W. Kellogg. Her involvement with AVS spanned forty years and included a stint, from 1970 to 1974, as chair of the group's executive committee. She was also a generous donor to AVS, giving it $15,000 in 1973.

Few individuals left more of an imprint on the sterilization movement than Helen Edey. After obtaining a bachelor's degree from Vassar in 1934 and raising her children, Edey graduated with a medical degree from New York University in 1951. From 1957 to 1970, she practiced psychiatry and psychoanalysis in Manhattan, but her most passionate interest was sterilization as a form of family planning. While working with poverty-stricken women in New York City tenements, she reported that they would "come in and beg, you know, to have something so they wouldn't have any more children. I felt terribly bad for them." "Furious at the lack of fairness" to these women, Edey joined the Human Betterment Association of America (HBAA) in 1958.[2] Ten years later, now convinced that reducing family size would also help to solve environmental problems, she, John Rague, Larry Lader, and others at AVS promoted the "desirability of the two-child family." In 1972, she and the AVS executive committee backed "the one-child family as an American average" in order to "demonstrate America's commitment to save the planet and to save the people, Americans of all races, economic status, age range, and educational background."[3]

Edey's first major achievement in the sterilization field was her role in helping Medora Bass and others start the first vasectomy clinic at the Margaret Sanger Bureau, in 1969, where Edey did all the screening of applicants for the operation. Her second key accomplishment was to help shift the focus of AVS from "public relations" advocacy of sterilization to scientific research and public education about population. This change in organizational direction was triggered by the financial crisis facing AVS. By the early 1970s, success had proven to be a mixed blessing for the group. As the U.S. annual sterilization rate reached 1 million, as more and more Americans relied on contraception, and as barriers to legalized abortion tumbled, the sense of urgency felt by philanthropists about birth control began to dissipate, and contributions fell off significantly. Hugh

Moore's death, in 1972, robbed AVS of one of its most generous bene-factors and effective fundraisers. In America's countercultural climate of the late 1960s and early 1970s, AVS had thrived because it had faced powerful adversaries; it appeared to be the plucky "little guy" struggling for reform and social justice against entrenched interest groups such as organized medicine and the Catholic Church. Yet by the Watergate era its legal victories led AVS to be viewed as a defender of the status quo, while its new opponents—the right-to-life movement and radical minority and women's groups—represented the forces for change. By the time of Jimmy Carter's presidency, AVS was no longer part of the "radical chic" as it had been in the late 1960s; it was part of the establishment.

With AVS in this uncustomary position, Edey and others cast their gaze toward new fields of endeavor, notably the global scene. "Look, there is the rest of the world," she exhorted her AVS colleagues, "we have to start all over again." Starting all over again meant working with govern-ment and other nongovernmental organizations (NGOs) to shape global attitudes toward birth control in general and sterilization in particular. Edey wrote, "[I]t sounds grandiose, but we [at AVS] want to become the 'Population Council' of the sterilization field, not just a publicity outfit."[4]

Edey's advice that AVS become the " 'Population Council' of the ster-ilization field" was not exactly new. Back in the 1960s, AVS officials, under Hugh Moore's leadership, had laid the groundwork for an In-ternational Association for Voluntary Sterilization (IAVS). A friend of Moore's, public health expert Homer Calver (1892–1970) (see insert), led the effort to launch the IAVS. After volunteering for medical duty during World War I, Calver edited the *American Journal of Public Health* (1925–1932) and served as the American Public Health Association's executive secretary. A consultant on health education for the Office of Inter-American Affairs during World War II, Calver became a well-known environmental journalist and population control proponent. Like many public health professionals, he harbored a distrust of organized medicine, an attitude that fit the lay, activist atmosphere of the Hugh Moore years at AVS. Calver viewed population control as "the number one public health problem" and believed that the involvement of physicians such as Alan Guttmacher would slow progress due to their long-standing professional desire to define contraception as a purely medical matter.[5]

Calver's efforts convinced luminaries such as Brock Chisholm, Mar-garet Sanger, C. P. Blacker, and Sripati Chandrasekhar to serve on the board of the newly organized IAVS. The potential of sterilization to make a bigger impact than other methods of contraception was a major selling point for the IAVS. As Calver observed in 1968, vasectomy offered the only type of birth control that recognized "that men too are potential partners."[6] That same year, the United Nations declared family planning a human right, buoying spirits at AVS. The decision of the United States Agency for International Development (USAID) to begin funding population control projects, in 1965, also augured well for AVS, which received $29 million from USAID between 1972 and 1980. By 1980, USAID's $185 million contribution to population control activities had increased eighty-eight times since 1965, and it reached $250 million during the Reagan administration (Sweden and Norway ranked a distant second and third among countries whose foreign aid included assistance to population control). These totals do not count the considerable sums spent on population assistance by the Ford Foundation, the Rockefeller Foundation, and the World Bank. In 1975, for example, Ford contributed over $10 million to population programs around the world, a sum that surpassed the combined total spent by Australia, Belgium, and Japan.[7] Thus, in the 1970s, AVS, alongside other nonprofit groups such as the Population Council, the Pathfinder Fund, and International Planned Parenthood Federation (IPPF) could reasonably expect to tap federal dollars to help pay for the advice and technical assistance it sought to provide governments in developing countries.[8]

Demographic Chic

However, the effort to launch the IAVS got bogged down in the late 1960s. In 1967, the World Health Organization denied AVS NGO status, and the Brush and Rockefeller Foundations turned down AVS requests for funding. The IAVS was officially launched in 1968, but it proved to be stillborn. Third World anti-Americanism was increasingly rife, making the times inhospitable for such an ambitious undertaking. IAVS officials encountered resistance from developing countries, whose citizens often viewed its efforts as paternalistic and imperialistic.[9] As the Population Crisis Committee's Phyllis Piotrow noted in 1971, "[O]ne of the difficulties of a population policy is the lurking suspicion of ulterior motives: that one socioeconomic, ethnic, or racial group may be trying to dissuade the others from childbearing."[10] Anti-Americanism with regard to family planning peaked in 1974, designated by the United Nations as World Population Year. In August, the World Population Conference in Bucharest, Rumania, threw "a wet blanket over population control efforts," remarked a Pathfinder Fund official.[11] Many of the delegates in Bucharest from Third World countries attacked the reigning theory that the way to alleviate poverty and disease was to promote contraception. Poor countries in Asia, Africa, and Latin America followed the lead of the People's Republic of China, whose communist delegation denounced "the hegemonism of the superpowers" and advocated national autonomy as the first step toward concrete action on population matters. At the same time, a resurgence of anti-Malthusianism—dubbed "demographic chic" by one disgruntled Western social scientist—also threatened to reverse whatever gains international family-planning agencies had managed to achieve. According to the United Nations Fund for Population Activities (UNFPA), in 1974, world poverty could be cured most effectively through programs aimed at economic development and wealth distribution, not population control. "Development is the best contraceptive," a delegate to Bucharest exclaimed.[12] Despite the objection that such views created "a false dilemma—population control or development," they proved to be popular in a day and age when international faith in state-run economies still ran high and "the echo of an old argument between Malthus and Marx" could still be heard across the continents.[13] The call at Bucharest for "a new economic order" that questioned the primacy of population control policies, as one Algerian delegate noted, marked "the end of the IPPF generation" (pp. 179–183).[14]

Third World critics of Western population-control strategies were heartened by the shift in John D. Rockefeller 3rd's own thinking away from population control to an emphasis on the global health, education, and social status of women. In his keynote address to the delegates at the Bucharest conference, Rockefeller effectively repudiated Population Council policy since 1952, stating that "we of the industrialized nations should be extremely cautious in advising others how to proceed . . . [and should] become more sensitive to the fact that each nation must solve its development and fertility problems in its own way, and stand ready to assist substantially in those processes." Influenced by the feminist perspective of his associate Joan Dunlop, Rockefeller added that "any modern development program" was incomplete unless it assigned a large role to the emancipation of women and validated their influence over reproduction. Rockefeller's growing sympathy for issues such as sex education, abortion rights, and women's economic independence discouraged many of the people in the population control movement he had been working with closely since 1952. One remarked, "I've seldom been as blue" (pp. 178–180, 185).[14]

Within this shifting international climate, in 1974 AVS relaunched its international sterilization organization, consisting of nongovernmental national associations dedicated to promoting scientific and medical recognition of sterilization. The aim of stimulating demand for sterilization in "poverty pockets" around the world remained the same, but in the meantime AVS had learned some hard lessons about tactics. "We can not come in with the answer but have to be asked to help," its executive director admitted in 1974, and the best way to ensure that such requests were forthcoming was to found "sister organizations" in other countries under a single international umbrella group, thereby paving the way for official NGO status from the World Health Organization (WHO).[15] The IAVS was renamed the World Federation of Associations for Voluntary Sterilization (WFAVS), and its first international conference was held in June, 1974, in Washington, D.C., where sixteen countries, including South Korea, Bangladesh, Colombia, Indonesia, Pakistan, and Thailand, produced a draft statement in favor of voluntary sterilization. At the third international WFAVS meeting, in Tunis, Tunisia, in February, 1976, sixty-six nations sent delegates, including three ministers of health. The year before, in Geneva, Switzerland, the emphasis had been on the technical side of sterilization, but at Tunis the delegates agreed on the need to promote the expansion of voluntary sterilization by "fostering international coordination and cooperation between the various governments and groups involved in the sterilization field."[16] Thus, by the late 1970s, the sterilization movement, having sunk roots in numerous developing countries, stood poised to sweep the world.

The Lovely Swan

By the time the WFAVS was up and running, the sterilization movement had gained a key convert and spokesman in Reimert T. Ravenholt, director of USAID's Office of Population between 1966 and 1979. Born in 1925 in Milltown, Wisconsin, Ravenholt grew up during the Depression in a family of ten children, struggling to make ends meet. At six feet three inches tall and over 200 pounds, he was a physically intimidating individual with few social skills—"not a company man," in the words of a colleague. Sometimes Ravenholt went so far as to engage in fistfights and shoving matches when others disagreed with him, notably over population control. A more pugnacious version of Sripati Chandrasekhar, Ravenholt, like Margaret Sanger, thrived in adversarial situations. A former official at USAID claimed that "if there wasn't something to fight about, sometimes he made up something. He'd beat people just to see the cut of their jib, to see how they'd react."[17]

Ravenholt's professional career began when, after graduating with a medical degree from the University of Minnesota in 1952, he plunged into the field of public health, highlighting the dangers of smoking at a time when most Americans worried less about chronic illnesses and more about infectious diseases such as polio, influenza, and diphtheria. Before his career move to USAID in 1965, he "had never thought about population per se," but once acquainted with the topic he embraced with his typical gusto the view that "population growth was one of the great issues of our time" (p. 100).[1] From his bully pulpit at USAID's Office of Population, Ravenholt, over the next fifteen years, preached the virtues of family planning to a world whose inhabitants, for the most part, were initially cool to his message. Yet the world increasingly listened: when he joined USAID in 1966, the global fertility rate was almost five children per woman; by the end of the twentieth century, it had dropped to three, thanks in part to his tireless efforts to get people to practice birth control.

In the 1960s, Ravenholt, like most international family-planning advocates, tended to favor the Pill and IUD for use in developing countries.[18] Yet by the end of the decade, Ravenholt, like Alan Guttmacher, was beginning to believe that rapid population growth had created an emergency situation in the Third World and that sterilization might be the best method for reducing family size, at least in the short term. Sometime in the early 1970s, his doubts about sterilization melted away, so it was no coincidence that, in 1972, USAID began funding AVS.[19] In 1974, Ravenholt received the Hugh Moore Award, a sign that his views on sterilization were becoming more sympathetic.[20] Ravenholt was also growing less and less patient with voluntary birth control. In 1976, as reports circulated in the media that the Indian government was considering compulsory sterilization measures, Ravenholt rejected "coercion," but in the next breath he urged 15 million sterilizations in India over the next five years to relieve the average peasant's "overdose of coercion from the exigencies of a harsh nature."[21] Without mass sterilization, he seemed to be saying, coercive birth control was inevitable in either natural or man-made forms. As guest speaker at AVS's annual meeting in 1976, he praised the group's work and noted that with 65 million couples around the world already depending on sterilization, eventually a quarter of all couples in the developing world would do the same. When he announced the need for four hundred sterilization training centers and

10,000 service clinics for Asia, Africa, and Latin America, his AVS audience applauded warmly.[22]

Once converted, Ravenholt became a vigorous defender of sterilization, telling the *St. Louis Post-Dispatch* in 1977 that the United States should pay for the sterilization of a quarter of all fertile women worldwide.[23] Two years later, at the Fourth International Conference on Voluntary Sterilization in Seoul, South Korea, with roughly five hundred social scientists, government officials, and family-planning and public health professionals in attendance, Ravenholt estimated that, internationally, 90 million couples of reproductive age had already been sterilized, and he predicted that this rate would go much higher in the coming years due to "worldwide demand for reduced child-bearing." These numbers had been possible thanks to USAID's spending $100 million for sterilization services, research, equipment, and training, including the purchase in 1978 of 1,000 simplified laparoscopes (p. 247).[24] According to Ravenholt, sterilization, once the "ugly duckling" of contraceptive methods, had become the " 'lovely swan' of the seventies" (pp. 241–247).[24]

Ravenholt's increasing outspokenness about sterilization, combined with his legendary abrasiveness and impatience, led to his departure from USAID in 1979. Accused of ethnocentrism, insensitivity toward individual rights—notably those of women—and an in-your-face form of showmanship (his business cards were printed on condoms), Ravenholt was a public-relations liability in an era when ever intensifying media coverage pounced on outbursts such as those he seemed incapable of stifling. Despite his talk of widespread "demand" for sterilization, Ravenholt tended to emphasize the supply side of population control: he thought flooding countries with contraceptives—what he called his "heavy artillery"—was the best first step in the battle against population.[25]

However, a new era in reproductive politics was dawning, first characterized by a Congress that in 1977 denied federal funding for abortions (except in cases of rape or incest or when the life of the mother was endangered) and (after 1980) a White House that openly courted the votes of the right-to-life movement and the "Moral Majority." Already under attack from leftist critics who complained that it was an arm of Western imperialism and paid far too little attention to women's health issues, the population control movement was dismayed to learn, at the 1984 United Nations–sponsored population conference, in Mexico City, that socially conservative supporters of the Reagan administration enjoyed considerable political leverage on Capitol Hill. Informed by the pronatalist theories of the University of Maryland economist Julian

Simon, the U.S. position in Mexico City echoed the declaration of the Bucharest conference ten years earlier (without, of course, its anti-Americanism).[26] So observers would get the message loud and clear, the official U.S. statement was presented by conservative James Buckley, former senator of New York, former undersecretary of state, and brother of William F. Buckley, editor of the right-leaning *National Review*.[27] According to the American delegation, population growth was "a neutral phenomenon" and could best be addressed through the spread of capitalist development and science and technology, not state-run economic and social policies. If John D. Rockefeller 3rd's speeches in the 1970s had stunned population control advocates, the events at Mexico City confirmed that the consensus that had held the movement together for three decades might be unraveling.[28]

The signals emitted by the U.S. delegation in Mexico City paved the way for Reagan administration funding cuts to USAID population programs. The White House had been contemplating such cuts since 1981, but furious lobbying by interest groups such as AVS and Congressional opposition maintained funding at consistent levels. Nonetheless, in 1984, IPPF was defunded due to its support of abortion. More ominously for AVS (by now AVSC), UNFPA was defunded in 1986 because of its involvement in the People's Republic of China's family-planning program.[29] In 1978, the Chinese government, home to one-quarter of the world's people and faced with a birth rate of six children per woman, jettisoned the orthodox Marxist theory that science and technology could provide enough food, commodities, services, and resources to support increases in population. Instead, the government instituted a policy designed to restrict couples to a single child. Because it exercised totalitarian control over the country, the communist leadership applied systematic pressure on China's families, penalizing couples with loss of jobs and housing if they had more than one child. Pregnant women who broke the one-child law sometimes were involuntarily sterilized or forced to abort their fetuses.[30]

Press accounts of China's use of forced sterilization to solve its population problems coincided with media accounts of the victims of (then defunct) U.S. state sterilization laws, notably in Virginia and California. Critics alleged that the old eugenics movement had survived, and revived, in organizations such as AVS and the Pathfinder Fund, thanks to millions of dollars in USAID funding.[31] Reporters pointed to the role of AVS in spearheading the mounting use of sterilization as a population control method in developing countries.[32] With these stories circulating on

Capitol Hill, a chilly funding climate descended on the international family-planning community, and sterilization yet again became a "dirty word" in the American lexicon. In response, AVS, in 1984, changed its name for the first time in twenty years, dropping the word "sterilization" and reintroducing itself as the Association for Voluntary Surgical Contraception (AVSC), in a deliberate effort to divert attention from both the organization's past and its present. The defiant spirit of Marian Olden and Hugh Moore gave way once again to pragmatic considerations as AVS and its supporters attempted to adapt to the new conservatism sweeping Capitol Hill and the White House. Nothing less than millions of taxpayers' dollars was at stake.

Pushing the Frontiers

Frosty relations between the White House and the sterilization movement in the 1980s stood in stark contrast to conditions during Ravenholt's tenure at USAID, when he had proven to be an invaluable ally for groups like AVS with less respectable credentials than Population Council or IPPF. Ravenholt had a special affection for AVS and Clarence Gamble's Pathfinder Fund because they appeared more innovative than mainstream groups, more infused with a "can-do and will-do spirit," and better able to cut through red tape and circumvent congested official channels, a crucial consideration in a country like India where (in Ravenholt's opinion) decision making was sclerotic in comparison with Western, developing countries.[33] The Pathfinder Fund viewed itself as a group particularly able to "act very quickly and flexibly, giving prompt field trial to new ideas, new procedures, or new methods."[34] Many of the Pathfinder programs are "pioneering and controversial," the organization's chairman[35] admitted:

> Persons who work with and are funded by Pathfinder often work on the fringe of what is currently socially acceptable or even legally permissible, be it family planning as was often the case in the past or today's efforts on behalf of abortion, women's rights, explicit population control and even sterilization. Pathfinder's long history of working in less developed countries and responding sympathetically, flexibly and with continuing commitment to the needs of people as they themselves perceive them are widely recognized. This record of achievement is extremely helpful as we seek allies and colleagues to join us in pushing the frontiers even further.

AVS, with its commitment to "mapping new directions," was a natural ally of Pathfinder, as both sought to "push the frontiers." As AVS stated in 1983, "[I]n many places voluntary sterilization is still controversial, and established family planning organizations are reluctant to risk their hard-won gains by advancing sterilization. AVS and the groups it collaborates with have nothing to lose and are able to take the heat."[36]

Thus, as AVSC attempted to cleanse its public image in the 1980s, behind the scenes it was still committed to pushing a "controversial" agenda. It was willing to "take the heat" because it sensed that no matter what abuses occurred in India or other localities, developing countries would, sooner or later, out of necessity, have to adopt sterilization as their favored method of contraception. Indeed, Indira Gandhi's government had barely fallen before the sense of urgency surrounding family planning in India returned as strong as ever; as one Indian official remarked, "[T]here is no hedging about family planning any longer." Between March, 1978, and March, 1979, 1.3 million sterilizations were performed, while payments to motivators, acceptors, and physicians were restored and the central government once again set sterilization targets for the individual states.[37] The government continued to privilege sterilization over other contraceptive methods. Reelected in 1980 and committed as ever to population control, a somewhat chastened Indira Gandhi announced that birth control was no longer viewed as an end in itself. Yet the alarming news that, between 1971 and 1981, India's population had grown by almost 136 million served as the backdrop to Gandhi's announcement of the Sixth Development Plan (1980–1985) and its $1.15 billion budget for family planning. Contraception was to be conceived of as only a single part of a broad public health strategy centered on improving women's health. Likewise, whereas prior to the 1980s the emphasis had been on vasectomy, the new decade witnessed growing government support for tubal ligation. Improving the quality of life of women was the new leitmotif of India's population control campaign, yet the continued state promotion of sterilization suggested that not much had changed. If, as the 1980s wore on, India's government had not exactly forgotten the sterilization scandals of the previous decade, they did gradually become a distant memory.[38]

Sterilization Works

The official Indian attitude toward sterilization was shared by a growing number of developing world countries, many of which launched aggressive sterilization campaigns in the 1980s and 1990s. Facing similar population pressures, national governments in Asia, Africa, and South America worked with family-planning NGOs to lower fertility rates and discovered what sterilization proponents had been preaching since the 1960s: nothing beat sterilization for rapidly reducing the size of poor families. Many national leaders concluded that, like India, their countries could not wait for long-term forces such as urbanization, education, economic development, and the spread of women's rights and opportunities to have an effect on birth rates. Feeling the need to act right away, they introduced crash sterilization programs resembling India's and China's. In the process, they realized that sterilization did in fact work, as fertility rates plunged dramatically. Yet, like Indira Gandhi, they also learned that sterilization advocacy sometimes came with a steep political price.

By the end of the twentieth century, the sterilization movement had reason to congratulate itself. In 1990, one in five married women around the world of reproductive age and using contraception had been sterilized. Both forms of sterilization (male and female) together accounted for 45% of contraceptive use in developing countries, and tubal sterilization had satisfied one-half of the demand for contraception to limit family size in the Dominican Republic, El Salvador, Sri Lanka, and Thailand. Sterilization rates remained "modest" in most of sub-Saharan Africa, but even there the rates, like those in most of Asia and Latin America, were on the rise as the 1990s began.[39] The percentage of all contraceptive users who were sterilized varied from Nepal (85.5%) to India (68.8%), the Dominican Republic (66.1%), South Korea (62.5%), Sri Lanka (41.3%), and Mexico (37%). In 1996, in Brazil, the most populous nation in Latin America, more than half of all contraceptive users relied on sterilization. By 2002, sterilization prevalence in at least thirteen countries ranged from one-third to almost one-half of all couples of reproductive age. Estimates were that 222 million women in union worldwide had been sterilized. Sterilization's use was increasing "gradually," family-planning proponents noted approvingly, creating a "very strong momentum" that "casts a long shadow into the future" due to the fact that "future adoptions by younger couples continuously shore up that momentum by adding yet more users to the pool who will remain members of it for a long time." In other words, the cumulative effect of sterilization as time went on eclipsed any other type of contraceptive method and continued to depress birth rates for years to come.[40]

By the end of the twentieth century, millions and millions of people around the world had been sterilized; but what impact did sterilization have on global fertility rates? How many births did it actually prevent? How effective was it in comparison with other birth control methods? Back in the 1950s and 1960s, when the operation was still the "ugly duckling" of all contraceptive methods and resistance to vasectomy was widespread, critics maintained that sterilization's impact on birth rates was minimal. Those who chose sterilization, it was argued, tended to be older men and women with large families already who normally wanted no more children. However, as sterilization became more popular and fears of the "population bomb" gripped many politicians around the world, opinions about the operation's effectiveness shifted. Environmentalists argued that couples should "stop at two" for the good of the planet, and women's rights activists claimed women ordinarily wanted no more than two or three children anyway. From these vantage points, the finality of sterilization appeared more and more attractive to Third World governments hard-pressed to alleviate mass poverty and resource depletion.

In the 1980s and 1990s, the reputation of sterilization as a virtually foolproof contraceptive method swiftly grew among demographers, environmentalists, family planners, and elected officials. Adumbrating Bill McKibben, Senator Bob Packwood (R-Oregon), in an open letter to "environmentalists," asserted "sterilization works" by preventing "nearly three times as many unwanted pregnancies as any other method."[41] Years earlier, advocates such as Sripati Chandrasekhar, A. R. Kaufman, and John Rague had argued forcefully that each sterilization prevented multiple births. As Chandrasekhar told the *New York Times* in 1967, "[W]hen your house is on fire, you choose the method that you think will put out the fire most quickly."[42] Studies since then have largely verified their theories.[43] By 1990, sterilization had "contributed to the realization of large declines in fertility in Brazil, South Korea, Thailand, and Kenya," thanks to AVSC "interventions" that included funding, training, counseling, technical assistance, the supply of surgical equipment, and "the encouragement of greater use of vasectomy."[44] One key to preventing births was to lower the average age of women at the time of their operations: the older a sterilized woman, the less impact on fertility.[45] At the height of the U.S. sterilization boom, in the 1970s, family-planning analysts estimated that from 1971 to 1973, 800,000 unwanted births in America (out of a total of 8.7 million actual births) were averted due to sterilization. This was partially due to the fact that among sterilized, once-married, white U.S. couples, about 45% of the wives had been sterilized before the age of thirty.[46] In Bangladesh, where the government called for 3.4 million sterilizations between 1980 and 1985, the mean age of women undergoing tubectomy was 29.1 years, slightly lower than in other Asian countries, including Indonesia, Nepal, and Thailand. In El Salvador, the average age had fallen to 27.6 by the late 1980s.[47] For both men and women sterilized in Bangladesh over the same period, 65% were under thirty years of age (in contrast to Tunisia, where 86% were older than thirty).[48] Each Bangladeshi tubectomy was estimated to prevent 1.2 births. In 1986, demographers calculated that in twelve developing countries "anywhere from 1.0 to 2.5 births" were averted by each sterilization, with a high of 2.7 for the Philippines. In India, sterilization prevented at least three times the number of births as IUD use. With worldwide trends pointing toward "an increase in reliance on sterilization among younger women with smaller families," the prospect for an even bigger demographic impact in densely populated Third World countries such as Brazil, Panama, Sri Lanka, Thailand, and Costa Rica grew as the 1990s dawned.[49]

The lowering of the mean age at the time of sterilization, generally hailed by sterilization advocates, raised a question: how satisfied were individuals with their operations? Unsurprisingly, U.S. studies discovered that women, when asked if they still thought tubal sterilization had been a good choice for them, were far more likely to regret their operation the younger they were at the time of the surgery. In the 1995 National Survey of Family Growth, almost a quarter of the 9.2 million married women with tubal ligations said that they or their husbands or partners wished to reverse the operation. Of the 3.7 million married women whose husbands or partners had had vasectomies, 11% expressed a similar desire. Regret was highest among Hispanic and low-income women. Investigators concluded that "a surprisingly high percentage of women sterilized at a young age in the United States will regret their decision at some point."[50] Findings about sterilization regret in developing countries were comparable. In Bangladesh between 1993 and 1994, 14% of all married women under fifty years of age regretted their tubal ligations, while about three in ten regretted their husbands' vasectomies. Sterilization advocates argue that these numbers "imply that a large majority of women . . . express no regrets" about their contraceptive surgeries, but the percentage of those who do express regret, though a minority, still translates into tens of thousands of individuals. Additionally, in societies where death rates were higher than in developed countries, the extensive use of a permanent method of birth control that foreclosed the possibility of further pregnancies after the death of a child or partner was a cause of considerable soul-searching for family-planning workers about what constituted informed consent. If sterilization prevented only unwanted pregnancies, why did so many people regret their operations later? How many actually knew at the time of the operation that it prevented them from having any more children?[51] The ability of sterilization to terminate fertility for good, however, tended to overshadow such concerns and made its application in Third World countries particularly impressive in the eyes of population control enthusiasts.

Cairo and Beyond

As global enthusiasm for sterilization climbed in the last years of the twentieth century, Democratic Arkansas governor William Jefferson Clinton was elected president in 1992, boosting hopes that the years of enmity between the White House and the family-planning movement were coming to an end. By 1992, Clinton and First Lady Hillary Clinton, as well as Vice-President Albert Gore Jr., a former U.S. senator from Tennessee, were open supporters of abortion rights and generally friendly toward birth control groups such as Planned Parenthood Federation of America (PPFA) and National Association for the Repeal of Abortion Laws (NARAL). To no one's surprise, domestic spending on family-planning supplies and services jumped by 11% in the first two years of the Clinton presidency, with funding for sterilizations in 1994 amounting to $148 million (out of a total of $715 million for all birth control expenditures). Clinton also moved quickly to appoint two pro-choice justices to the U.S. Supreme Court, Stephen Breyer and Ruth Bader Ginsburg. Most significantly for population control groups, in early 1993 the White House overturned the Reagan/Bush ban on federal funding for international birth control organizations that performed or counseled for abortions (pp. 220–221).[52]

The upbeat mood of the international family-planning community in the wake of Bill Clinton's presidential victory was evident at the 1994 Cairo International Conference on Population and Development, the United Nations' third decennial conference on population issues. Hailed as a "milestone in population policy and politics" by global family planners, the Cairo Conference's 4,000 delegates from one hundred and eighty national governments produced a "programme of action" intended to serve as a blueprint for population policy for the next twenty years.

The "Cairo consensus" suggested that family planning NGOs had learned the lesson from the Reagan years that discussion of population, still regarded as "a top-ranking issue" for many governments around the world, had to be couched within the context of economic development and women's rights if expectations of U.S. public spending on international birth control were to be met. Ravenholt's supply-side theory of population control, with its crash programs in which agencies flooded developing countries with contraceptive devices, was no longer fashionable. In its place were demand-side approaches that stressed stimulating desire for artificial contraception by providing women and their partners with the information, resources, and services necessary for fertility control. "Basic education" and "the empowerment of women" were to be the cornerstones of the post-Cairo-era population movement. Gone was talk of incentives and disincentives to meet population goals, replaced by "condemnations of coercion." In the words of a Nigerian official delegate, the aim of family planning was to "allow people to count . . . not count people." "Top-down" solutions were out; "bottom-up" solutions were now in vogue, prompting family-planning advocates to marvel at "how far the population issue has come since the days when talk centered on the 'population bomb' " (p. 277).[52]

The Cairo "programme of action" also reflected the dawning awareness among family-planning NGOs of the global dimensions of the AIDS epidemic (pp. 272–277).[52] First identified in 1981, AIDS (acquired immune deficiency syndrome) quickly became the leading killer of men between the ages of twenty-five and forty-four in the Northeast United States, exacting a fearsome toll on the male homosexual population in particular. By the time the human immunodeficiency virus (HIV), said to have originated in sub-Saharan Africa, had been isolated and demonstrated, in mid-1984, to be the cause of AIDS, thousands had already died. In the early twenty-first century, HIV/AIDS was a global pandemic, with almost 40 million people living with the disease. In 2006, the WHO estimated that AIDS had killed more than 25 million people since 1981, with a third of the death toll occurring in sub-Saharan Africa. As the alarm over the HIV/AIDS epidemic spread, family-planning groups realized that many of their resources had to be allocated to the prevention of AIDS and other sexually transmitted diseases.

However, the resounding Republican victory in the 1994 midterm congressional elections revealed that even Clinton's winning the White House again in 1996 had not turned the tide. Between 1965 (when USAID began funding overseas birth control) and 1995, Congressional appropriations to international family-planning programs generally increased, but between 1995 and 1996 they tumbled 35%. Additionally, Congress delayed release of fiscal-year 1996 funds until July 1, 1996 (nine months into the fiscal year), and placed limits on how much funding could be apportioned per month. Intervention on the part of the Clinton White House softened the negative impact of USAID funding delays, but with the United States contributing almost one-half of all donor funding to more than sixty countries with a combined population of 2.7 billion people, the implications of the cutbacks for global family-planning programs were staggering.[53]

The news for the family-planning community got even worse when George W. Bush won the presidency in 2000 and 2004. It did not take long before the Bush administration, following the example of the Reagan presidency, again slashed funding for UNFPA because of its connections to China's population policy of coercive abortions and sterilizations. Noted pro-life Congressman Chris Smith (R-New Jersey) led the Republican attack on UNFPA. To EngenderHealth, like the rest of the family-planning community, U.S. denial of funding for UNFPA was a deplorable "decision to treat the UNFPA as a political pawn," "imperil[ing] the lives of countless women and their families" around the world. Despite EngenderHealth's claim that fact-finding teams had found no evidence that UNFPA supported any coercive activities in China, the widespread perception that sterilization was associated with involuntary birth control was yet another reminder that the movement's eugenic and population-control past remained a vivid memory in the minds of many voters.[54]

Running Amok

By slashing spending on international birth control programs, the Bush administration was not simply bowing to pressure from its core supporters on the pro-life, Christian right. It was also reacting to the scandals that continued to dog the family-planning movement in general and the sterilization movement in particular up to the turn of the century, proving that the 1975–1977 sterilization abuses of Indira Gandhi's government were less isolated incidents than systemic examples of what could go wrong when governments, under the influence of population control ideology, moved to cut birth rates. By the end of the 1990s, news about the human rights violations caused by China's one-child population policy was matched by disturbing reports out of Peru that aggressive government attempts between 1996 and 2000 to popularize contraceptive sterilization had "run amok," in the words of the *New York Times*.[55] As had been the case in India, intense pressure in the form of quotas, publicity campaigns, financial incentives, misleading information about the operation's reversibility, and outright threats of loss of food and medical benefits meant informed consent was absent in most of the more than 200,000 operations performed on poor, indigenous women in Peru's rural areas. Another similarity to India's sterilization programs was the Peruvian government's use of "festivals" to round up large numbers of women in one place for mass operations. Investigations revealed that frequently there had been inadequate evaluation before surgery, and little aftercare. Less than half of the operations were carried out with a proper anesthetist. Evidence pointed to the conclusion that Peru's sterilization program had been designed, encouraged, and monitored at the highest government levels, including the office of President Alberto Fujimori, who ruled Peru from 1990 to 2000. In 2000, Fujimori fled Peru for Japan to escape allegations of corruption and human rights abuses, only to return in 2005 with the open intention of running again for president in 2006, but a February, 2001, decision by the Peruvian Congress banning Fujimori from holding office for ten years blocked his political comeback.[56]

Peru's sterilization program should have come as no surprise because, in 1995, Fujimori's government had decriminalized vasectomy and tubal ligation. Two months later, in September, he appeared at the Beijing Conference on Women's Rights, where he announced his government's firm intentions to tackle the country's population growth. Amid applause from leading family-planning NGOs, Fujimori declared his opposition to the Vatican's condemnation of artificial contraception and pledged to provide Peru's 23 million (mostly Catholic) citizens with birth control education and family-planning services. Fujimori's remarks about family planning were couched in the language of women's reproductive rights and socioeconomic opportunities, but his overall goal to widen access to surgical contraception as a means to cut Peru's birth rate, especially in the countryside, where family size tended to be higher than in urban areas, should have sparked concerns that a replay of India's 1975–1977 sterilization tragedy was imminent.[57]

In the event, by 1998, when a Peruvian delegation traveled to Washington, D.C., to testify before a Congressional Subcommittee on International and Human Rights Operations, numerous stories about thousands of involuntary sterilizations in Peru were already circulating in the media, including in the *New York Times*, *Washington Post*, and *Miami Herald*. One Peruvian doctor told the subcommittee that physicians who disagreed with the sterilizations went along with the program for fear of losing their jobs.[58] Thanks to Congressman Chris Smith's prodding, U.S. official attention focused on whether or not USAID money had been spent on the Peruvian program. The subcommittee's chief counsel, after a fact-finding visit to Peru, determined that no U.S. funds went directly to the Peruvian government's campaign, but conceded that some foreign aid in the form of food might have been used to bribe women to undergo sterilizations, since U.S.-sponsored food programs operated at the local, rural level from the same Peruvian government posts that administered family planning. The pro-life Population Research Institute disputes this interpretation, asserting that USAID officials were involved directly in Fujimori's sterilization campaign from the start.[59] What is beyond dispute is that AVSC International itself had been active in Peru since the early 1990s, thanks to USAID funding. AVSC provided donations, training, and equipment to Instituto Peruano de Paternidad Responsable (INPARRES), International Planned Parenthood's Peruvian affiliate and a key player in the country's sterilization program, but significantly cut back its activities in Peru by the end of the decade. AVSC stated in 1998 that it continued to work with governments such as Peru's "to identify and overcome barriers" to informed choice, including incentives, quotas, and target goals.[60] However, if it was engaged in efforts to stem the rampant involuntarism of the Peru program, it made little difference.

Equally disquieting were the reports of forced sterilization in East Timor, which gained its independence in 2002 and changed its name to the Democratic Republic of Timor-Leste. Between 1975 and 1999, East Timor, the eastern half of a tiny South Pacific island with a population of about 1 million (90% of whom are Catholic), was occupied by Indonesia's armed forces. Indonesia considered East Timor its twenty-seventh province, and when a guerilla movement arose seeking self-rule, the Indonesian government retaliated with harsh measures. In January, 2002, the United Nations called for an international tribunal to investigate allegations of massive human rights violations, including mass rape and coercive sterilization by the Indonesian occupiers. The reproductive oppression in East Timor, which also included compulsory injections of the contraceptive drug Depo-Provera, had been documented by the East Timor Human Rights Centre in Australia. By the early twenty-first century, many allegations still awaited verification, but the perception that international family-planning organizations had cooperated with the Indonesian military to coercively reduce the birth rate of East Timorese women was disturbing and was enough to convince the World Bank and USAID to drastically cut their funding to the Indonesian Association for Secure

Contraception (PKMI) and the Indonesian Planned Parenthood Federation (PKBI), the groups that had spearheaded the campaign to cut birth
rates in East Timor. Since 1977, AVSC had been PKMI's chief donor,
but the U.S.-based group terminated its contacts with these organizations
in the 1990s as the allegations of forced sterilization multiplied.[61]

The Birth Dearth

The reports of forced sterilizations in Peru and East Timor shook the
international community, but other troubling news was starting to emerge
as the century wound to a close, casting even more doubt on the sterilization movement's agenda. In 1987, U.S. journalist Ben Wattenberg
coined the phrase "birth dearth" and became the first pundit to warn that
a "depopulation bomb," rather than overpopulation, constituted the real
threat to international prosperity and stability. As Wattenberg observed,
"[N]ever have birth and fertility rates fallen so far, so fast, so low, for so
long, and in so many places, so surprisingly" (p. 5).[62] Inspired by Julian
Simon's pronatalist theories, Wattenberg, a 2006 Senior Fellow at the
American Enterprise Institute in Washington, D.C., warned that plummeting birth rates would wreak havoc on future generations by shrinking
the pool of young workers whose taxes were necessary to support the
"baby boom" generation, born during the post–World War II era, as
it entered retirement. This imbalance between retirees and taxpaying
workers, Wattenberg predicted, would jeopardize costly government
programs such as Social Security and Medicare. The overall effect of the
"grayby boom," as Wattenberg calls it, on economies based on growth
is likely to be disruptive. To Pat Buchanan, the conservative broadcast
journalist who ran for the U.S. presidency in 2000, low fertility rates in the
developed world are part of an even more disturbing process that will
lead to the "death of the West," the end of Western civilization in a
fashion reminiscent of the fall of the Roman Empire 1,500 years ago.[63]

More optimistically, Wattenberg believes that immigrants (both low-
and high-skilled) will continue to supply the taxpaying laborers necessary
for the U.S. economy in the years to come (pp. 191–206).[62] As he puts it,
"[S]omeone has to empty those bedpans" (p. 196).[62] From the other side of
the political spectrum, Philip Longman, Senior Fellow at the Washington,
D.C., New America Foundation and author of *The Empty Cradle* (2004),
agrees with Wattenberg about the birth dearth, but he is less confident that
heavy immigration will offset the aging of society. He argues that as other

regions of the world experience their own fertility declines, there will be a smaller and smaller pool of immigrants to choose from, exacerbated by the mounting competition from other developed countries equally hungry for alien labor. By the same token, a country like India with a surging economy of its own will try to keep skilled workers at home rather than export them. These factors, when combined with the average advanced age of newcomers and the national security risks associated with heavy immigration, convince Longman that reliance on immigration is not prudent. Instead, Longman recommends that governments compensate parents for providing the next generation of taxpayers in the form of special tax breaks. He points to numerous surveys showing that women throughout the industrialized world ultimately bear fewer children than they intended. The key, to Longman, is for governments to ensure that the high costs of raising children do not diminish the "desire" of men and women to produce them.[64]

Longman, no political conservative, has warned Democratic Party voters and socially progressive Americans that the birth dearth could tip the country's political balance toward the Republicans. Besides the birth dearth's many economic disadvantages, there is the distinct prospect that, based on the statistical correlation between churchgoing and family size, religiously motivated, socially conservative Americans could outbreed Americans whose politics are comparatively secularist and liberal.[65] Longman unhappily predicts that "conservatives will inherit the earth" and "patriarchy" will make a comeback in U.S. families as socially conservative values become more popular.[66] If Longman's forecasts are correct, the constituencies involved in the family-planning movement ought to sit up and take notice, because traditionally they have mainly depended on Democratic Party politicians and lobbyists. Longman's interpretation of the birth dearth suggests that the issue could enjoy bipartisan support in the new millennium, in the process forging a new, pronatalist consensus on population and further undercutting support for birth control organizations such as EngenderHealth.

Wattenberg, Longman, and other social scientists might disagree over the remedies for the birth dearth, but by the early twenty-first century what had once been a "stunning silence" surrounding the issue had become a major official concern in capitals around the world.[67] Elected leaders throughout the European Union have repeatedly expressed their alarm over low national birth rates, such as Germany's 1.4 and Italy's and Spain's 1.3 children per childbearing woman (the replacement level is 2.1). Russian president Vladimir Putin, whose country was shedding

750,000 citizens a year by 2004, has called Russia's shrinking population a "national crisis," yet other Eastern European nations, including Romania, Bulgaria, and Estonia, are little better off.[68] In 2006, Russia's Duma even considered a proposal to reintroduce a Stalin-era "sterility tax" on the country's 21 million childless singles. Meanwhile, Japan's birth rate has plunged to 1.3, and with a national average age of forty-three years old, its Minister of Gender Equality and Social Affairs said she felt "a sense of crisis" surrounding the country's future. Singapore, Hong Kong, Taiwan, Thailand, and Burma, as well as Latin American countries Cuba, Uruguay, and Brazil, were all reporting sub-replacement fertility in the early twenty-first century. At the same time, South Korea announced it would spend $20 billion to increase its birth rate, a "turnabout" that abruptly reversed its decades-old policy of promoting smaller families, notably through sterilization (Korea, China, India, and Canada have the highest prevalence rates of sterilization in the world).[69]

Similarly, by 2006, the People's Republic of China's one-child program was beginning to look like a "monumental demographic mistake," in the words of the *New York Times*. China's population, too, was aging, while a shortage of cheap labor loomed ominously on the horizon.[70] Additionally, in China, as in India, years of propaganda about the need for family limitation have dovetailed with the introduction of sophisticated medical technology to produce a gender imbalance skewed in favor of males.[71] Prenatal gender screening enables couples to determine whether their fetuses are male or female, and where boys are preferred and governments promote strict family planning, the result has been the abortion of millions of females.[72] Some observers predict that the millions of unmarried, underemployed, and rootless men in the world's two most populous nations will threaten domestic law and order and endanger international security.[73] The magnitude of this trend assumes even greater proportions in view of the fact that 40% of the world's population resides in India and China. UNFPA has denounced sex-selection abortion, and governments (such as India's and China's) have responded by making it illegal, but a black market for such services survives, and the total number of "lost daughters" around the world remains high.[74]

Long Shadows

Throughout its history, the sterilization movement has been buffeted by events that have questioned its very *raison d'être*, but nothing has the potential to affect the movement's future as much as the birth dearth, which could rival climate change as a central issue of global concern in the new century. Indeed, by the early twenty-first century, the growing number of governments intent on boosting their birth rates, as well as the ripple effects from the Peruvian and East Timorese sterilization scandals, had produced a major change in USAID's approach to foreign assistance. The agency officially moved toward an eventual phase-out of population assistance, representing a quarter of its total budget on health, causing NGOs like AVSC International (which between 1988 and 2005 received $312 million from USAID) to adapt to this shift in foreign aid priorities. The 2001 name change to EngenderHealth was based on the realization, EngenderHealth's president admitted, that AVSC's name "closed rather than opened doors to new opportunities and funding."[75] The name "EngenderHealth" reflected the group's decision to "broaden its agenda to all contraceptive methods. . . . We felt it wasn't appropriate for us to offer sterilization services and not make certain we were meeting other needs as well," board member and Dean of Columbia University's Mailman School of Public Health Allan Rosenfield remarked in 2001. The old name of AVSC International "caused confusion, conveyed implications about the focus of our work that are no longer accurate, and failed to communicate what we do or the passion with which we do it." "EngenderHealth" mirrored the "definition of reproductive health" articulated by the 1994 "Cairo consensus," a viewpoint that sought to "empower" women and integrate family planning with reproductive health services such as postabortion care and the prevention of sexually transmitted diseases, including HIV/AIDS. The journey from the 1970s to the twenty-first century had seen the organization go "from a primary focus on sterilization to the partnership of family planning and reproductive health," including support for "women's equity and opportunity." Yet there was "no cause for alarm," Rosenfield added, because the new orientation grew naturally out of the work the group had been doing for years.[76] To Rosenfield and the rest of EngenderHealth, the group's tasks in the twenty-first century were not a fundamental departure from its activities in previous decades, especially in "the area of sterilization counseling and clinical services." "This is not a legacy we either want or intend to lose," the group's Web site announced in 2001.[77]

Indeed, as the new millennium unfolds, continuities stand out as much as discontinuities in the history of the sterilization movement. Rationales for vasectomy and tubal ligation may have changed over the years, but the overall justification for spreading sterilization around the world is a fairly

consistent galaxy of motives, including the expansion of personal autonomy, the reduction of the birth rate in overpopulated regions, the liberation of women from the health consequences of uncontrolled childbearing, the protection of the environment and conservation of natural
resources, and the sexual fulfillment of men and women the world over.
As this book shows, there is a recognizable present-day resonance to what
pioneers in the sterilization movement, including Robert Latou Dickinson, Emily Mudd, Helen Edey, Lonnie Myers, and Mary Calderone,
had to say about the virtues of the operation. Their advocacy of women's
reproductive rights and sexual fulfillment was not simply a rhetorical
gambit and has proven to be remarkably durable, spanning both the early
and recent stages of the sterilization movement. Thus scholars who draw
invidious distinctions between one era in the history of family planning
dominated by eugenic, antifeminist, and population control imperatives
and another (more recent) era during which women have finally begun to
exercise the reproductive choices denied them by the earlier birth control
movement ignore the evidence that such neat differences do not accord
with historical reality.

A good example of how EngenderHealth was blending old and new by
the turn of the twenty-first century was its "men as partners" program,
designed to break down the long-standing attitude that women bear sole
responsibility for contraception. As this book has shown, on and off since
the 1940s, the sterilization movement has promoted vasectomy as a means
of relieving women of the dread of unwanted pregnancy, thereby enabling
them to express themselves sexually. AVSC International's 1998 launch
of a campaign aimed, in the group's own words, at "increas[ing] access to
vasectomy by low-income and minority men" in Pinellas County, Florida,
the state's most densely populated county, fits this historical pattern. The
campaign featured the distribution of a kit designed by AVSC and a New
Mexico marketing firm. The kit, whose slogan was "You'd Be Surprised,"
contained posters, brochures, and temporary tattoos aimed at dispelling
fears and misconceptions about vasectomy. Area beer drinkers also no-
ticed that beneath their mugs in various county bars were coasters that
read "Make My Next One a Vasectomy," complete with the Pinellas
County Department of Health (DOH) phone number and the promise of
"low cost/no cost vasectomies." Alongside funding by the David and
Lucille Packard Foundation, the campaign enjoyed the full cooperation
of the county DOH, whose health educator described the kit as "a very
clever, lighthearted way of addressing a topic that many couples are
not comfortable discussing." The three-month campaign resulted in

twenty-five vasectomies at the DOH, compared with none in Pinellas County in the last quarter of 1997.[78]

The Pinellas County initiative was matched by similar projects in economically underprivileged parts of the country, including New York City's Washington Heights, "a predominantly Hispanic and low-income neighborhood," or the Navajo Nation Reservation, covering 25,000 square miles of Arizona, Colorado, New Mexico, and Utah.[79] According to AVSC, its "work with a health facility in Colorado taught us that low-income men were not accessing [vasectomy] services," and the group took steps that "specifically responded to the needs expressed by this population." In the twenty-first century, EngenderHealth views its efforts to encourage vasectomies as a key component of an overall policy aimed at improving women's reproductive health by stressing gender equity and rights, an approach that includes the attempt to convince men to "access" sterilization services. Such an approach assumes that without Engender-Health's programs, the "needs" of various communities are not met. Yet who determines whose needs? Historically, family-planning programs have operated with the assumption "that service providers know what is best for an individual client"[80]—for example, "that unplanned means unwanted."[81] So how does a group like EngenderHealth balance choice and advocacy? The targeting of clients according to socioeconomic and ethnic status runs the risk of "exaggerat[ing] the links between fertility and poverty" and revives memories of the sterilization movement's eugenic period.[82] This chronic tendency of the movement to look eugenic even when it forswears such intentions likely has something to do with the decision, made in 2005, to "temporarily close until further notice" EngenderHealth's U.S. program.[83]

What is striking is how these boundaries between birth control and population control remain blurred even after EngenderHealth's decades of practical experience in the field, partnerships with numerous mainstream NGOs, and multimillion-dollar contributions from USAID and prominent private foundations. This may be because, as historian James Reed has noted, the distinction between birth control and population control for examining the motives of the "political coalitions supporting both the welfare state and family planning since World War II" is "not a very useful analytical tool."[84]

Overseas, the same imprecision regarding the differences between birth control and population control lingers as the attractiveness of sterilization as a quick-fix solution to population problems refuses to disappear. India, for example, has continued to experiment with mass sterilization schemes despite the mounting historical evidence that such policies routinely violate global standards of informed consent and universal human rights. In 2000, the Indian government, facing a population expected to grow beyond 1.5 billion before it stabilizes, announced "a new initiative on population growth."[85] India, having added 181 million citizens in the 1990s and expecting to overtake China in population size by 2020, once again became the scene of "hard sell" sterilization policies. In the wake of the 1994 Cairo Conference, the country's central government had abandoned numerical sterilization targets and had embraced "an agenda for improving health and education for women and children." Yet it has given the individual states considerable leeway in trying to reduce birth rates. In Andhra Pradesh, the nation's fifth largest state and in which half the women are still illiterate and married before the age of fifteen, specific targets for the sterilization of couples with two or more children are backed by the full weight of the government. As one official put it, "[I]f you get operated quickly, you get goodies quickly"—"goodies" such as priority for antipoverty benefits including housing, land, and loans. Lotteries for sterilized couples have drawn the ire of religious groups and social activists, who have called them "a macabre metaphor of the lottery that is the life of the poor." Another critic, when informed about women being offered gold chains to undergo a tubal sterilization, said, "[I]f that isn't coercion, what is?"[86]

In 2004, in Uttar Pradesh, India's largest and most populous state, outrage surfaced over the state's plan to issue guns as an incentive to undergo sterilization. Reports of rich farmers rounding up unwitting agricultural laborers for vasectomies and claiming a gun license shocked the press, but state administrators were unapologetic, stating, "[W]e have to meet our [sterilization] goals."[87] Meeting sterilization goals was also the reason that, in 2006, teachers in Uttar Pradesh were ordered to each find two "volunteers" for sterilization or face disciplinary action.[88]

Despite the troubling data from around the world that such radical experiments in population control are often coercive and backfire a generation later in sub-replacement birth rates, India seems intent on repeating the past. Yet what does this say about EngenderHealth, active in India since 1988 in providing information, training, and technical assistance at the district, state, and national levels regarding reproductive health and family planning? In the group's own words, it has occupied a "significant presence" there, especially in the state of Uttar Pradesh. With the help of USAID, EngenderHealth seeks to "reduce the overall fertility rate" in Uttar Pradesh by trying to improve the reproductive health of women.[89] The group insists it defends the principles of "client rights" and "informed consent," which it defines as the free and voluntary choice of the patient to agree to sterilization based on extensive counseling regarding the operation's nature and all the available options. Yet how, in fact, do providers, intent on cutting birth rates, empower men and women with reproductive choice without compromising voluntarism? No organization has wrestled historically with this issue more than EngenderHealth. From its origins to the present day, EngenderHealth has tried to widen access to sterilization and motivate people to accept the operation. Events in the past decade and a half suggest that it has yet to reconcile these two goals successfully without compromising choice.

If this form of success still eluded EngenderHealth by the early twenty-first century, the group nonetheless could take some credit for the fall in global fertility rates, as well as the drop in the number of countries restricting access to sterilization, from twenty-eight to eight. A 1998 RAND study estimated that 40% of the observed decline in fertility in the developing world from the 1960s to the 1990s was due to the impact of family-planning programs alone, distinct from other factors such as economic development and the changing status of women.[90] Given that sterilization is the leading contraceptive method around the world, EngenderHealth could be forgiven for congratulating itself at the end of the twentieth century on its ability, through its own programs, to shape the course of modern history. Yet with a birth dearth looming and threatening to choke future prosperity, such congratulations may be premature and are likely destined to wear thin as the years go by. Sterilization appears poised to cast its "long shadow" well into the twenty-first century, the capstone to a series of achievements that began sixty years ago in the Princeton, New Jersey, home of Marian Olden. Were she still alive today, she might well believe that God's plan for her had indeed been fulfilled.

Notes

1. Donaldson PJ. *Nature Against Us: The Untied States and the World Population Crisis, 1965–1980*. Chapel Hill and London: University of North Carolina Press, 1990.
2. "A loss to the AVSC community." *AVSC News*, 36, 1998. Available at http://www.avsc.org/avscnews/wn98.
3. "Edey-Lader Ad Hoc Committee Draft: Resolutions of the Two-Child Family," September 9, 1969; "The Davis-Edey-Rague Proposal: Resolution on the Desirability of the One-Child Family," February 9, 1972, LL, Box 12.

4. Helen Edey to Hugh Moore, November 9, 1970, HM, Series 3, Box 17, folder 11.

5. Homer Calver to Howard Ennis, October 22, 1963; Homer Calver to Hugh Moore, July 29, 1965, AVS, Box 87, Calver folder.

6. Homer N. Calver, "Six Concepts for Survival," 1968 Hiscock Lecture at the University of Hawaii School of Public Health, AVS, Box 87, Calver folder.

7. Donaldson PJ. *Nature Against Us: The United States and the World Population Crisis, 1965–1980.* Chapel Hill and London: University of North Carolina Press, 1990, pp. 46–51. Donaldson writes that it is "impossible to produce completely accurate figures on the amount of [population control] aid that specific countries received, because a large proportion of foreign assistance funds pass through a variety of organizations, making careful tracking of who gave what to whom and when very difficult" (p. 46).

8. William H. Draper to Homer Calver, March 19, 1969, AVS, Box 87, Calver folder.

9. "World group for VS is formed." *New York Times,* Jan. 9, 1968; AVS, Box 87, IAVS folder. When H. Curtis Wood publicly called for "less conservative and bolder actions among the Latin Americans," an IPPF official said the aim was to avoid "any idea that we are trying to tell the South American doctors what they should do." Sidney Swensrud to Frances Ferguson, April 22, 1970, AVS, Box 89, General Correspondence folder.

10. Phyllis Piotrow, testimony before the Commission on Population Growth and the American Future, April 14, 1974, AHC, MSB, Box 40.

11. Sarah Gamble to Stuart and Emily Mudd, October 10, 1974, EM, Carton 11, folder 490.

12. *Times of India,* August 21, 1974. Cited in Vicziany M. Coercion in a soft state: The family-planning program of India. Part 1: The myth of voluntarism. *Pacific Affairs.* 1982;55:397.

13. Stycos JM. Demographic chic at the UN. *Family Planning Perspectives.* 1974;6:160–164.

14. Critchlow DT. *Intended Consequences: Birth Control, Abortion, and the Federal Government in Modern America.* New York and Oxford: Oxford University Press, 1999.

15. Ira Lubell, "Report of the Executive Director," AVS annual meeting, March 13, 1974, AVS, Box 110, 1974 Board Minutes folder.

16. Marilyn Schima, *Final Report of the Third International Conference on Voluntary Sterilization,* Tunis, Tunisia, February 1–4, 1976, AVS, Box 113, Tunis Conference folder.

17. This and others details about Ravenholt are the result of interviews conducted by Peter J. Donaldson. See Donaldson PJ. *Nature Against Us: The United States and the World Population Crisis, 1965–1980.* Chapel Hill and London: University of North Carolina Press, 1990, pp. 97–112. See also "Rei Ravenholt: fighter for world-population control." *The Seattle Times,* May 28, 1978.

18. His initially low opinion of sterilization sparked a terse reply in 1968 from John Rague, who informed Ravenholt that while the IUD's success rate was 60%, sterilization's was 99%. Reimert Ravenholt to John Rague, February 16, 1968; Rague to Ravenholt, February 20, 1968; AVS, Box 54, Ravenholt folder.

19. In 1974, Ravenholt was interviewed by *Equilibrium*, a Zero Population Growth publication, in which he claimed that family-planning programs were having a big impact on worldwide fertility rates, the IUD had "not really lived up to the expectations of a decade ago," and few women in the developing world wanted more than three children. In answer to the question "What new developments in contraceptive technology seemed to be most promising?" he replied that the development of newer and simpler surgical techniques has created "very intense" demand for female sterilization in India, Nepal, Pakistan, Thailand, Indonesia, and other countries. To Ravenholt, sterilization appeared to be the future face of population control. "Interview with Dr. Ravenholt." *Equilibrium*. 1974;2(April):12–16.

20. Population Crisis Committee. "Ravenholt Wins Hugh Moore Award." Press release, June 20, 1974.

21. Reimert Ravenholt to the editor of *The Washington Post*, January 13, 1976, AVS, Box 110, 1976 Board Minutes folder.

22. Minutes of March 24, 1976, AVS meeting, AVS, Box 110, 1976 Board Minutes folder.

23. Wagman P. U.S. goal: Sterilize millions of world's women. *St. Louis Post-Dispatch*, April 22, 1977.

24. Landman LC. Fourth International Conference on Voluntary Sterilization. *Family Planning Perspectives*. 1979 9:11.

25. Sarah Gamble's notes of Jack Sullivan's comments at the Harvard University seminar on AID, February 5, 1975, EM, Carton 11, folder 480.

26. Simon JL. *The Ultimate Resource*. Princeton: Princeton University Press, 1981.

27. "U.S. policy on population causes outcry at Mexico conference." (London) *Times*, August 10, 1984; Buckley JL. All alone at the U.N. *National Review*. 1984;36(December 14):25–28.

28. Donaldson PJ. *Nature Against Us: The United States and the World Population Crisis, 1965–1980*. Chapel Hill and London: University of North Carolina Press, 1990, pp. 129–132; Kasun J. *The War Against Population: The Economics and Ideology of World Population Control*. San Francisco: Ignatius Press, 1988, pp. 170–172.

29. "China assails U.S. on population funds." *New York Times*, February 10, 1985, p. A3; "U.S. assailed on population aid." *New York Times*, July 22, 1985; Schiffer RL. Hostages to U.S. abortion politics. *New York Times*, November 11, 1985, p. A19.

30. Donaldson PJ. *Nature Against Us: The United States and the World Population Crisis, 1965–1980*. Chapel Hill and London: University of North Carolina Press, 1990, pp. 131–132; Burns JF. In China these days, an only child is the only

way. *New York Times*, May 12, 1985, p. A24; Cooney RS, Li J. Sterilization and financial penalties imposed on registered peasant couple, Hebei Province, China. *Studies in Family Planning*. 2001;32:67–78; for the Chinese population control policy and its ties to eugenics and euthanasia, see Dikötter F. *Imperfect Conceptions: Medical Knowledge, Birth Defects, and Eugenics in China*. New York: Columbia University Press, 1998. For a retrospective analysis of China's population policy, see Hesketh T, Lu L, Xing ZW. The effect of China's one-child family policy after 25 years. *New England Journal of Medicine*. 2005;353:1171–1176.

31. "California sterilized 20,000 with no outcries, paper says." *Minneapolis Star*, March 27, 1980; "Changes eyed in 'misfit' law." *Richmond Times-Dispatch*, December 29, 1980.

32. "30 million sterilized." *Toronto Sun*, March 30, 1980; "U.S. programs sterilized 'millions' in Third World." *Richmond Times-Dispatch*, March 30, 1980; "U.S. helped sterilize 'millions' abroad." *Minneapolis Tribune*, March 30, 1980.

33. Reimert Ravenholt to the editor of *The Washington Post*, January 13, 1976, AVS, Box 110, 1976 Board Minutes folder; Ravenholt to Stuart Mudd, December 22, 1969, EM, Carton 11, folder 480.

34. The Pathfinder Fund, "1973–Year End," December 27, 1973, "The Pathfinder Fund and its Board of Directors," January 1974, EM, Carton 11, folders 485, 486.

35. The Pathfinder Fund. "General Support Proposal." n.d. but likely the late 1970s, EM, Box 11, folder 492.

36. AVSC, *1983 Annual Report*, p. 11. Cited in Kasun J. *The War Against Population: The Economics and Ideology of World Population Control*. San Francisco: Ignatius Press, 1988, p. 178.

37. "India's family planning program recovering slowly from setbacks–voluntarism emphasized." *Family Planning Perspectives*. 1979;5:162–163.

38. "In India, birth control focus shifts to women." *New York Times*. March 7, 1982, p. A6.

39. Rutenberg N, Landry E. A comparison of sterilization use and demand from the demographic and health surveys. *International Family Planning Perspectives*. 1993;19:4–13.

40. Ross JA. Sterilization: past, present, future. *Studies in Family Planning*. 1992;23:197; "More than half of all Brazilian contraceptive users rely on sterilization." *International Family Planning Perspectives*. 1997;23:184–186; "EngenderHealth releases new factbook about contraceptive sterilization," May 29, 2002, www.managingcontraception.com/new/engender.html; *Contraceptive Sterilization: Global Issue and Trends*. New York: EngenderHealth, 2002, pp. 17–44.

41. Sen. Bob Packwood. "Dear Environmentalist." n.d. This letter, endorsing AVS, was distributed by AVS to raise funds for the group.

42. "India, dissatisfied with progress on birth control, plans shift of emphasis." *New York Times*, March 31, 1967.

43. For example, see "Mexican fertility falls as female sterilization becomes more popular." *International Family Planning Perspectives.* 1990;16:36–38.
44. Halpern JH. "Fertility reductions in four countries: Voluntary sterilization plays a role." *AVSC News,* July 1990, pp. 3–4.
45. Measham AR, et al. The demographic impact of tubectomy in Bangladesh. *International Family Planning Perspectives.* 1982;8:18–21.
46. Westoff CF, McCarthy J. Sterilization in the United States. *International Family Planning Perspectives.* 1979;11:147–152.
47. "El Salvador: Fertility decline mainly result of female sterilization." *International Family Planning Perspectives.* 1988;14:35–37.
48. Ross J, Huber DH, Hong S. Worldwide trends in voluntary sterilization. *International Family Planning Perspectives.* 1986;12:35.
49. Ross JA, Wardlaw TM, Huber DH, Hong S. Cohort trends in sterilization: Some international comparisons. *Inernational Family Planning Perspectives.* 1987;13:52–60, especially p. 58. See also Rutenberg N, Ferraz EA. Female sterilization and its demographic impact on Brazil. *International Family Planning Perspectives.* 1988;14:61–68, in which the authors assert that sterilization had a "significant impact on fertility in Brazil."
50. "Women who are sterilized at age 30 or younger have increased odds of regret." *Family Planning Perspectives.* 1999;31:308–309; "Most U.S. couples who seek surgical sterilization do so for contraception; fewer than 25% desire reversal." *Family Planning Perspectives.* 1999;31:102–103; "Women sterilized before age 25 are most likely to regret their decision." *Family Planning Perspectives.* 1991;23:236–237.
51. Population Council, Bangladesh, "Regret after sterilization: Can it be averted?" *Policy Dialogue,* No. 4, December 1996, pp. 1–9.
52. Cohen SA, Richards CL. The Cairo Consensus: Population, development, and women. *Family Planning Perspectives.* 1994;20:150–155.
53. United States General Accounting Office, Report to Congressional Requesters. *Foreign Assistance: Impact of Funding Restrictions on USAID's Voluntary Family Planning Program.* April 1997.
54. "EngenderHealth regrets U.S. denial of UNFPA funding." EngenderHealth News Release, July 27, 2004. Available at http://www.engenderhealth.org/news/releases/040804.html.
55. "Using gifts as bait, Peru sterilizes poor women." *New York Times,* February 15, 1998, pp. A1, A12.
56. "Fujimori to contest Peru election." *BBC News,* October 6, 2005. Available at http://news.bbc.co.uk; "Peru asks Chile to extradite Fujimori to face a range of charges." *New York Times,* January 4, 2006, p. A5.
57. "At women's forum, Peru's leader defies church." *New York Times,* September 13, 1995.
58. Bosch X. Former Peruvian government censured over sterilizations. *British Medical Journal.* 2002;325:236.

59. Population Research Institute. "USAID supported Fujimori's sterilization campaign; seeks to cover up involvement." *Weekly Briefing*, 5, September 22, 2003. Available at http://www.pop.org.

60. "Final evaluation of USAID's cooperative agreement (1993–1998) with AVSC International." April 1998, pp. 51–52. Available at http://www.poptechproject.com/pdf/avsc59.

61. Eaton T. East Timor: Raping the future. *Mother Jones Online*, August 26, 1999. Available at http://www.motherjones.com/news/special_reports/east_timor/features/women.html; Sissons M. From one day to another: Violations of women's reproductive and sexual rights in East Timor. Available at http://www.hartford-hwp.com/archives/54b/052.html.

62. Wattenberg B. *Fewer: How the New Demography Will Shape Our Future*. Chicago: Ivan R. Dee, 2004.

63. Buchanan P. *The Death of the West: How Dying Populations and Immigrant Invasions Imperil Our Country and Civilization*. New York: Thomas Dunne, 2001.

64. Longman P. The global baby bust. *Foreign Affairs*, May/June 2004. Available at http://www.foreignaffairs.org.

65. Longman P. Political victory: From here to maternity. *Washington Post*, September 2, 2004, p. A23.

66. Longman P. The return of patriarchy. *Foreign Policy*, March/April 2006. Available at http://www.foreignpolicy.com/story/cms.

67. Varga-Toth J, Singer SM. Labour pains: Stunning silence around issue of birth rates in Canada. *The Hill Times*, September 18, 2006, p. 16.

68. Samuelson RJ. Behind the birth dearth. *Washington Post*, May 24, 2006, p. A23.

69. Sieg L. Land of the Rising Sun fails to raise enough sons and daughters. *National Post*, December 29, 2005, p. A11; "South Korea, in turnabout, now calls for more babies." *New York Times*, August 21, 2005.

70. French HW. As China ages, a shortage of cheap labor looms. *New York Times*, June 20, 2006, p. A1; Lim BK. China's 1.3 billionth citizen born into population maze. *National Post*, January 7, 2005, p. A2.

71. "China's boy trouble." *Globe and Mail*, December 11, 2004, p. F5.

72. Sheth SS. Missing female births in India. *The Lancet*. 2006;367:185–186; Rahman SA. Where the girls aren't. *Globe and Mail*, October 16, 2004, p. F2; Katyal S. Aborting female fetuses distorts India's sex ratio. *National Post*, August 5, 2005, p. A11; Foster P. India cracks down on sex selective abortions. *National Post*, March 30, 2006, p. A10.

73. Hudson V, Den Boer A. *Bare Branches: The Security Implications of Asia's Surplus Male Population*. Cambridge, MA: MIT Press, 2004.

74. Even industrialized, developed countries such as Canada are not immune to the practice. See Mrozek A. Canada's lost daughters. *Western Standard*, June 5, 2006, pp. 33–39.

75. "Letter from the President." Available at http://www.engenderhealth.org/pubs/ehnews/sp01.html.

76. "A view from our board: Becoming EngenderHealth." *EngenderHealth Update*, n.d. Available at http://www.engenderhealth.org/pubs/ehnews/sp01.html.

77. "AVSC is now EngenderHealth!" Available at http://www.engenderhealth.org/about/announcement.html.

78. Becker R. Toast of the town. *AVSC News*, 38, 2000. Available at http://www.avsc.org/avsc_news/sp00.

79. "Navajo Nation expands family planning services." *AVSC News*, 34(2), Summer 1996.

80. Visaria L, Jejeebhoy S, Merrick T. From family planning to reproductive health: Challenges Facing India. *International Family Planning Perspectives*. 1999;25:S47.

81. Gordon L. *Woman's Body, Woman's Right: A Social History of Birth Control in America*. New York: Penguin, 1980, p. 403.

82. Merrick TW. Population and poverty: New views on an old controversy. *International Family Planning Perspectives*. 2002;28:45.

83. "Country by country: United States." Available at http://www.engenderhealth.org/ia/cbc/united_states.html.

84. Reed J. Misconstruing social change. *Family Planning Perspectives*. 1987;19:89–90.

85. "New Indian initiative on population growth," February 15, 2000. Available at http://www.bbc.co.uk/hi/eglish/world/south_asia/643894.stm.

86. Dugger CW. Relying on hard and soft sells, India pushes sterilization. *New York Times*, June 22, 2001.

87. "Outrage at guns for sterilization policy." *The Guardian*, November 1, 2004. Available at http://www.guardian.co.uk/html.

88. "Find students for sterilization, Indian teachers ordered." *National Post*, February 25, 2006, p. A14.

89. "Country by country: India." Available at http://www.engenderhealth.org/ia/cbc/india.html; "Meeting the need for permanent contraception in India." Available at http://www.engenderhealth.org/itf/india.html.

90. Middleberg MI. Family planning: Great success, greater needs. *EngenderHealth Update: A Quarterly Newsletter*. Available at http://www.engenderhealth.org/pubs/ehnews/wt02.

Bibliography

Allitt, Patrick. *Religion in America Since 1945*. New York: Columbia University Press, 2003.

Bachrach, Peter, and Bergman, Elihu. *Power and Choice: The Formulation of American Population Policy*. Lexington: Lexington Books, 1973.

Blanshard, Paul. *American Freedom and Catholic Power*. Boston: Beacon, 1950.

Bordahl, Per E. Tubal sterilization: A historical review. *Journal of Reproductive Medicine*. 1985;30:18–24.

Braslow, Joel. *Mental Ills and Bodily Cures: Psychiatric Treatment in the First Half of the Twentieth Century*. Berkeley: University of California Press, 1997.

Briggs, Laura. *Reproducing Empire: Race, Sex, Science and U.S. Imperialism in Puerto Rico*. Berkeley: University of California Press, 2002.

Broberg, Gunnar, and Roll-Hansen, Nils (eds.). *Eugenics and the Welfare State: Sterilization Policy in Denmark, Sweden, Norway, and Finland*. East Lansing: Michigan State University Press, 1996.

Burch, Guy Irving, and Pendell, Elmer. *Population Roads to Peace or War*. Washington: Population Reference Bureau, 1945.

Carlson, Allan. *The Swedish Experiment in Family Politics: The Myrdals and the Interwar Population Crisis*. New Brunswick and London: Transaction, 1990.

Cassidy, Keith. The right to life movement: Sources, development, and strategies. In Critchlow, Donald T. (ed.), *The Politics of Abortion and Birth Control in Historical Perspective* (pp. 128–159). University Park: Pennsylvania State University Press, 1996.

Chatterjee, Nilanjana, and Riley, Nancy E. Planning an Indian modernity: The gendered politics of fertility control. *Signs*. 2001;26:811–845.

Chesler, Ellen. *Woman of Valor: Margaret Sanger and the Birth Control Movement in America*. New York: Simon and Schuster, 1992.

Critchlow, Donald T. *Intended Consequences: Birth Control, Abortion, and the Federal Government in Modern America*. New York/Oxford: Oxford University Press, 1999.

Critchlow, Donald T. (ed.). *The Politics of Abortion and Birth Control in Historical Perspective.* University Park: Pennsylvania State University Press, 1996.

Davis, Kingsley. Population and power in the Free World. In Spengler, Joseph J., and Duncan, Otis Dudley (eds.), *Population, Theory, and Policy.* Glencoe, IL: Free Press, 1956, pp. 342–356.

Davis, Kingsley. Population policy: Will current programs succeed? *Science.* 1967;158:730–739.

Dawley, Alan. *Struggles for Justice: Social Responsibility and the Liberal State.* Cambridge: Harvard University Press, 1993.

D'Emilio, John, and Freedman, Estelle B. *Intimate Matters: A History of Sexuality in America.* New York: Harper and Row, 1988.

Dikötter, Frank. *Imperfect Conceptions: Medical Knowledge, Birth Defects, and Eugenics in China.* New York: Columbia University Press, 1998.

Dolan, Jay P. *The American Catholic Experience: A History from Colonial Times to the Present.* Notre Dame: University of Notre Dame Press, 1992.

Donaldson, Peter J. *Nature Against Us: The United States and the World Population Crisis, 1965–1980.* Chapel Hill and London: University of North Carolina Press, 1990.

Dowbiggin, Ian. "A rational coalition": Euthanasia, eugenics, and birth control in America, 1940–1970. *Journal of Policy History.* 2002;14:223–260.

Dowbiggin, Ian. *Inheriting Madness: Professionalization and Psychiatric Knowledge in Nineteenth-Century France.* Berkeley and London: University of California Press, 1991.

Dowbiggin, Ian. *Keeping America Sane: Psychiatry and Eugenics in the United States and Canada, 1880–1940.* Ithaca: Cornell University Press, 1997 (paperback edition, 2003).

Dowbiggin, Ian. *A Merciful End: The Euthanasia Movement in Modern America.* New York and Oxford: Oxford University Press, 2003.

Dowbiggin, Ian. Sterilization, American freedom, and Catholic power: A revisionist interpretation of eugenics. *History and Philosophy of Psychology Bulletin.* 2004;16:4–9.

Dreifus, Claudia (ed.). *Seizing Our Bodies: The Politics of Women's Health.* New York: Random, 1977.

Franks, Angela. *Margaret Sanger's Eugenic Legacy: The Control of Female Fertility.* Jefferson, NC: McFarland and Co., 2005.

Gallagher, Nancy L. *Breeding Better Vermonters: The Eugenics Project in the Green Mountain State.* Hanover, NH: University Press of New England, 1999.

Garrow, David J. *Liberty and Sexuality: The Right to Privacy and the Making of Roe v. Wade.* Berkeley and Los Angeles: University of California Press, 1998.

Gillham, Nicholas W. *A Life of Sir Francis Galton: From African Exploration to the Birth of Eugenics.* New York: Oxford University Press, 2001.

Gordon, Linda. *The Moral Property of Women: A History of Birth Control Politics in America.* Urbana and Chicago: University of Illinois Press, 2002.

Gordon, Linda. *Woman's Body, Woman's Right: A Social History of Birth Control in America.* New York: Penguin, 1980.

Greer, Germaine. *Sex and Destiny: The Politics of Human Fertility.* London: Martin Secker and Warburg, 1984.

Haller, Mark H. *Eugenics: Hereditarian Attitudes in American Thought.* New Brunswick: Rutgers University Press, 1963.

Harrison, Paul. *The Third Revolution: Population, Environment and a Sustainable World.* London: Penguin, 1992.

Hudson, Valerie, and Den Boer, Andrea. *Bare Branches: The Security Implications of Asia's Surplus Male Population.* Cambridge: MIT Press, 2004.

Hunter, James Davison. *Culture Wars: The Struggle To Define America.* New York: Basic Books, 1991.

Jones, James H. *Alfred C. Kinsey: A Public/Private Life.* New York and London: W. W. Norton, 1997.

Junod, Suzanne White, and Marks, Lara. Women's trials: The approval of the first oral contraceptive pill in the United States and Great Britain. *Journal of the History of Medicine.* 2002;57:117–160.

Kasun, Jacqueline. *The War Against Population: The Economics and Ideology of World Population Control.* San Francisco: Ignatius Press, 1988.

Kevles, Daniel J. *In the Name of Eugenics: Genetics and the Uses of Human Heredity.* New York: Knopf, 1985.

Kline, Wendy. *Building a Better Race: Gender, Sexuality, and Eugenics from the Turn of the Century to the Baby Boom.* Berkeley and Los Angeles: University of California Press, 2001.

Konner, Melvin. *Becoming a Doctor: A Journey of Initiation in Medical School.* New York: Viking, 1987.

Kühl, Stefan. *The Nazi Connection: Eugenics, American Racism, and German National Socialism.* New York and Oxford: Oxford University Press, 1994.

Ladd-Taylor, Molly. Eugenics, sterilization and modern marriage in the USA: The strange career of Paul Popenoe. *Gender and History.* 2001;3:298–327.

Lader, Lawrence. *Breeding Ourselves to Death.* New York: Seven Locks Press, 2002.

Lader, Lawrence (ed.). *Foolproof Birth Control: Male and Female Sterilization.* Boston: Beacon Press, 1972.

Largent, Mark A. "The greatest curse of the race": Eugenic sterilization in Oregon, 1909–1983. *Oregon Historical Quarterly.* 2002;103:188–209.

Larson, Edward J. *Evolution: The Remarkable History of a Scientific Theory.* New York: Modern Library, 2004.

Larson, Edward J. *Sex, Race, and Science: Eugenics in the Deep South.* Baltimore and London: The Johns Hopkins University Press, 1995.

Ledbetter, Rosanna. Thirty years of family planning in India. *Asian Survey.* 1984;24:736–758.

Leon, Sharon M. "Hopelessly entangled in Nordic pre-suppositions": Catholic participation in the American Eugenics Society in the 1920s. *Bulletin of the History of Medicine.* 2004;59:3–49.

Lerner, Barron H. Constructing medical indications: The sterilization of women with heart disease or tuberculosis, 1905–1935. *Bulletin of the History of Medicine.* 1994;49:362–379.

Littlewood, Thomas B. *The Politics of Population Control.* Notre Dame and London: University of Notre Dame Press, 1977.

Longman, Philip. *The Empty Cradle: How Falling Birthrates Threaten World Prosperity and What To Do About It.* New York: Basic Books, 2004.

Macklin, Ruth, and Gaylin, Willard. *Mental Retardation and Sterilization: A Problem of Competency and Paternalism.* New York: Plenum, 1981.

Marks, Lara V. *Sexual Chemistry: A History of the Contraceptive Pill.* New Haven and London: Yale University Press, 2001.

May, Elaine Tyler. *Homeward Bound: American Families in the Cold War Era.* New York: Basic Books, 1988.

McCann, Carole R. *Birth Control Politics in the United States, 1916–1945.* Ithaca: Cornell University Press, 1994.

McGreevy, John T. *Catholicism and American Freedom: A History.* New York and London: W. W. Norton, 2003.

McKibben, Bill. *Maybe One: A Case for Small Families.* New York: Plume, 1999.

McLaren, Angus, and McLaren, Arlene Tigar. *The Bedroom and the State: The Changing Practices and Politics of Contraception and Abortion in Canada, 1880–1997.* Oxford and Toronto: Oxford University Press, 1997.

Morantz-Sanchez, Regina. *Conduct Unbecoming a Woman: Medicine on Trial in Turn-of-the-Century Brooklyn.* New York: Oxford University Press, 1999.

Moscowitz, Eva. "It's good to blow your top": Women's magazines and discourse of discontent, 1945–1965. *Journal of Women's History.* 1996;8:67–98.

Nathanson, Bernard H., and Ostling, Richard N. *Aborting America.* New York: Doubleday, 1979.

Neuhaus, Jessamyn. The importance of being orgasmic: Sexuality, gender, and marital sex manuals in the United States, 1920–1963. *Journal of the History of Sexuality.* 2000;9:447–473.

Ordover, Nancy. *American Eugenics: Race, Queer Anatomy, and the Science of Nationalism.* Minneapolis: University of Minnesota Press, 2003.

Osborn, Fairfield. *Limits of the Earth.* Boston: Little, Brown, 1953.

Osborn, Fairfield. *Our Plundered Planet.* Boston: Little, Brown and Co., 1948.

Paul, Diane B. *Controlling Human Heredity: 1865 to the Present.* Atlantic Highlands, NJ: Humanities Press, 1995.

Pernick, Martin S. *The Black Stork: Eugenics and the Death of "Defective" Babies in American Medicine and Motion Pictures Since 1915.* New York and Oxford: Oxford University Press, 1996.

Pernick, Martin S. Public health then and now: Eugenics and public health in American history. *American Journal of Public Health.* 1997;87:1767–1772.

Piotrow, Phylis Tilson. *World Population Crisis: The United States Response.* New York: Praeger, 1973.

Porter, Roy. *The Greatest Benefit to Mankind: A Medical History of Humanity*. New York: W. W. Norton, 1998.

Presser, Harriet B. *Sterilization and Fertility Decline in Puerto Rico*. Berkeley: Institute of International Studies, 1973.

Proctor, Robert N. *Racial Hygiene: Medicine Under the Nazis*. Cambridge: Harvard University Press, 1988.

Rafter, Nicole Hahn. *Creating Born Criminals*. Urbana and Chicago: University of Illinois Press, 1997.

Ramirez de Arellano, Annette B., and Seipp, Conrad. *Colonialism, Catholicism, and Contraception: A History of Birth Control in Puerto Rico*. Chapel Hill and London: University of North Carolina Press, 1983.

Reed, James. *From Private Vice to Public Virtue: The Birth Control Movement and American Society Since 1830*. New York: Basic Books, 1978.

Reilly, Philip R. *The Surgical Solution: A History of Involuntary Sterilization in the United States*. Baltimore and London: The Johns Hopkins University Press, 1991.

Robitscher, Jonas (ed.). *Eugenic Sterilization*. Springfield, IL: Charles C. Thomas, 1973.

Rosen, Christine. *Preaching Eugenics: Religious Leaders and the American Eugenics Movement*. New York and Oxford: Oxford University Press, 2004.

Rosenberg, Charles E. *The Care of Strangers: The Rise of America's Hospital System*. New York: Basic Books, 1987.

Schoen, Johanna. "A great thing for poor folks": Birth control, sterilization, and abortion in public health and welfare in the twentieth century. University of North Carolina: Unpublished doctoral dissertation, 1995.

Schoen, Johanna. Between choice and coercion: Women and the politics of sterilization in North Carolina. *Journal of Women's History*. 2001;13:132–156.

Schoen, Johanna. *Choice and Coercion: Birth Control, Sterilization, and Abortion in Public Health and Welfare*. Chapel Hill: University of North Carolina Press, 2005.

Shorter, Edward. *Bedside Manners: The Troubled History of Doctors and Patients*. New York: Viking, 1985.

Shorter, Edward. *From Paralysis to Fatigue: A History of Psychosomatic Illness in the Modern Era*. New York: The Free Press, 1992.

Shorter, Edward. *A History of Psychiatry: From the Era of the Asylum to the Age of Prozac*. New York: Wiley, 1997.

Shorter, Edward. *A History of Women's Bodies*. New York: Basic Books, 1982.

Sidel, Victor W., and Sidel, Ruth (eds.). *Reforming Medicine: Lessons of the Last Quarter Century*. New York: Pantheon, 1984.

Simon, Julian L. *The Ultimate Resource*. Princeton: Princeton University Press, 1981.

Stage, Sarah. *Female Complaints: Lydia Pinkham and the Business of Women's Medicine*. New York: Norton, 1979.

Stern, Alexandra Minna. *Eugenic Nation: Faults and Frontiers of Better Breeding in Modern America*. Berkeley and Los Angeles: University of California Press, 2005.

Tone, Andrea. *Devices and Desires: A History of Contraceptives in America.* New York: Hill and Wang, 2001.

Trombley, Stephen. *The Right to Reproduce: A History of Coercive Sterilization.* London: Weidenfeld and Nicholson, 1988.

Vanessendelft, William Ray. *A history of the Association for Voluntary Sterilization, 1935–1964.* University of Minnesota: Unpublished doctoral dissertation, 1978.

Vicziany, Marika. Coercion in a soft state: The family-planning program of India. Part One: The myth of voluntarism. *Pacific Affairs.* 1982;55:373–402.

Vicziany, Marika. Coercion in a soft state: The family-planning program of India. Part Two: The sources of coercion. *Pacific Affairs.* 1982;55:557–592.

Vogel, Amy. Regulating degeneracy: Eugenic sterilization in Iowa, 1911–1977. *The Annals of Iowa.* 1995;54:119–143.

Vogt, William. *Road to Survival.* New York: Sloane, 1948.

Warwick, Donald P. *Bitter Pills: Population Policies and Their Implementation in Eight Developing Countries.* Cambridge: Cambridge University Press, 1982.

Wattenberg, Ben J. *The Birth Dearth.* New York: Pharos Books, 1987.

Wattenberg, Ben J. *Fewer: How the New Demography of Depopulation Will Shape Our Future.* Chicago: Ivan R. Dee, 2004.

Weikart, Richard. *From Darwin to Hitler: Evolutionary Ethics, Eugenics, and Racism in Germany.* New York: Palgrave Macmillan, 2004.

Weindling, Paul. *Health, Race and German Politics Between National Unification and Nazism, 1870–1945.* Cambridge: Cambridge University Press, 1989.

Westoff, Charles F., and Ryder, Norman B. *The Contraceptive Revolution.* Princeton: Princeton University Press, 1977.

Abbreviations

ACLU	American Civil Liberties Union
ACOG	American College of Obstetricians and Gynecologists
AHC	American Heritage Center, University of Wyoming
AJPH	*American Journal of Public Health*
AMA	American Medical Association
AVS	EngenderHealth Records, Social Welfare History Archives, University of Minnesota
BC	Brock Chisholm Fonds, National Archives of Canada, Ottawa, Canada
EM	Emily Borie (Hartshorne) Mudd Papers, Schlesinger Library, Radcliffe Institute for Advanced Study, Harvard University, Cambridge, Massachusetts
FDA	U.S. Food and Drug Administration
HBAA	Human Betterment Association of America
HBAVS	Human Betterment Association for Voluntary Sterilization
HEW	U.S. Department of Health, Education, and Welfare
HM	Hugh Moore Collection, Seeley G. Mudd Library, Princeton University, Princeton, New Jersey
IAVS	International Association for Voluntary Sterilization
LL	Lawrence Lader Papers, Manuscript and Archives Division, New York Public Library, New York, New York
MSB	Medora S. Bass Collection, American Heritage Center, University of Wyoming

NARAL   National Association for the Repeal of Abortion Laws
(Now known as NARAL Pro-Choice America)

NOW   National Organization for Women

OEO   Office of Economic Opportunity

PP   Planned Parenthood

PPFA   Planned Parenthood Federation of America

RLD   Robert Latou Dickinson Papers, Francis Countway
Library, Rare Books Department, Harvard University
Medical School, Boston, Massachusetts

RPS   Ruth Proskauer Smith Papers, Schlesinger Library,
Radcliffe Institute for Advanced Study, Harvard
University, Cambridge, Massachusetts

SC   Sripati Chandrasekhar Papers, Ward M. Canaday
Center, University of Toledo, Ohio

SIECUS   Sex Information and Education Council of the
United States

USAID   United States Agency for International Development

ZPG   Zero Population Growth

Index

243